ARAMAIC LIGHT ON EZRA THROUGH THE SONG OF SOLOMON

Aramaic Old Testament Series
Volume 4

Books in print by Rocco A. Errico

Setting A Trap for God: The Aramaic Prayer of Jesus
Let There Be Light: The Seven Keys
And There Was Light
The Mysteries of Creation: The Genesis Story
The Message of Matthew: An Annotated Parallel Aramaic-English Gospel of Matthew
Classical Aramaic – Book 1

Spanish publication

La Antigua Oración Aramea de Jesús: El Padrenuestro

German publications

Das Aramaische Vaterunser
Es Werde Licht

Italian publication

Otto accordi con Dio: il Padre Nostro originario

Books in print by Rocco A. Errico and George M. Lamsa
Aramaic New Testament Series: Volumes 1 – 7

Aramaic Light on the Gospel of Matthew
Aramaic Light on the Gospels of Mark and Luke
Aramaic Light on the Gospel of John
Aramaic Light on the Acts of the Apostles
Aramaic Light on Romans through 2 Corinthians
Aramaic Light on Galatians through Hebrews
Aramaic Light on James through Revelation

Aramaic Old Testament Series: Volumes 1 – 4

Aramaic Light on Genesis
Aramaic Light on Exodus through Deuteronomy
Aramaic Light on Joshua through 2 Chronicles
Aramaic Light on Ezra through Song of Solomon

Books in print by George M. Lamsa

The Holy Bible from the Ancient Eastern Text
Idioms in the Bible Explained & A Key to the Original Gospels
New Testament Origin
The Shepherd of All – The 23rd Psalm
Dr. George M. Lamsa: A Life

ARAMAIC LIGHT ON EZRA THROUGH THE SONG OF SOLOMON

A commentary based on the Aramaic language
and ancient Near Eastern customs

Aramaic Old Testament Series
Volume 4

Rocco A. Errico / George M. Lamsa

The Noohra Foundation, Inc
Smyrna, Georgia

 For information, address Noohra Foundation, 4480 South Cobb Drive SE, Ste H PMB 343, Smyrna Georgia 30080, www.noohra.com, email: info@noohra.com.

First Printing June 2010

ISBN: 978-0-9760080-6-4

To

Mrs. Donalyn Kling

with my deepest and most sincere appreciation for your generous help and interest in the Aramaic work and for making the publication of this commentary possible.

CONTENTS

(There are no comments in chapters that are not listed below)

Book of Ezra

Book of Nehemiah

Book of Esther

Book of Job

Book of Job (Cont.)

Book of Psalms

The Proverbs

The Proverbs (Cont.)

Ecclesiastes

Song of Solomon

FOREWORD
by Rocco A. Errico

A Distinctive Commentary

Aramaic Light on Ezra through Song of Solomon is an unusual and incomparable commentary for many reasons. First, it provides a unique understanding of the ancient Semitic customs and culture. It illuminates difficult and puzzling passages of the Old Testament and offers unparalleled insight into the character and behavior of the people. This is possible because of the late Dr. George M. Lamsa, who was born in that part of the world where the very old Semitic world's customs and manners were kept.

Dr. Lamsa, the originator and coauthor of this present commentary, was a native Aramaic speaking Assyrian, who came from an area of the Near East where the people were still living and practicing much of their past cultural religious traditions. He grew up in that part of the age-old biblical land from which Abraham migrated to Canaan. His family lived a simple pastoral life, as did his ancestors during the time of the Hebrew patriarchs. Even to this day, these Aramaic speaking people converse in idioms and parables, some of which would be difficult for Westerners to comprehend. His people were direct descendants of the Assyrians, who also mixed with some of the dispersed northern ten tribes of Israel in the mountains of ancient Assyria. This area, which during Dr. Lamsa's time was a part of Turkey, is today also a part of Iraq.

Dr. W. A. Wigram, a noted English scholar, spent over ten years as a missionary and researcher in Kurdistan in that region of Turkey. Concerning the survival of the descendants of the ancient Assyrians and their cultural customs, Dr. Wigram writes:

> A strange survival in an isolated corner of the world, these last representatives of the ancient Assyrian stock have hitherto kept up the most primitive of Semitic customs to an extent that can hardly be paralleled elsewhere, even in Mesopotamian marsh districts. As an ancient and fossilized Church, they had also preserved ecclesiastical

rites and ceremonies which have either perished altogether elsewhere, or else have survived only in almost unrecognizable form. . . .Here are a people who, in the time of the beginning of the Christian era, are found living in the lands where, in the year 600 BC, the Assyrian stock had been established since history began; nor is there any record of any considerable immigration into, or emigration from, that land in the interval.

Their own traditions affirm that they are of the old Assyrian blood, with a possible intermixture of certain Babylonian or Chaldean elements . . . It was only natural that this old Semitic stock, living where nothing had ever occurred to disturb their habits of life, should keep up the old Semitic customs. **They still lived, or did live till the changes of the Great War brought about an alteration, the life of the Old Testament.** Bible customs or those that we call such, were, of course, not peculiar to the Hebrew, but were the common heritage of all the stock to which he belonged and a part of the atmosphere of the land.[1]

Dr. Lamsa's Original Commentary

When Dr. Lamsa wrote *Old Testament Light,* a commentary on Genesis to Malachi, 976 pages, his publisher and his friends advised him to comment only on the most difficult and important verses. They especially asked him to elucidate passages of Scripture that had become obscure through translation and misunderstanding of Near Eastern, Semitic word meanings, idioms, and culture. While he was preparing *Old Testament Light*, Dr. Lamsa was constantly aware of the size of the book. He did not want to create a very large volume that would burden the reader, nor did he wish to duplicate what one might find from other commentaries.

When *Old Testament Light* was published in 1964, it received much acclaim and publicity. This recognition brought requests from various regions in the United States and Canada for a more expanded exposition on many passages that he only lightly explained and for

---

[1]Dr. W. A. Wigram, *The Assyrians and Their Neighbors,* pp. 177-178, 185. The bold lettering was put by me for emphasis in this study of the Old Testament.

further enlightenment on others in which he made no comments. These requests were made during the time, 1965 to 1972, when Dr. Lamsa and I were collaborating. So in the early 1970s we drafted additional material on the Old Testament; however, these new works were not completed.

Now with the kind and generous permission of Dr. Lamsa's niece, Mrs. David (Nina) Shabaz and the entire Shabaz family, I have been editing, expanding, annotating and preparing Dr. Lamsa's previous volume in a new format. I have also added more comments derived from my continual research in the Aramaic language and completing the comments that Dr. Lamsa and I had only drafted.

Formation of this Commentary

Dr. Lamsa and I had worked together for ten years before he passed from this earthly life on September 22, 1975. I have been lecturing, writing, teaching, and continuing the Aramaic approach to holy Scripture since his passing. Before Dr. Lamsa became ill, he told me how he wanted the new commentaries on the Aramaic Old Testament Series to be published in separate volumes to aid Bible students and ministers who were interested in this approach to Holy Scripture.

Aramaic Light on Ezra through Song of Solomon is not a commentary founded on contemporary academic analysis of Scripture nor on modern interpretations. It does not employ critical source/historical and literary methods of interpretation. Occasionally, however, I do refer in the footnotes to some of the modern, scholarly material on the various books of the Old Testament.

The reader must keep in mind that this commentary works with the received text—that is, with the Old Testament as we now have it in its present form—and does not attempt to provide the reader with source/critical studies. Nor is this volume a verse by verse commentary. We only commented on those verses that were difficult to understand, bridging the ancient Near Eastern world for people in the Western world.

As much as possible, each comment is written in story form, using laymen's language and not theological, specialized terminology. Its basic premise is the clarification of Aramaic word meanings, cultural and religious customs, and misunderstood idiomatic expressions of speech. This style will be maintained throughout the *Aramaic Old Testament Series* beginning with Genesis and ending with Malachi.

Concerning Translations

All scriptural excerpts are from the King James Version of the Old Testament. The comments also contain scriptural passages from *The Holy Bible from the Ancient Eastern Text* by Dr. George M. Lamsa. Whenever there are phrases such as "It should read," "The Aramaic text reads," and "The Eastern Aramaic text reads," these statements indicate that the scriptural quote is from the "Eastern Aramaic Peshitta Text, Lamsa Translation." There are other citations of Scripture in the body of the comments that I translated directly from the Aramaic Peshitta text. These citations are identified as "Aramaic Peshitta text, Errico."

I have attempted as much as possible to avoid a collision with denominational interpretations and theological implications. However, in certain passages cited in this volume, it became unavoidable. Apparently, some biblical interpreters have unwittingly formed and established monumental dogmas and confusing notions on verses that were only idioms, metaphors, or cultural customs.

According to Scripture, God, through revelation, had told the prophets to write in a plain and simple language.[2] But, because of translating from one language to another, adding and omitting from Scripture, and a lack of translators, many passages of scripture have suffered losses. Thousands of these verses that were once clear in their original state became obscure and the subject of theological controversies. Both the literalist interpreter and the modern thinker have contributed to a misunderstanding of Scripture, not through a fault of their own, but because the Bible comes to us from a culture distinct from our forms of thinking and reasoning.

---

[2]See Dt. 27:8 and Hab. 2:2.

A Note on the Term "Semitic"

In modern times in the West, the term "Semites" has been used exclusively to refer to Jewish people. In this commentary, the terms "Semitic" and "Semite" refer, in most instances, to the behavior and beliefs that apply to Near Eastern Jews and other Near Eastern Semites who kept the customs and manners of the ancient Near East, such as Assyrians, Syrians (Arameans), Chaldeans, and Arabs. (It does not apply to Westernized Semitic peoples.)

Acknowledgments and Final Word

My deep appreciation and sincere gratitude to the entire Shabaz family as proprietors of the Lamsa estate for their kind and most gracious permission to edit, revise, expand, annotate, and prepare Dr. Lamsa's previous commentary *Old Testament Light* in this new format.

My very genuine and heartfelt thanks and gratefulness to Ms. Sue Edwards and Ms. Linetta Izenman for their constructive suggestions and assistance in preparing this manuscript for publication. In addition, the board of the Noohra Foundation and I are extremely thankful to Mrs. Donalyn Kling, whose generosity and dedication to the Aramaic work made this publication possible. We also wish to acknowledge Mr. Hans-Jürgen Mauer, of Frankfurt, Germany, for his help in preparing and copying *Old Testament Light* into the computer program for the present volume, *Ezra through Song of Solomon.*

To readers of this commentary I say: *Tybootha washlama dalaha nehwoon amhon hasha walmeen!* "The grace (loving-kindness) and peace of God are with you now and always!"

Rocco A. Errico
June 2010

ABBREVIATIONS

Hebrew Bible (Old Testament)

Gen.	Genesis
Ex.	Exodus
Lev.	Leviticus
Num.	Numbers
Dt.	Deuteronomy
Josh.	Joshua
Judg.	Judges
1 Sam.	1 Samuel
2 Sam.	2 Samuel
2 Ki.	2 Kings
1 Chron.	1 Chronicles
Neh.	Nehemiah
Ps.	Psalms
Prov.	Proverbs
Ecc.	Ecclesiastes
Sol.	Song of Solomon
Isa.	Isaiah
Jer.	Jeremiah
Lam.	Lamentations
Ezk.	Ezekiel
Dan.	Daniel
Hab.	Habakkuk
Zech.	Zechariah
Mal.	Malachi

New Testament

Mt.	Matthew
Mk.	Mark
Lk.	Luke
Jn.	John
Rom.	Romans
1 Cor.	1 Corinthians
Eph.	Ephesians
Phil.	Philippians
1 Tim.	1 Timothy
Heb.	Hebrews
1 Pet.	1 Peter
2 Pet.	2 Peter
Rev.	Revelation

Other Abbreviations

BCE	Before the Common Era (BC)
CE	Common Era (AD)
K.J.V.	King James Version

INTRODUCTION TO EZRA

The book of Ezra, like those of Nehemiah and Esther, is a postexilic work. The Eastern Aramaic Peshitta text contains Second Ezra, as does the Vulgate and the Septuagint, but this book is not read in churches. According to Scripture, Ezra, Daniel, and Nehemiah were in government service. The books of Ezra and Nehemiah contain the narratives of the two most zealous and pious Jews. Both Ezra and Nehemiah were born during the captivity and educated in Babylon (Chaldea). They contributed a great deal to the second Jewish commonwealth, playing a very prominent role in the restoration of the remnant and the rebuilding of Jerusalem and the temple.

All of these post-exile books were written in Chaldean (Southern Aramaic), which was the literary and imperial language, and were translated or transcribed into what was thought to be the original Hebrew. The Hebrew language was lost during the 70 years of the exile, and Aramaic, a sister tongue, had become the vernacular of the Jews.

Some portions of these scrolls still remain in Aramaic, which was the imperial language in the western provinces of the far-flung Persian Empire. The letters written against the Jews were written and interpreted in Aramaic.[3] The Persians could not dispense with Aramaic in the provinces west of the River Tigris and in Egypt. Aramaic was well established by the Assyrians and Babylonians, who ruled over the same provinces.

The books of Ezra and Nehemiah begin where Chronicles ends. Therefore, these books were written as a continuation of Chronicles. There is much controversy and debate over authorship and dating. Most scholars date Ezra and Nehemiah to the fourth century BCE. Hebrew tradition teaches that Ezra is the author of both books. Other scholars believe that the editors and authors of Chronicles were responsible for these two books. They also teach on the unity of these books, but this is also disputed and has come under much scholarly debate and criticism.

Ezra was a scribe and a teacher of the Mosaic law. In part of the book, he speaks in the first person.[4] In other sections of the book, however, he is placed in the third person by the scribes. In Jewish rabbinical teaching, Ezra is known as the second Moses because he was the one who brought the Torah to the Jews returning from exile.

---

[3]Ezra 4:7.

[4]Ezra 7:27-28.

CHAPTER TWO

Cyrus' Proclamation

Now these are the children of the province that went up out of the captivity, of those which had been carried away, whom Nebuchadnezzar the king of Babylon had carried away unto Babylon, and came again unto Jerusalem and Judah, every one unto his city. Ezra 2:1.

The return of the first Jews from captivity in Babylon under the leadership of Zerubbabel and Jesuha was in the first year of the reign of Cyrus, the king of Persia, about 538 BCE.[5] Another group came up with Ezra about 458 BCE. The third group came with Nehemiah in 443 BCE.

All these people who returned comprised the remnant of Israel and Judah which was destined to return to Jerusalem and Judah. But because of strong opposition from enemies, the restoration was gradual.[6]

Confusion in Names

The children of Solomon's servants: the children of Sotai, the children of Sophereth, the children of Peruda. Ezra 2:55.

The Eastern Aramaic text reads: "The descendants of Ebar, the descendants of Satim, the descendants of Aspherot, the descendants of Peruda."

This should read *benai Abar,* "the sons, children, or descendants of Abar," and *benai Shalim,* "the sons, children, or descendants of Shalim." The error is caused by the confusion of *abar,* "crossing," with *abad,* "a servant." Solomon's servants were registered among their own families and by their own tribes as the servants of the kings of Judah.

Tirshatha

And the Tirshatha said unto them, that they should not eat of the most holy things, till there stood up a priest with Urim and with Thummim. Ezra 2:63.

---

[5]Ezra 1:1, Neh. 7:6.
[6]Ezra 4:4-5.

The Eastern Aramaic text reads: "And the leaders of Israel said to them that they should not eat of the most holy things until there should rise up a high priest who would make an inquiry and see about the matter."

The Peshitta text reads *resheh di Israel,* "the headmen, leaders, or chieftains of Israel." The Hebrew word *hatiershatha* that appears in the Masoretic text should read *resheh*, "chieftain, prince." Apparently the term *tirshatha* is a confusion of *resheh* or *reshaneh.* The Hebrew word for "leader" is *neged*, and the Hebrew word for "chief" is *rosh* (Aramaic, *resha*).

CHAPTER FOUR

Hinderers

And hired counselors against them, to frustrate their purpose, all the days of Cyrus king of Persia, even until the reign of Darius king of Persia. Ezra 4:5.

The Aramaic word *malkaneh,* "counselors," has been confused with the Aramaic word *mawkaneh,* which refers to "objectors, hinderers" who persuaded the king of Persia to revoke the royal decree and stop the work. The first part of the verse reads: "And hired objectors against them to frustrate their purpose . . ."

The reference here is to *Rehum*, *Shimshai*, and the rest of the native people west of the River Euphrates. These men were hindering the work of rebuilding the temple.[7]

Letters Interpreted

And in the days of Artaxerxes wrote Bishlam, Mithredath, Tabeel, and the rest of their companions, unto Artaxerxes king of Persia; and the writing of the letter was written in the Syrian tongue, and interpreted in the Syrian tongue. Ezra 4:7.

"Syrian" is a misnomer. It should read "Aramaic." This ancient language was called Syrian because it was the language of Sur (Tyre), a city on the Mediterranean coast that was visited by Greek sailors and later conquered by Alexander the Great about 332 BCE.

Aramaic was the language of the Fertile Crescent and the imperial

---

[7]See Ezra 4:4, 8-16, Eastern Aramaic Peshitta text, Lamsa translation.

language of the two great Semitic empires, Assyria and Babylon. The Persians could not dispense with Aramaic in their far-flung provinces west of the River Tigris. Then again, the Jews who had returned from Babylon and other parts of the Persian Empire spoke and wrote in Aramaic.

In the Near East, it was not unusual to interpret a king's letter or a government decree. Such letters were generally written by court scribes, who used difficult words and abstruse terms of speech unfamiliar to ordinary readers and illiterate people, and which were couched in diplomatic language that ordinary people could not understand. This is true of laws and treaties in our own day. They have to be interpreted in order to clarify qualifying clauses and ambiguous terms of speech.

The letter was interpreted in order to elucidate all the issues that were involved so that there should be no more misunderstanding and delay in the rebuilding of the temple.

CHAPTER SIX

Erecting a Cross

Also I have made a decree, that whosoever shall alter this word, let timber be pulled down from his house, and being set up, let him be hanged thereon; and let his house be made a dunghill for this. Ezra 6:11.

The Eastern Aramaic text reads: "Also I have made a decree that whosoever shall alter this ordinance, let a beam be pulled down from his house, and they shall make it a cross for him and they shall crucify him upon it; and let his house be made a dunghill for this."

Crucifying was a Persian custom for certain crimes. The victims were crucified and left alive on the cross as an example to all evildoers and to those who did not comply with the laws and ordinances. This custom might have been used by the Egyptians and other peoples who had come under Persian rule. Joshua had crucified the king of Ai and five other rulers.[8]

Jesus of Nazareth, a Galilean Jew, was crucified and nails were driven into his hands and feet. Paintings that depict Jesus just hanging on the cross without being nailed to the cross are not accurate. Italian artists did not know how people were crucified, but they had seen bandits and other malefactors hanged on trees.

---

[8]See Josh. 8:29 and 10:26. He did not hang these kings but crucified them.

Roman governors in Judea and other countries used native customs for punishing criminals. The Romans themselves might have borrowed this custom of crucifixion from the Near East.

CHAPTER NINE

A Remnant

And after all that is come upon us for our evil deeds, and for our great trespass, seeing that thou our God hast punished us less than our iniquities deserve, and hast given us such deliverance as this. Ezra 9:13.

The Eastern Aramaic text reads: "And after all these things that have come upon us for our evil deeds and for our great sins, seeing that thou our God hast purposed to forgive our sins and to give us a remnant in the world."

The Aramaic word *sharqanah,* "a remnant," has been confused with *porqanah,* "salvation, deliverance." Ezra states that despite all the evil works of the people, the Lord had forgiven them and spared a remnant.

Only a small number of the people returned from Babylon. But this remnant served as a nucleus for a new Jewish commonwealth through which God's promises to humankind were fulfilled and God's lamp was kept burning—that is, divine laws and spiritual principles were still practiced.

INTRODUCTION TO NEHEMIAH

Nehemiah was a great Jewish leader with deep religious convictions. His devotion and concern for his people and religion transcended his political and material interest in life.

Nehemiah was living at Shushan Palace (465 BCE). He had risen to the high position of cupbearer to Artakhshisht, king of Persia, an office that was greatly desired by princes and nobles of the realm because the cupbearer stood in the presence of the king daily. No one else could enter into his presence without being summoned—not even the queen or his children.

Nehemiah must have been a handsome and educated youth and a man of integrity and trustworthiness to have been appointed as cupbearer to the great king of Persia. In those days cupbearers often were bribed, and kings were murdered by poisoning the wine that they were to drink.

When Nehemiah heard the sad report concerning the state of Jerusalem and the misery of the people who were living in Judah, he was so grieved that he fasted and prayed fervently. He made sincere and powerful supplications to God, confessing the sins of his forefathers who had broken God's covenant and transgressed the commandments. The Lord God answered his prayers and he found favor in the eyes of the Persian King.

In April of 445 BCE, Nehemiah obtained permission from Artakhshisht to go to Jerusalem to rebuild the walls of the city and to supply the timber for the gates and other materials. The king not only granted all his requests but also granted him power never allowed to any other Jewish leader who had gone to Jerusalem before him. Nehemiah could issue commands to the army and order food supplies from the king's treasurers beyond the River Euphrates. Because of his high position, he was looked upon as a prince of the realm, and all governors and army commanders both revered and feared him.

The first edict to rebuild Jerusalem and the temple was issued by King Cyrus in 538 BCE and resulted in many Jews returning to the land of Judah with Zerubabel and later with Ezra. But the work of rebuilding the city and the temple was greatly hampered by enemies of the Jews—the Samaritans, and the Gentiles in Galilee. Sanballat, Tubiah, and Geshem the Arabian, made every effort to stop the work of rebuilding the walls. These men even conspired to kill Nehemiah, who was also accused of the rebellion against the king of Persia.[1]

The book of Nehemiah and the book of Ezra are seemingly one book. Some scholars believe that Ezra went to Jerusalem after Nehemiah. Dr. Lamsa believed that Ezra preceded Nehemiah by a number of years. However, both of them went during the reign of Artakhshisht, king of Persia.

Indeed, Nehemiah was mainly responsible for overcoming the opposition against the returning Jews, the establishment of the second Jewish commonwealth, and the rebuilding of Jerusalem, which was completed in 445 BCE. Moreover, Nehemiah, being well versed in Jewish law and religion, helped with the reorganization work and, as the governor of the city, made new laws and ordinances. Nehemiah was a pious and just man and hospitable toward the poor and oppressed. Some people considered him as a messiah and savior of the Jewish people, but being a humble person, Nehemiah refused such honors and preferred to live in a simple way and not as a prince or governor.[2]

CHAPTER TWO

Nisan

And it came to pass in the month Nisan, in the twentieth year of Artaxerxes the king, that wine was before him: and I took up the wine, and gave it unto the king. Now I had not been beforetime sad in his presence. Neh. 2:1.

Nisan is another name for *Abib,* "April," the month of the blossoms and greens. This is the name of the first Hebrew month, in which the feast of the Passover was celebrated on the fifteenth day. It was in this month that the Hebrews left Egypt, and Pharaoh and his army were drowned in the Sea.[3]

Abib, in Aramaic, is called *hababeh*, "blossoms." The term *nisan* must have been a later adaptation, which might mean *bethnesaney*, "spring."

---

[1]Ezra, all of chapter 4.
[2]Neh. 5:14.
[3]Ex. 23:15.

A Cupbearer's Position

Wherefore the king said unto me, Why is thy countenance sad, seeing thou art not sick? this is nothing else but sorrow of heart. Then I was very sore afraid. Neh. 2:2.

The Persian kings lived in complete isolation. The monarch's person was so sacred that no one, not even the queen or one of his children, could approach him without being royally summoned. The Persian court etiquette was very rigid in this respect. The rulers, being despots and living lavishly, had many enemies. No one was trusted, not even the members of the king's household and his ministers.[4]

Cupbearers were carefully selected from among the most faithful men. Using poison to do away with people in the Near East was a common practice. Our English word "assassin" is derived from the Persian word *hashashin,* a kind of poisonous drug. The cupbearer was the most trusted person in the palace and the only one who could freely come before the king's presence. And, being faithful and close to the king, he indulged in conversation and jokes with him.

This is why Nehemiah was so bold as to make such a request from the emperor and also why the request was speedily granted. Had the monarch been petitioned by a Jewish delegation, the matter would have been referred to one of the ministers and the appeal delayed or even discarded.

The building of Jerusalem was stopped by Emperor Artaxerxes. The Gentiles in Galilee and Syria had complained to the king, warning him against the rebuilding of such a strategic city as Jerusalem.[5]

The Persian monarch was deeply moved by the sincere appeal that his faithful cupbearer made before him and the deep concern he had for the city and the graves of his fathers, so evidenced in his sad face. The king promptly granted the request. Therefore, Nehemiah wrote another glorious chapter in the history of Israel.

Nehemiah Prayed

Then the king said unto me, For what dost thou make request? So I prayed to the God of heaven. Neh. 2:4.

---

[4]Esther 4:16.
[5]Ezra 4:5.

Wsalet means "and you have prayed." The Eastern Aramaic text reads: "Then the king said to me, For what did you make supplications and pray before the God of heaven?" In the Aramaic text, the scribe placed the dot over the "t," which would properly read, "you have prayed. A dot under the "t" would read, "I have prayed." The entire phrase was addressed to Nehemiah by the king.

CHAPTER THREE

Hundred Tower

Then Eliashib the high priest rose up with his brethren the priests and they builded the sheep gate; they sanctified it, and set up the doors of it; even unto the tower of Meah they sanctified it, unto the tower of Hananeel. Neh. 3:1.

It should read: ". . . as far as the tower of the Hundred; and they sanctified it as far as the tower of Hananael." *Maa*, in Aramaic, means "one hundred," that is, the one hundredth tower. Ancient cities had small towers around the wall.

Herbs as Medicines

After him repaired Malchiah the goldsmith's son unto the place of Nethinims, and of the merchants, over against the gate Miphkad, and to the going up of the corner. Neh. 3:31.

The Eastern Aramaic text reads: "After him repaired Melachiah the son of Zepaniah as far as the house of Nethanites and of the dealers in herb drugs. Opposite the gate at the extreme end and as far as the ascent of the corner which turns toward the sheep gate repaired the goldsmiths and the dealers in herb drugs."[6]

Near Eastern cities were divided into various quarters. For example, the silversmiths would ply their trade in one sector, saddle makers in another area, and dealers in herbs and medicines in another section. Cities had neither names for streets nor numbers for homes. Some notable streets had names, but they were not written anywhere on a marker. Writing names and numbers of streets is a Western custom.

---

[6]Neh. 3:31-32, Eastern Aramaic Peshitta text, Lamsa translation.

Prior to the introduction of modern drugs by Europeans into the Near East, herbs were used as medicines. Herbs were collected in the summer time, dried, and stored in large reeds. Some herbs were used for clotting blood, others to stop infections and to restore flesh on a wound and to dry a wound while healing.[7]

CHAPTER FOUR

Weak Wall

Now Tobiah the Ammonite was by him, and he said, Even that which they build, if a fox go up, he shall even break down their stone wall. Neh. 4:3.

These words were spoken sarcastically, meaning that the wall, being so weak, could not serve as a defense. A fox walks very carefully when climbing walls to prey on animals or chickens.

The people were very poor and the work was done hastily. Their wall could hardly be compared with the strong and wide wall of Jerusalem which, in former days, was built by the kings of Judah.

Forgive Not

And cover not their iniquity, and let not their sin be blotted out from before thee: for they have provoked thee to anger before the builders. Neh. 4:5.

The Aramaic word *tishbook* means "forgive." It should read: "And forgive not their offenses, and let not their sins be blotted out from before thee . . ." "Cover" is incorrect.

Sanballat and Tobiah the Ammonite had hindered the rebuilding of the temple of God. Nehemiah invokes God not to forgive them or to blot out the offenses and sins that they had committed.

---

[7]In human terms, a plant is very wise. It knows how to store the rays of the sun, provide food for itself, birds, and humans. When people learn to store solar energy, many problems will be solved. There will be no shortages of gas, oil, and other raw materials. All these things come from four elements: heat, water, air, and soil. A leaf is a great chemist because it knows how to combine these elements and put them to work. The ancients knew that plants could heal human physical afflictions.

CHAPTER FIVE

King Loaned Money

There were also that said, We have borrowed money for the king's tribute, and that upon our lands and vineyards. Neh. 5:4.

The Aramaic word *Nezap* means, "Let us borrow." The verse should read: "There were those who said, Let us borrow money from the king's tribute, and work our fields and our vineyards that we may live." The Aramaic word *Neplokh* means, "Let us work our fields and vineyards." The italics in the King James Version show that the translators were not sure of the meaning of the words.[8]

In the Near East, kings loaned money to farmers during famines and disasters. In most cases, the loans were repaid in kind, and the produce that was sold to the people was stored in government storehouses. In those days Persian kings were magnanimous toward their subjects.

CHAPTER SEVEN

Bethlehem of Zebulon.

The men of Bethlehem and Netophah, an hundred fourscore and eight. Neh. 7:26.

There is a good possibility that another town called Bethlehem existed in northern Israel. It was in the region of Neophah not far from Nazareth. Whenever there were two cities or towns with the same name, the state is also mentioned with the city to distinguish it from other towns with the same name. This might be the reason that the prophet Micah says: "And you, Bethlehem Ephratah, though you are little among the thousands of towns of Judah, yet out of you shall come forth a ruler to govern Israel; whose goings forth have been predicted from of old, from eternity."[9] The name "Bethlehem" means the House of Bread.

---

[8]One must read the King James Version of this verse to see the italics. It cannot be done by reading the verse in this comment because the entire verse is in italics.

[9]Micah 5:2, Eastern Aramaic Peshitta text, Lamsa translation.

CHAPTER EIGHT

Citrons or Citrus

And that they should publish and proclaim in all their cities, and in Jerusalem, saying, Go forth unto the mount, and fetch olive branches, and pine branches, and myrtle branches, and palm branches, and branches of thick trees, to make booths, as it is written. Neh. 8:15.

The Eastern Aramaic text reads: "And that they should hear everything which Moses wrote in the book of the law; and the heralds proclaimed throughout all towns in Jerusalem, saying, Go up to the mountain and bring olive branches and walnut branches and palm branches and branches of citrons and branches of willow trees, and make booths, as it is written in the book of the law of Moses."

The Aramaic word *etrogeh* means "citron, orange tree" and "fruit." Oranges were known in biblical days. The term "citrons" occurs twice in the Peshitta. There is no mention of this fruit in other Bibles.

CHAPTER NINE

Shoes Lasted Long

Yea, forty years didst thou sustain them in the wilderness, so that they lacked nothing; their clothes waxed not old, and their feet swelled not. Neh. 9:21.

The Aramaic word *mesaneh* means "shoes." The last phrase of the scripture in Aramaic reads: ". . . and their shoes had no holes in them." The Aramaic word for "feet" is *rigleh*, but this word is not in the Eastern Aramaic text of this verse. The Assyrians, until World War I, wore woolen shoes called *rashikeh*, which lasted for many years because they were easily mended. Some tribal people continue to wear this style of shoes.

The reference here is to the total care of God, who provided daily needs, clothes, and protection. Those who trusted in God lacked nothing.[10]

---

[10]Dt. 8:4.

CHAPTER THIRTEEN

Mixed Marriages

In those days also saw I Jews that had married wives of Ashdod, of Amman, and of Moab. And their children spake half in the speech of Ashdod, and could not speak in the Jews' language, but according to the language of each people. Neh. 13:23-24.

During the Babylonian captivity in 596 BCE, some of the Jewish peasant classes were left in the land to take care of the vineyards and the trees.[11] Many of these Jews married foreign wives. The temple was destroyed and the national unity broken up. The people who remained in the land became the prey of pagan people and many of them gave up hope of any restoration.

Children born of these mixed marriages spoke the languages of their mother, which were dialects of the Hebrew language. The Moabites, Ammonites, and Edomites were akin to the early Hebrews, and they spoke different Semitic dialects. Both Nehemiah and Ezra were opposed to these mixed marriages and the departure from the language of their forefathers, the ancient Hebrew.

Remember Me

Remember them, O my God, because they have defiled the priesthood, and the covenant of the priesthood, and of the Levites. Neh. 13:29.

The Eastern Aramaic text reads: "Remember me, O my God, concerning the rest of the priesthood and concerning the rest of the priests and the Levites." The Aramaic word *li,* "to me," is the objective case of "I." The Aramaic word for "them" is *Ion.*

Nehemiah prayed to God to remember him for the work he had done in cleansing the priests and the Levites. Only a remnant of the priests and the Levites had returned from exile and participated in the rebuilding of the temple.

---

[11]2 Ki. 25:22.

INTRODUCTION TO ESTHER

Esther is a Persian name, *Histar*, "Star," that is, Venus, one of the prominent Babylonian goddesses, whose cult had spread throughout the Near East and Greece. Queen Esther is the principle character in the book which was named for her.

Esther is admired more than all other Jewish heroines. Therefore, there are more scrolls of this book that bears her name than of any other book in the Holy Writ. This is because Queen Esther was willing to die for her people. It was her devotion to the cause of the Jews that saved them from complete annihilation. The book of Esther was written about 520 BCE,[1] during the reign of Akhshirash, a Persian king.

Interestingly, the term God is not mentioned in the book of Esther. One reason for its omission is the fact that the queen's husband, Akhshirash, was the god of the empire. Had the book been written later than the Persian period, the Jews would have mentioned God's name in it.

Had Esther refused or been afraid to intervene on behalf of her people, there might have been no Jewish race, no second temple, and no Christianity. The Jews could have perished completely.

But, while Haman was planning to destroy the Jewish people in the vast Persian realm, Mordecai and Esther were being prepared to act as God's agents in saving the remnant, so that the messianic promises might be fulfilled and the world blessed by the faith of Abraham.

CHAPTER ONE

Couches

Where were white, green, and blue hangings, fastened with cords of fine linen and purple to silver rings and pillars of marble: the beds were of gold and silver, upon a pavement of red, and blue, and white, and black marble. Esther 1:6.

The Eastern Aramaic text reads: "There were curtains of white cotton and wool, and hangings of violet, fastened with cords of fine linen and purple

---

[1]Modern biblical scholars, both Jewish and Christian, date the scroll of Esther between 400 and 300 BCE. They also teach that the book is a pseudo-historical tale written in Near Eastern humor and exaggeration. The book provided the biblical authority for the celebration of the feast of Purim.

to silver rings and pillars of marble; the couches were of gold and silver, upon a pavement of marble, and the carpets were of fine white linen and silk."

Arsatha in Aramaic means "couches" on which the king, princes, and high state dignitaries reclined. It should not be confused with the word "beds" on which people slept at night.

Persia, now known as Iran, has always been famous for its couches, carpets, draperies, and for the arts that made their palaces and divans famous and conspicuous.

In that part of the ancient world, the glory and the fame of a king was manifested by the extravagant palaces, vessels of gold and silver, and couches and rugs. Persia inherited all of the Assyrian and Babylonian culture. Moreover, Persian kings were interested in beauty and progress and entertained lavishly.

Drinking Wine

And the drinking was according to the law; none did compel: for so the king had appointed to all the officers of his house, that they should do according to every man's pleasure. Esther 1:8.

Near Easterners seldom indulged in wine or strong drink; however, during wedding feasts and banquets, it was required to drink until all the men were drunk. The people considered it a great honor to the bridal couple for the male guests to be totally intoxicated during these festivities. Even those who refused to drink were compelled to do so. Only holy men were exempted.

The emperor of Persia had to rescind the unwritten law that stated there must be compulsory drinking. Only the ruler could allow the guests to drink as they wished. He had the power to do away with an ancient custom that in the Near East was looked upon as law.

Although wine and strong drinks were commonly used in weddings and feasts and were approved by the people, there always had been wise men, prophets, and kings who realized the danger of indulging in too much drinking. It was a bad habit even when wine and strong drinks were used moderately.

The king of Persia was wise in rescinding the law at such an important state banquet. Many conspiracies and revolutions were conceived and carried out when men were drunk with wine. Holy Scripture condemns excessive drinking and drunkenness.

Mehemneh, "Eunuchs"

On the seventh day, when the heart of the king was merry with wine, he commanded Mehuman, Biztha, Harbona, Bigtha, and Abagtha, Zethar, and Carcas, the seven chamberlains that served in the presence of Ahasuerus the king. Esther 1:10.

The Eastern Aramaic text reads: "On the seventh day, when the heart of the king was merry with wine, he commanded the eunuchs, Biztha, Rahbona, Bigtha, and Abagtha, Terash, Zethar, and Carcash, the seven eunuchs who served in the presence of Akhshirash the king." *Mehemneh,* "eunuchs," has been left untranslated. The translators apparently thought it was the name of one of the palace attendants.

Eunuchs were employed in kings' harems until the twentieth century. The office of the eunuch still prevails in some countries. The Aramaic word *mehemnah* means "a trustworthy person, a faithful one." Eunuchs were entrusted with the care of women in the royal palace.[2] Most of the eunuchs were men who had been castrated, though some of them were born eunuchs—that is, without the usual sexual powers and characteristics of males.

Near Eastern Women Are Shy

But the queen Vashti refused to come at the king's commandment by his chamberlains: therefore was the king very wroth, and his anger burned in him. Esther 1:12.

Until the 1940s and 50s, no stranger could see the face of an Iranian princess or a woman of nobility, not even princes and noble guests. Even peasant women covered their faces with their black veils and would run away when they saw a stranger. Covering of the face is an ancient Near Eastern custom going back to time immemorial. When Rebekah saw her future husband, Isaac, in the field, she covered herself as a token of respect and dignity.[3]

---

[2]See Esther 2:8 in the Eastern Aramaic text, Lamsa translation.

[3]Gen. 24:65.

Kings' wives were always veiled. They also shunned the presence of strangers. Their faces could only be seen by eunuchs, who were appointed by the king to take charge of them.

Queen Vashti was mindful of her dignity as a queen of the world's largest and most powerful empire. She refused to lower herself and to act as an entertainer in the presence of provincial governors, princes, and servants.

Vashti stands as the greatest example of chastity and dignity. For centuries in the Near East, women were considered inferior to men. They were presented to honorable guests and princes, and, at times, were asked to act as striptease dancers at banquets. Vashti would not have any of that.

On the other hand, it was fate that Vashti should refuse to obey the imperial command of her husband, who was the human god of the empire, so that Esther might become the queen in her place and thus save her people from the slaughter. Both Vashti and Esther were courageous women. Vashti was willing to sacrifice her crown for the sake of womanhood, and Esther was willing to lay down her life, if necessary, for the sake of her people.

Women must Obey

If it please the king, let there go a royal commandment from him, and let it be written among the laws of the Persians and the Medes, that it be not altered, That Vashti come no more before king Ahasuerus; and let the king give her royal estate unto another that is better than she. Esther 1:19.

In lands where polygamy was practiced, men were afraid to give their wives freedom. Women had to obey their husbands' every wish and must never question their wisdom. This was especially true of the wives of princes and noblemen.

The princes were afraid that Vashti's act would become an example to millions of women in the vast empire, who craved freedom and equality, and who were ready to revolt against the tyranny of their husbands, especially those who had large harems.

CHAPTER TWO

Hadassah

And he brought up Hadassah, that is, Esther, his uncle's daughter: for she had neither father nor mother, and the maid was fair and beautiful; whom Mordecai, when her father and mother were dead, took for his own daughter. Esther 2:7.

Hadassah is an Aramaic name meaning "a bud." The Hebrew word *hadas* means "a myrtle tree." Hadassah was born in captivity, and her parents had given her a native name. Esther is a Persian name which means "star," or Venus, a Babylonian goddess (see Introduction).

Mordecai, being a palace servant, knew most of the king's servants and eunuchs. That is why Esther was left in the custody of the keeper of the women, the chief eunuch. The Lord gave Esther favor in the eyes of the keeper of women, who helped her to become the queen of Persia and wear the coveted crown.[4]

Execution in Persia

And when inquisition was made of the matter, it was found out; therefore they were both hanged on a tree: and it was written in the book of Chronicles before the king. Esther 2:23.

Capital punishment was carried out by means of crucifixion. The criminals were stretched on their crosses so that people could look at them and become fearful about attempting to commit crimes.

Apparently the translators of the book of Esther into Greek were unfamiliar with the manner of execution in the Persian empire.[5] Such acts were recorded every day. The term "chronicles," *barmu,* refers to the recording of daily events.

CHAPTER THREE

Haman

After these things did king Ahasuerus promote Haman the son of Hamedatha the Agagite, and advanced him, and set his seat above all the princes that were with him. Esther 3:1.

Haman is a Semitic name. The last part of Haman, *"man,"* in Aramaic

---

[4]See verse 15.

[5]See the commentary on Ezra 6:11, "Erecting a Cross," p. 4-5.

means "what, why," from *manna,* meaning "what is it?" The first two letters of his name might derive from the definite article "the," which in Hebrew is "*ha.*" Another example of this is in the name *Hamelek; ha* means "the" and *melek* means "king."

The term "Agagite" means that Haman is a descendant of King Agag, the Amalekite king whom Samuel had commanded King Saul to slay. But Saul did not follow through with Samuel's orders, and he lost his kingship over his disobedience to the prophet Samuel.[6] The storyteller refers to the ancient enmity between Israel and Amalek that points to the relationship between Haman and Mordecai.The enmity between the Jews, Arabians, Syrians, Edomites, Moabites, and Amalekites was smoldering in the Persian Empire as well as in Israel.[7]

Some biblical authorities believe that Haman was a Greek and that he hated the Jews.[8] But this theory cannot be true. During this period the Greeks were hardly known in the Near East. The Persian armies had subjugated a part of Greece and crushed all Greek resistance in other provinces that remained independent. The Greek conquest of the Near East and the destruction of the Achaemenian Empire began in 311 BCE after the battle of Essus.

Human Deities

And when Haman saw that Mordecai bowed not, nor did him reverence, then was Haman full of wrath. Esther 3:5.

Bowing to anything or anybody besides God, the Creator of the heavens and the earth, was idolatry in the eyes of the Jews.[9] Haman was a pagan high official in the realm of King Akhshirash of Persia, a mortal man made a deity by the princes of the realm and the people.

Mordecai was requested not only to salute the pagan prime minister, Haman, but also to worship him. *Barak osagid* in Aramaic means "to kneel and worship." This is why Mordecai refused to obey the command. Being a Jew, a worshiper of the only true God, Mordecai would not acquiesce to Haman's request or accept the counsel of his fellow officials and servants.

---

[6]See 1 Sam. 15:8.

[7]Neh. 6:1-10.

[8]Dr. Lamsa believed that Haman was an Edomite, a descendant of Esau.

[9]Ex. 20:3.

In the book of Daniel, Shadrach, Meshach, and Abednego refused to bow and worship the statue of Nebuchadnezzar and his gods.[10] Daniel also refused the command of the king of Persia and was willing to die rather than violate the ordinances of his religion.

Much of humankind's difficulties have sprung from infidelity and worship of human personalities and false material gods.

CHAPTER FOUR

A Drastic Ordinance

All the king's servants, and the people of the king's provinces, do know, that whosoever, whether man or woman, shall come unto the king into the inner court, who is not called, there is one law of his to put him to death, except such to whom the king shall hold out the golden sceptre, that he may live: but I have not been called to come in unto the king these thirty days. Esther 4:11.

This drastic ordinance was enacted to protect the lives of kings from usurpers and rivals. In those days, kings were often assassinated by their wives, sons, and other relatives. At times, conspirators would also plot with one of the king's wives to murder the ruling monarch. In addition to this, jealousy between wives in large harems would engender hatred against a king who took sides and who favored some and punished others.

Akhshirash had many wives and concubines as well as many servants. Therefore, he was always in danger of being assassinated. But the Lord touched the king's heart so that he held out to Esther the golden scepter that was in his hand.[11]

Esther's Destiny

For if thou altogether holdest thy peace at this time, then shall there enlargement and deliverance arise to the Jews from another place; but thou and thy father's house shall be destroyed: and who knoweth whether thou art come to the kingdom for such a time as this? Esther 4:14.

"For such a time as this" means, "You have come to the kingdom for this

---

[10]Dan. 3:1-20.

[11]Esther 5:2.

cause." Esther was an orphan girl who was prepared for a great mission. Even though it was unlawful for Queen Esther to appear before the king to petition him on behalf of her people, nevertheless, she risked her life and appeared before him.[12] Just as the wicked Haman was preparing to destroy the Jews, the Lord was preparing Esther to be a deliverer of her people.

CHAPTER FIVE

An Idiom

Then said the king unto her, What wilt thou queen Esther? And what is thy request? it shall be given unto thee to the half of the kingdom. Esther 5:3.

"It shall be given unto thee to the half of the kingdom." Such utterances were not taken literally. Near Eastern monarchs, princes, and nobles were magnanimous in their promises and rewards. This Near Eastern idiom is similar to the English idiom, "The sky is the limit."

In the New Testament, we are told that on his birthday (which became a state occasion), Herod gave a banquet for his officials, captains, and prominent Galilean leaders. During the celebration, the daughter of Herodias, a little girl, entertained the guests with dancing. Herod was so pleased with her that he promised to give her half of his kingdom. What would a little girl do with half of the kingdom?[13] It was an idiomatic expression of speech meaning, "ask what you will."

In biblical days, when a king died his kingdom was divided among his sons. A king was sole owner of the kingdom and all his possessions went to his heirs. Constantine appointed his sons to rule in various sections of his vast empire just as Herod the great had done with his sons. Kings and emperors had absolute power.

CHAPTER SIX

A Sign of Condemnation

And Mordecai came again to the king's gate. But Haman hastened to his house mourning, and having his head covered. Esther 6:12.

---

[12]Esther 4:10-11.

[13]See Mk. 6:21-23.

When a man was sentenced to death, his face was covered as a sign of his treacherous act. In such cases people would spit on the condemned person and could also beat him.[14] Covering one's head entirely was also a sign of mourning.

CHAPTER NINE

King's Scribe

But when Esther came before the king, he commanded by letters that his wicked device, which he devised against the Jews, should return upon his own head, and that he and his sons should be hanged on the gallows. Esther 9:25.

The Eastern Aramaic text reads: "When Esther came before the king, the scribe would say, Let the wicked plots which were devised against the Jews return upon the head of him who had devised them, and let him and his sons be hanged on the gallows."

The Aramaic word *sapra,* "scribe," is omitted in the King James Version but is retained in the Hebrew text. The error is caused by the translator, who evidently overlooked the word. Without the noun "scribe," the antecedent is missing. According to the King James Version, the reference is made to the king himself; that is, instead of condemning Haman's evil devices and putting his sons to death, the king condemns his own devices and commands that his own sons be put to death. This is misleading.

When Queen Esther appeared before the king, she first saw the scribe, who informed the king of her coming to the king's house. As the queen waited in the scribe's office, the scribe condemned Haman's evil acts as well as those of Haman's sons, who later were hanged by the command of the king.

CHAPTER TEN

Seeking Welfare

For Mordecai the Jew was next unto king Ahasuerus, and great among the Jews, and accepted of the multitude of his brethren, seeking the wealth of his people, and speaking peace to all his seed. Esther 10:3.

---

[14]See Lk. 22:63-65.

The last portion of the verse in Aramaic reads differently: ". . . and he sought the good of his people and spoke on behalf of all his race." The Aramaic word *tabta* means "good, favor, welfare, interest." It has nothing to do with material wealth or monetary gains. Mordecai was not that type of man. He had been willing to die for his people if necessary. Moreover, Jewish leaders interceded on behalf of their people without any remuneration.

INTRODUCTION TO JOB

It is assumed by some authorities that Job was not a Hebrew from Canaan. Nevertheless, Job was a prophet who believed and communed with the living God, the God of Abraham. Job might have been a Hebrew descendant of Abraham, who lived on the other side of the River Euphrates.

Job was from the land of Uz in Mesopotamia or southeast Arabia. Uz was a son of Aram, and the Arameans were a kindred people of the Hebrews. The Arameans also revered the Lord, the God of Israel, and for a long time preserved their racial ties with the Hebrews, a branch of their families which had crossed the River Euphrates with Abraham. Isaac married Rebekah, a sister of Laban the Aramean. Jacob married his Uncle Laban's daughters, Leah and Rachel.[1]

Job's trials took place in Padan-Aram (Mesopotamia). We are told that Job's donkeys, camels, sheep, and cattle were raided by the Sabeans and Chaldeans.[2] Had Job been born in the land of Canaan, the author of the book would have mentioned the name of his father and his tribe. Uz is mentioned in the book of Jeremiah.[3]

Job, no doubt, was one of the richest patriarchs on the other side of the River Euphrates; his fame had spread all over the Near East, and his conduct and faith had been emulated by those who revered God. Wealthy men in the Near East were known even in foreign lands. Merchants, wayfarers, and caravans carried their fame from one place to another. Their possessions and gold and silver became common topics in towns, cities, and camps. Evidently, Job was familiar with mining, astronomy, and other sciences that were discovered by the Babylonians (Chaldeans).

This book is entitled "Job" because it is written about him, but it was not written by Job himself. In the opening verse of the book Job is placed in the third person: "There was a man in the land of Uz."[4] However, there is a possibility that Job might have dictated the work.

In the Near East, a book about a ruler was called by the name of the ruler, and the name of the scribe may never appear in it. Sometimes the scribe places his name at the end, as a writer or a copyist.

---

[1]Gen. 29:15-28.

[2]Job 1:15-17.

[3]See Jer. 25:19-21.

[4]Job 1:1.

Job must have lived around 800 BCE. He is also mentioned in the book of Ezekiel.[5] Some biblical authorities place the date at 1520 BCE. If this were the case, Moses and Joshua would have written about him. The book, indeed, is inspired and is a narrative of a pious and wise man whose faith and loyalty to God had never been questioned.

The style of the book of Job has never been duplicated or surpassed. It still stands as a great work of ancient Near Eastern wisdom. The book is noted for its depth and sublimity. Indeed, the book was written by an author who was inspired by God to produce such a poetic and dramatic dialogue depicting ancient belief systems in debate form. For the ancient world it is a book of great magnitude dealing with some scientific work without equal in thought or in diction for that time. The writer knew that the earth was round and floating in the air.[6]

The book of Job answers one of the oldest human riddles: Why does a pious or righteous person suffer? A partial answer is: There is no such thing as a perfect, pious or righteous individual. No human being can attain absolute perfection and righteousness. God is the only righteous and perfect one; a human being is constantly learning and maturing. A human reaps what he or she sows whether it is good or bad. Moses had told Israel that doing good brought its own blessings and doing evil its own curses.[7] Nonetheless, the book of Job's final argument is that no one really understands why some suffering just exists without any explanation.

The first two chapters of Job deal with a heavenly drama between God and the accuser. This creates the setting for the narrative and belief systems that were to be argued and debated. It is very difficult to read and understand how a loving and compassionate God would take counsel from Satan and then grant him power to torment Job, a pious man, with such tremendous suffering. But in a drama, anything can happen, at any time, and in any place.[8]

Many modern biblical scholars propose that Job was a fictitious character and that he did not really exist at all. However that may have been, whether Job was an actual person or merely a fictional character in this great

---

[5]Ezk. 14:14.

[6]Job 26:7.

[7]Dt. Chapter 28.

[8]Modern scholars have diverging notions about the dating of the book and how it was written. Some suggest that it was composed during the time of the patriarchs but more material was gradually added to the book of Job over time.

narrative, written by a wise man or a group of wise men, is not important. One thing we know is that Satan can neither sit in the presence of God nor tempt the divine with evil devices. God is purity, goodness, and love. The Divine cannot be tempted with evil. The most important idea in the book is the fact that there have always been such upright men in the world as Job, who revere God above their possessions, children, and even their own lives.

The contents of the book show that it was written as a dialogue in a most vivid and dramatic style. This is a story and must not be understood in a literal manner. The writer tells us that whenever God's sons presented themselves before the deity, Satan came, too. And God, instead of carrying on a conversation with the sons of God, conversed with Satan only.

What the book reveals is that there is no such thing as a perfect man, that no one is perfect but God. Even Jesus, who was good, refused to be called good. The central teaching of the book informs the reader that those who trust in God cannot be shaken or utterly destroyed by material losses, calamities, and disease. Job is an example of a pious and wise man who revered God above everything else in his life.

CHAPTER ONE

Job, a Wealthy and Upright Man

There was a man in the land of Uz, whose name was Job; and that man was perfect and upright, and one that feared God, and eschewed evil And there was born unto him seven sons and three daughters. His substance also was seven thousand sheep and three thousand camels, and five hundred she asses, and a very great household; so that this man was the greatest of all the men of the east.
Job 1:1-3.

During the time of Job, sickness was commonly believed to be a punishment from God for sin. People held the notion that even natural blindness was the result of sin. In the first century CE, Jesus of Nazareth challenged this belief when he healed a blind man. His disciples asked him the question: "Who did sin, this man or his parents, that he was born blind?" Jesus, as a Torah teacher and prophet, replied: "Neither did he sin nor his parents."[9] Nevertheless, at other times Jesus did imply that some

[9]Jn. 9:3, Eastern Aramaic Peshitta text, Lamsa translation.

sickness could be caused by sin but never as a punishment from God. For example, when Jesus healed a man who had been sick for 38 years, he said to him: "Behold, you are healed; do not sin again, for something worse might happen to you than at first."[10] In those New Testament days, various illnesses were also attributed to evil forces. Medical terms describing many forms of mental illness were unknown. This is why people believed that the insane were supposed to be possessed by evil spirits.

Job was a decent and innocent man, and according to the story, he endured severe punishment and affliction. But there is not even the slightest suggestion that he was afflicted because of his sins. The author of the book of Job tells us that Job was innocent[11] and upright and one who revered God and turned away from evil. Therefore, Job could not have been justly punished by a good and loving God, nor could Satan have tempted God.

Sons of God

Now there was a day when the sons of God came to present themselves before the Lord, and Satan came also among them. Job 1:6.

The phrase "sons of God" in this passage refers to "good men," that is "believers in God." There were always a remnant of men and women who remained loyal to God. In the Near East, these people were called "sons of God"—spiritual sons—to distinguish them from sons of men—materialists, or descendants of Cain.[12] The sons of God were pious men like Job who had been steadfast in the way of God. Job was probably the most pious among them. This is why Satan, opponent to truth, singled him out.

Satan represents the old adversary, the enemy, who caused humans to transgress against their fellow creatures. Satan, the antagonist, is included in this episode simply because he is the author of sin. According to the storyteller, Satan is envious and despises Job. He hates seeing such an

---

[10]Jn. 5:14, Eastern Aramaic Peshitta text, Lamsa translation.

[11]In the Aramaic text the phrase in the first verse reads: ". . .And that man was innocent and upright." In the King James Version, the word "perfect" is incorrect.

[12]Gen. 6:1-2.

upright man as Job trying to do good and refraining from evil.[13]

In this wonderful narrative, we see that there were some men who were envious of Job and thought that he was a hypocrite. They also suspected that he used his religious life and piety to camouflage his improper business activities. Even the so-called friends who came to comfort him tried to make him confess his evil deeds.

Sabeans

And the Sabeans fell upon them, and took them away; yea, they have slain the servants with the edge of the sword; and I only am escaped alone to tell thee. Job 1:15.

Sabeans are a Mesopotamian people, descendants of the ancient Babylonians. There is a community of these people that live in Iraq. They are also known as the people of St. John the Baptist. They practice water baptism and believe in the teaching of John the Baptist.

The Sabeans are a very peaceful people, whose occupation for centuries has been silver work. They are noted silversmiths, engravers, and craftsmen in the Near East.

In the ancient days, the Sabeans, like many other nomad tribes in southwestern Mesopotamia and the Arabian desert, at times raided peaceful, agricultural communities. Until the rise of Islam, Arabian tribes raided each other, killing, plundering herds and flocks, and carrying away other booty.

Job Mourns

Then Job arose, and rent his mantle, and shaved his head, and fell down upon the ground, and worshiped. Job 1:20.

To rip one's mantle and shave one's head were symbolic acts of mourning over a great calamity. Even in the modern Near East, men tear their clothes and women cut off their hair and inflict wounds on their faces as an expression of their deep grief over losing their dear ones or similar

---

[13]Actually, the term "Satan" is symbolic of the men who envied Job and accused hin of impiety and of being a worker of evil deeds. They believed he only worshiped God for the blessings.

calamities.

There are many portions of the Bible that show how the Israelites practiced this custom of tearing their clothing. For example, when Israel was crushed and defeated by the Philistines, a messenger brought the sad and terrible news to Eli, who was the high priest at that time. Upon hearing the messenger, Eli immediately tore his clothes and put earth upon his head.[14] On another occasion, priests were commanded by Moses not to rend their clothes as a sign of mourning over two of Aaron's sons, who were burned in the tabernacle of the congregation.[15]

A great calamity had befallen Job. His wealth was plundered, his sons and daughters were dead. And by shaving his hair and tearing his clothes, he showed his humility and deep grief to the people around him.

CHAPTER TWO

A Father Visiting with His Children

Again there was a day when the sons of God came to present themselves before the Lord, and Satan came also among them to present himself before the Lord. And the Lord said unto Satan from whence comest thou? And Satan answered the Lord, and said, From going to and fro in the earth, and from walking up and down in it. And the Lord said unto Satan, Hast thou considered my servant Job, that there is none like him in the earth, a perfect and upright man, one that feareth God and escheweth evil? and still he holdeth fast his integrity, although thou movedst me against him, to destroy him without cause. Job 2:1-3.

Near Eastern kings and princes married many women, and some of them had numerous children. In the book of Judges, the biblical writer tells us that Gideon had seventy sons. Also, in the book of Second Kings, Jehu had the seventy sons of King Ahab slain.[16]

Although these famous leaders and kings loved their children, they had no time to see all of them or talk and play with them. Therefore, there was an appointed day when all the royal children would meet with their father in the large royal tent. Furthermore, during religious festivals, the family is united again. In some cases, the king knows neither the identity nor the

---

[14]1 Sam. 4:12.

[15]Lev. 10:6.

[16]See Judges 9:5, 2 Ki. 10:6.

names of some of his own sons. Most of the monarchs' sons were reared by governors in various regions of the country. "And Ahab had seventy sons in Samaria. And they were brought up by the nobles of the city. And Jehu wrote a letter and sent it to Samaria, to the princes of Jezreel, to the elders, and to those who brought up Ahab's children, saying . . ."[17]

The author of the book of Job likens God to a Near Eastern monarch who sets up an appointed day to see his many sons. As has been said in the introduction of this commentary, the book is a dialogue that was to answer an extremely difficult question: Why do good, righteous people suffer? The three men, the young man, and Job came to the conclusion that there is no one that is one hundred percent righteous except God.

The entire purpose of the book is to build up the dialogue between all the so called comforters and Job, arguing and debating various points of view. The opening two chapters establish the plot to show that God allowed all the calamities to happen. In reality, Satan could not come into the presence of God, who is pure light. Nor could the Lord have listened to the devilish envy and advice. How could Satan move or provoke God into doing evil? Nevertheless, for the sake of the story, the author puts God in that position.

Smitten with a Dreadful Disease

So went Satan forth from the presence of the Lord, and smote Job with sore boils from the sole of his foot unto his crown. And he took him a potsherd to scrape himself withal; and he sat down among the ashes. Job. 2:7-8.

The Aramaic word *shookhna* means "cancer." This malady creates intense burning that makes the flesh waste away.[18] Boils are not that serious an illness. Many people suffer from boils. During World War I, the Assyrians, who were living in the north but fled to the south, suffered from the disease known as *sakhara,* "boils." These skin eruptions appeared on the nose and other places of the body. At that time, these terrible boils were blamed on too much consumption of dates.

Job's disease was cancer, and it was destroying his body completely. One cannot rub a boil with a piece of potsherd, but one can rub the areas that are afflicted with cancer. Job had feared this dreadful disease and finally was overcome by it.

---

[17]2 Ki. 10:1, Eastern Aramaic Peshitta text, Lamsa translation.

[18]Job 33:21.

Job felt that he was a pious man and free from all evil things, but the writer reveals that there is no one totally pious but God. Job was reminded of the wickedness by the men who were arguing with him. He was told that if he had not done certain evils, then his servants must have done wrong. The men questioned the manner in which Job had accumulated his vast riches and wealth. What the book ultimately demonstrates is that there is no one righteous, and no one has all the answers to life's tragedies and complexities.

Job's Friends

Now when Job's three friends heard of all this evil that was come upon him, they came every one from his own place; Eliphaz the Temanite, and Bildad the Shuhite, and Zophar the Naamathite: for they had made an appointment together to come to mourn with him, and to comfort him. Job 2:11.

The three friends of Job were the wisest of men in those days, and because of their fame and wisdom, were known in all adjacent lands.

Eliphaz was a native of Teman (south), the Negeb, which was ancient Edom. During this period, the people in this place were renowned for their wisdom and counsel. But the prophet Jeremiah declared there was no more wisdom in Teman and that counsel perished from the prudent and their wisdom had been taken away.[19] Bildad the Shuhite and Zophar the Naamathite were members of the Aramean tribes who dwelt in the desert, also known as Naabatites. The descendants of these tribes were some of the first Arabs in Edom and northwestern Arabia to embrace Christianity. However, they later converted to Islam in the early part of the seventh century.

These wise men tried to induce Job to confess his guilt and seek forgiveness. They believed that Job's affliction was the result of his sins. Job had no guilt to confess; his conscience was clear. As far as he knew and understood, he had done nothing wrong.

Job Disfigured

And when they lifted up their eyes afar off, and knew him not, they lifted up their voice, and wept; and they rent every one his mantle, and sprinkled dust upon their

---

[19]See Jer. 49:7, Lamsa translation.

heads toward heaven. Job 2:12.

In this instance, "knew him not" means that he was so afflicted that they did not recognize him. The three friends could hardly believe that it was Job who sat in ashes scraping himself with a potsherd.

In the Near East, when a man is afflicted or reduced to poverty, his friends say: "I saw him, but I did not recognize him." Of course, the three friends who came to see him and comfort him expected to find him deep in grief, but Job's wounds were so great that they altered his physical appearance. That is why they wept and tore their garments.

As stated earlier, the tearing of garments was an ancient Near Eastern custom. Even in the modern world of the Near East, during funerals and great tragedies, men tear their garments and women cut off their hair as a token of deep mourning. It was recorded in Scripture that when Abner was slain by Joab, David ordered the army commanders and nobles to tear their clothes and put on sackcloth.[20]

Seven Days of Silence

So they sat down with him upon the ground seven days and seven nights, and none spake a word unto him: for they saw that his grief was very great. Job 2:13.

Seven is a sacred number that appears in the Bible quite often. For example: Near Eastern biblical writers refer to seven days in the creation epic, seven wells, seven virgins, and in the book of the Revelation, seven stars, seven candlesticks, seven churches, and seven angels.

The three friends of Job who had come to comfort and console him sat in silence for seven days. When entering a house of mourning, Near Easterners sit down in silence for a long time. On such occasions no greetings are exchanged. After a long period of quietness, the silence is broken; then one of the men starts to comfort the mourners. At times, the silence is broken by one of the mourners. The seven days and seven nights of silence showed that these wise men were deeply grieved for their friend Job.

---

[20]See 2 Sam. 3:31, Lam. 2:10.

CHAPTER THREE

Cursing the Day of Birth and the Night of Conception

After this opened Job his mouth, and cursed his day. And Job spake, and said, Let the day perish wherein I was born, and the night in which it was said, There is a man child conceived. . .let it not be joined unto the days of the year, let it not come into the number of the month. Job 3:1-3, 6.

According to ancient astrological beliefs, the particular day of one's birth or conception determines one's fate and future. Astrology, astronomy, and other studies of the heavenly bodies were common among the Assyrians and the Egyptians. They believed time was an important element in a human being's life and that it had something to do with the day of his or her conception, birth, and death. The whole universe, including humans, is one organism. These beliefs are still maintained in many regions of the world. But time and space have no place in the realm of the spirit.

Job thought he was conceived on a bad night and born on an unlucky day. That is why he cursed both the day and the night.

Jeremiah also cursed the day in which he was born.[21] Near Easterners, when mourning or despondent, often curse the day of their birth and wish they never had been conceived. On such dark occasions when life is bitter, death appears to be sweeter.[22]

Leviathan, A Great Evil

Let them curse it that curse the day who are ready to raise up their mourning. Job 3:8.

The Eastern Aramaic text reads: "Let them who curse it who curse the day, who are ready to stir up Leviathan. The Aramaic word *lewiathan* ("leviathan," sea monster, serpent, whale) metaphorically means "a great evil." It has been confused with *aoliathan* that means "lamentation, wailing, or mourning for the dead." The two words are similar in Aramaic. This is why the King James Version translates the word as "mourning" instead of Leviathan. It is another term for evil forces or trouble. Job here

---

[21]Jer. 20:14.

[22]See verses 4-7.

is speaking of the awakening of evil forces that were responsible for his afflictions.

Undoubtedly, the question of Job's piety and integrity was raised by many of his neighbors and associates. Job was a very wealthy man. The people wondered how he had accumulated so many possessions.

Childbirth

Why died I not from the womb? why did I not give up the ghost when I came out of the belly? Why did the knees prevent me? or why the breasts that I should suck? Job 3:11-12.

The Eastern Aramaic text reads: "Why did I not die from the womb? Why did I come forth at birth? Why was I reared at my mother's knee? Why did I suck the breasts?" Prior to World War II, hospitals and maternity wards were unknown in many cities and towns in the Near East, and especially in little villages, sheep camps, and the deserts. Most of the people knew no more about the nature of disease than their ancient ancestors had known.

The old methods of child delivery were still practiced. When a pregnant woman was ready to give birth, she was assisted by two midwives, who held her arms and helped her walk around the house or the tent. Some women, however, required no assistance.

In most houses, and especially in tents, privacy was lacking, and there were no beds on which the women might lie. When a child was delivered, the mother had to be careful to prevent the child from falling on the hard ground. This was the reason Job says: "Why was I reared at my mother's knee? Why did I suck the breasts?" Job wishes his mother's knees had let him drop on the ground so that he might have died.

Job's Misery

Wherefore is light given to him that is in misery, and life unto the bitter in soul. Job 3:20.

Job wonders why light, which is one of the most precious things in the world, should be given to a human being who is in trouble and misery? And why is life given to one who is bitter in soul. More plainly, Job is saying, "Why am I living?" He was stricken with cancer and his flesh was falling apart. He saw death as his only ally and comfort.

Hidden Future

Why is light given to a man whose way is hid, and whom God hath hedged in? Job 3:23.

In this passage "light" means "joy, happiness, delight." Here Job wonders why God gives men wealth and fame and the desire to enjoy life and yet hides his future and fences him in. Job's tragedy was very sudden. In the past, God had given him prosperity, children, and fame. But now he found himself trapped, his wealth gone, and his children slain.

Job wonders why human beings have no power over their destiny. Why can people not map their future and see the dangers that are ahead of them? Or, why do human beings, with all the knowledge with which God has endowed them, lose their direction? Then again, Job questions why people should suffer and pass away.

Such questions are not new. Throughout the centuries humans have been bewildered about certain unhappy events in their lives, in particular, sickness, suffering, and death. Today, we know that disease can be the result of erroneous thinking, errors in human judgment, and transgressions against God's natural laws. Yet, in spite of this knowledge, we are still left with many unanswered questions.

CHAPTER FOUR

Feeble Knees

Behold, thou hast instructed many, and thou hast strengthened the weak hands. Thy words have upholden him that was falling, and thou hast strengthened the feeble knees. Job 4:3-4.

"Feeble knees" is a Near Eastern saying that refers both to people with uncertain, weak, shaky, or unsteady feet and to those who are unsure of their lives. In these words, Eliphaz was reminding Job that he had strengthened many men who were falling and those who were uncertain of their faith in God and in the divine true path of life.

Many of the men whom Job had helped and strengthened had had experiences like his own. Some of them had suffered severe tragedies, some had been sick, and others had lost their possessions. And now Job was troubled because of the losses that he had suffered and because of his disease that was consuming him. Eliphaz seems to be suggesting that one who has been a counselor and instructor to others should practice what he preaches.

Fear Causes Sickness

Is not this thy fear, thy confidence, thy hope, and the uprightness of thy ways? Job 4:6.

The Aramaic word *adlaiah* means "blame, fault, censure." *Adal* means "to find fault." The Eastern Aramaic text reads: "Behold, your fear is to be blamed, and your trust in the integrity of your way."

Eliphaz claims that Job's fears were due to faults or blunders that he had committed. Eliphaz is sure that if Job were not guilty of some sin he would not suffer: ". . . whoever perished, being innocent?"[23]

The Law of Compensation

Remember, I pray thee, who ever perished, being innocent? or where were the righteous cut off? Even as I have seen, they that plow iniquity, and sow wickedness, reap the same. Job 4:7-8.

Eliphaz, like other Near Easterners, believed in the law of compensation, or cause and effect.[24] What one sows one reaps.

Job had been wondering why he was stricken and bereaved of his children. He thought that he had been innocent all of his life, that he had helped the poor, the widows, and had wronged no one.

Eliphaz was not quite sure of Job's innocence. He had seen Job's flocks, herds, camels, and other possessions increasing, and now he wondered if Job had acquired all of these earthly goods righteously. Like other rich men, Job's stewards and servants probably had loaned money at interest, had kept the pledges of those who had been unable to pay, and, at times, might have acted crookedly so that they could make more money for their master. In other words, Job might have been a pious man, but what did he

---

[23]See verse 7. Also see comment "The Law of Compensation" (Job 4:7-8).
[24]Ps. 7:14-17.

know about his servants, shepherds, and cameleers? Eliphaz believed that no mortal man can be justified before God.

Catastrophe

By the blast of God they perish, and by the breath of his nostrils are they consumed. The roaring of the lion, and the voice of the fierce lion, and the teeth of the young lions, are broken. The old lion perisheth for lack of prey, and the stout lion's whelps are scattered abroad. Job 4:9-11.

Eliphaz depicts the kings, rulers, and dictators of the world as lions, which symbolize power and dominion. He speaks metaphorically to indicate that the wicked rich men of his day were to be punished for their evil deeds. Their wealth would be plundered and taken from them. They would be like a lion whose teeth are broken and whose fierce voice is silenced; they would no longer be able to prey upon other animals. They would also be like a lioness whose cubs were scattered for the lack of prey.

Job had been one of the richest men of his day, but now he was reduced to poverty. His friends and acquaintances also had deserted him, and he was afflicted with the most dreaded disease in the Near East.

A Psychic Experience

Now a thing was secretly brought to me, and mine ear received a little thereof. In thoughts from the visions of the night, when deep sleep falleth on men Fear came upon me, and trembling, which made all my bones to shake. Then a spirit passed before my face; the hair on my flesh stood up: It stood still but I could not discern the form thereof: an image was before mine eyes, there was silence, and I heard a voice, saying, Shall mortal man be more just than God? Shall a man be more pure than his maker? Job 4:12-17.

Again, Eliphaz cited one of his experiences that he had seen in a night vision to Job. It was an experience that shook his body and made his hair stand on end. A great message was to be revealed to him.

In the vision, Eliphaz was told through the spirit that mortal man is neither righteous nor pure. Righteousness and purity belong to God alone. He wanted to persuade Job to confess that he had done some evil and that is why he was smitten. Job was reluctant to admit he had done anything wrong.

Eliphaz was also shocked when he heard the spirit telling him that no man was truly righteous. He also believed that men could attain the purity and righteousness of God. Even when Jesus of Nazareth was called a good master, he replied that no one was good.[25]

Wealthy Men's Dark Destiny

Behold, he put no trust in his servants; and his angels he charged with folly: How much less in them that dwell in houses of clay, whose foundation is in the dust, which are crushed before the moth? They are destroyed from morning to evening: they perish for ever without any regarding it. Doth not their excellency which is in them go away? they die, even without wisdom. Job 4:18-21.

The Eastern Aramaic text reads: "Behold, he put no trust in his servants; and his messengers he struck with amazement; Even those who dwell in decorated houses of clay, whose foundation is in the dust, shall be humbled before the thick darkness. They shall be afflicted from morning to evening, that they may not dwell for ever; yea, they shall perish. Behold, their possessions are taken away from them; and the rest of them shall die without wisdom."

This wise man portrayed a gloomy future for the wealthy and the prominent. He declared that they were plagued with many problems with the wealth they possessed. They did not trust their servants and ambassadors and had no confidence in anyone but themselves. Their servants were amazed when their masters revealed some of their hidden secrets.

Although these men lived in decorated palaces, their foundations were in the dust; that is, they had no firm foundation. Sooner or later, these men were plundered and humbled by disaster, and all they possessed was gone.

Job was not the only wealthy person who had been reduced to poverty or stricken by a terrible disease; thousands of men before and after him had met with the same fate.

CHAPTER FIVE

Wicked Reduced to Poverty

I have seen the foolish taking root: but suddenly I cursed his habitation. His children are far from safety, and they are crushed in the gate, neither is there any

---

[25]Lk. 18:19.

to deliver them. Job 5:3-4.

The Eastern Aramaic text reads: "I have seen the wicked prosper; but his habitation is suddenly destroyed. His children are far from salvation, and they are humiliated at the gate, and there is no one to deliver them."

Again, Eliphaz tells Job that the wicked prospered because of their evil deeds, greed, and confiscation of property from the weak and poor. But, this prosperity is only temporary. Sooner or later it is taken away from them and their children are not secure. They are also defeated by their enemies at the gate of the city or at the doors of their houses.

Job had lost not only his dear children but was reduced to poverty. His so called "comforter" hints to Job that his case is not unusual, that this always happens to the wicked.[26]

Falsehood Is Hidden in Man

Although affliction cometh not forth of the dust, neither doth trouble spring out of the ground. Job 5:6.

The Aramaic word *shookra* means "falsehood." The Eastern text reads: "For falsehood does not come forth from the dust, nor does iniquity spring out of the ground."

Humanity's troubles and difficulties come from within themselves; that is, human beings chart their own path. There is a Near Eastern parable that says: "The worm of a tree is within itself"; that is, an individual, through good thinking, receives good things and through bad thinking, receives bad things.

Troubles of Life

Yet man is born unto trouble, as the sparks fly upward. Job 5:7.

The last section of the Eastern Aramaic text reads: ". . . as sure as the wild birds fly." Job is saying that a human being is born into trouble, struggle, and hard labor. The span of life is full of sorrows, difficulties, and insecurities that befall people as suddenly as a bird flies.

In those ancient days, hard manual labor was looked upon as a curse and

[26]See Job 12:5-6.

the lot of slaves, the poor, and the weak. Most of the men and women of the higher classes shunned work.

Here Job speaks of the grinding toil that one has to go through in order to make a living. Even the rich were not free from trouble and toil,[27] nor is anyone sure of the future. Truth and righteousness are the only safe guides for directing a human being's course of life.

Nature on Man's Side

For thou shall be in league with the stones of the field: and the beasts of the field shall be at peace with thee. Job 5:23.

Such sayings are used metaphorically. "You shall be in league with the stones of the field" means, "Nature will be on your side, and whatever you do will prosper." In the Near East, it is often said: "Stones talked to him," or, "Asses gave him admonition."

When people are at peace with their Creator, universal forces are on their side, and they can overcome any problem or difficulty.

CHAPTER SIX

Job Seeks Healing

Even that it would please God to destroy me; that he would let loose his hand, and cut me off. Job 6:9.

The Eastern Aramaic text reads: "So that God would hearken to cleanse me, and to spread out his hand and make me whole."

Job is pleading with God for help that he might be healed and live. This is consistent with Job's patience and his firm faith in God. ". . . so that I may be restored to my strength without measure; for I have not lied against the words of the Holy One."[28] "Do not withdraw thy help from me; and let not thy dread terrify me."[29]

---

[27]Ecc. 2:22-23.

[28]Job 6:10, Eastern Aramaic Peshitta text, Lamsa translation.

[29]Job 13:21, Eastern Aramaic Peshitta text, Lamsa translation.

Peace and Good Deeds

To him that is afflicted pity should be showed from his friend; but he forsaketh the fear of the Almighty. Job 6:14.

The Eastern Aramaic text reads: "He who withholds peace from his friend, forsakes the worship of the Almighty." The Aramaic word *dikhlety* means "worship, reverence, fear." In this instance it means "worship." Worship without peace and good deeds is dead, as faith without works is dead. Peace always reigns in the house of the righteous. Like light, peace must be shared so it may lighten the path of those seeking the way of God.

Israel's prophets exhorted the people to extend kindness one to another and to strangers, widows, and orphans. Jesus of Nazareth, in his teaching, said: "For I was hungry, and you gave me food; I was thirsty, and you gave me drink; I was a stranger and you took me in."[30] Charity and good works are the manifestations of true religion. Jesus emphasized that meeting the basic needs of people reveals the kingdom of God in action.

Deceitfulness

My brethren have dealt deceitfully as a brook, and as the stream of brooks they pass away. Job 6:15.

During severe droughts in Arabia and other arid lands of the Near East, springs, streams, and brooks that once had been prolific suddenly dry up. The shepherds and travelers who visit the springs and streams are greatly disappointed when they find them dry.

The term "deceitful" is used because no one can tell when brooks and streams will dry up. This is also true of deceitful, ungodly men—no one knows how long their friendship will last. Job was disappointed with his friends. He expected comfort; instead, they heaped scorn upon him. Instead of bringing consolation, his comforters added mischief to his sorrows.[31]

Insincere Friends and Comforters

Which are blackish by reason of the ice, and wherein the snow is hid. What time

---

[30]Mt. 25:35, Eastern Aramaic Peshitta text, Lamsa translation.

[31]See verses 16-21 in the Lamsa translation.

they wax warm, they vanish: when it is hot, they are consumed out of their place. The paths of their way are turned aside; they go to nothing, and perish.
Job 6:16-18.

The opening verse 16 of the Eastern Aramaic text reads: "Those who were afraid of ice, much snow has fallen upon them." This is a Near Eastern saying that means, "When one was expecting just a little trouble, he received much." One can easily walk over the ice, but it is difficult to walk in deep snow. The reference here is to Job's comforters. He had expected some criticism from them, but they heaped too much on him.

On the other hand, Job had not sent for his comforters or asked them to do anything for him. When they came, however, he was eager to discuss his misfortune with them. But he found they were like dry brooks that disappoint the thirsty traveler.

CHAPTER SEVEN

Shadow Used for Clock

As a servant earnestly desireth the shadow, and as a hireling looketh for the reward of his work. Job 7:2.

In biblical times when clocks were unknown, time was determined by the declining shadows of the rocks and trees. The kings and princes used sundials like that of king Ahaz.[32] The Romans used sand containers to measure time.

The reference is to servants who worked long hours from early dawn to sunset. Being eager to go home, they frequently stopped to look at the shadows. The word "reward" is not correct in the last part of the verse. It should read, "as a hireling who looks to complete his job." Clocks and watches were rarely seen until World War I in some of the lands in the Near and Middle East. Time was determined by the crowing of the rooster and the shadows of the rocks.

Laborers in the Near East were paid in the evening. But, in some instances, when the employer was a government official or a rich person, the laborer's wages were held for months and even years, and in many cases, they were not paid at all. This custom prevailed until World War I.

---

[32]2 Ki. 20:9-11.

"Behold, the wage of the labourers who have reaped your fields, that which you have fraudulently kept back, cries; and the cry of the reapers has already entered into the ears of the Lord of Sabaoth."[33]

Life Is Eternal

O remember that my life is wind: mine eye shall no more see good. Job 7:7.

In Aramaic, the word that means "spirit" also means "wind." The Eastern Aramaic text reads: "O remember that the spirit is still alive; even yet my eye shall again see good." Job believed in the immortality of the spirit, life eternal. He knew that the spirit is indestructible.

Ruha has many meanings in Aramaic such as "spirit, wind, pride, rheumatism," and it is often mistranslated. Jesus said, "It is the spirit that gives life; the body is of no account . . ."[34] "Do not be afraid of those who kill the body . . ."[35]

Eternal life is compared to the spirit because spirit is indestructible. But temporal life is like the wind—it passes away.[36] James compares life to vapor, which appears for only a little while and then disappears.[37] Job was speaking of life hereafter.

Job's Help Delayed

When I say, My bed shall comfort me, my couch shall ease my complaint; Then thou scarest me with dreams, and terrifiest me through visions. Job 7:13-14.

The Eastern Aramaic text reads: "For I said that thou shalt comfort me, and I will be relieved of the pain of my sick bed. And, behold, thou dost scare me with dreams, and terrify me through visions."

Job complains to God because of his severe wound. He had been looking to God for comfort and for healing, but instead he is terrified with night visions and dreams. This is because the more he meditates on his troubles

---

[33]James 5:4, Eastern Aramaic Peshitta text, Lamsa translation. See also Lev. 19:13 and Mal. 3:5.

[34]Jn. 6:63, Eastern Aramaic Peshitta text, Lamsa translation.

[35]Mt. 10:28, Eastern Aramaic Peshitta text, Lamsa translation.

[36]See Ps. 78:39.

[37]James 4:14.

and sickness, the more he sees his past mistakes. Job is becoming more aware that he has brought this calamity upon himself.

God Stood by Job

So that my soul chooseth strangling, and death rather than my life. Job 7:15.

The Aramaic word *bakhar* means "to try" or "prove," and metaphorically, "to examine." The Aramaic word for "strangle" is *khenak*. Job here is speaking of his soul that has been purified and drawn out of destruction. The Eastern Aramaic text reads: "Thou hast drawn my life out of destruction, and my bones out of death."

Job's concern is the spiritual man—the spirit—and not the temporal man that passes away like a shadow.[38]

When silver and gold are purified, the impurities perish, but the fine gold and silver come out shining. At the end of Job's terrible trial and suffering, he came out happily and victoriously. At last, he was vindicated and his temporal losses were restored.

Job's Piety a Burden

I have sinned; what shall I do unto thee, O thou preserver of men? why hast thou set me as a mark against thee, so that I am a burden to myself? Job 7:20.

The Eastern Aramaic text reads: "If I have sinned; what have I done to thee, O thou Creator of men? Why hast thou caused me to encounter thee? Thou hast become a burden to me." The Aramaic word *hwet* (you have become) has been confused with *hwet* (I have become). The difference between these two words is merely in the position of a dot over or under the letter "t."

Job considered himself a pious man who had done nothing wrong to justify his afflictions; yet, seemingly, God had afflicted him just to test his loyalty. In other words, his righteousness and his loyalty to God had become a heavy burden upon him. He had been subjected to a harsh ordeal to prove his faith in God. Job did not expect to see a good man suffering.

---

[38]Ps. 8:4.

CHAPTER EIGHT

Spider's Web

Whose hope shall be cut off, and whose trust shall be a spider's web. He shall lean upon his house, but it shall not stand: he shall hold it fast, but it shall not endure. Job 8:14-15.

"Spider's web" is used figuratively, meaning "weakness" or "insecurity." Spiders' webs are so delicate that they are easily destroyed. This figure of speech is common in Near Eastern languages and literature. It was also used by Muhammad in the Koran.

The spider's web not only is weak but also becomes a trap to insects that take refuge in it. Such are the hopes and evil devices of the wicked. They are destroyed and cut off like a spider's web.

God Does Not Forsake the Righteous

Behold, God will not cast away a perfect man, neither will he help the evildoers. Job 8:20.

God does not cast away or reject the good or upright person who trusts in the divine ways. And when an individual suffers and is persecuted by evildoers, God is with that person and helps him or her overcome the difficulties. God does not forsake the righteous. The psalmist tells us: "Though he fall, he shall not be utterly cast down: for the Lord upholdeth him with his hand. I have been young, and now am old; yet I have not seen the righteous forsaken, nor his descendants begging bread."[39]

"Though he slay me, yet will I look for him . . . "[40] "Yea, though I walk through the valley of the shadow of death, I will fear no evil: for thou art with me . . . "[41] When Jesus was on the cross, he said: "My God, my God, for this I was spared."[42] God never forsook him while he was suffering on the cross. Even his enemies said he trusted in God and let God deliver him.

---

[39]Ps. 37:24-25, Eastern Aramaic Peshitta text, Lamsa translation.
[40]Job 13:15, Eastern Aramaic Peshitta text, Lamsa translation.
[41]Ps. 23:4, Eastern Aramaic Peshitta text, Lamsa translation. See also Ps. 34:8.
[42]Mt. 27:46, Eastern Aramaic Peshitta text, Lamsa translation.

CHAPTER NINE

The Bitterness of Job

How much less shall I answer him, and choose out my words to reason with him? Whom, though I were righteous, yet would I not answer, but I would make supplication to my judge. If I had called and he had answered me; yet would I not believe that he had hearkened unto my voice. For he breaketh me with a tempest, and multiplieth my wounds without cause. Job 9:14-17.

Job is so bitter because of his illness and loss of riches that even if God would say "I will heal you," Job would not believe the divine word. And if God would declare Job righteous, he would still make supplication to his deity. The reason for this is that humanly speaking, God's hand had been heavy on Job and he was crushed to the earth. Job thinks that God has accepted Satan's advice and turned against him.

Short Life

Now my days are swifter than a post: they flee away, they see no good. They are passed away as the swift ships: as the eagle that hasteth to the prey. Job 9:25-26.

The Aramaic word *rakhta* means a "runner" or "courier." The term "post," in this instance, means a "messenger" or "postman." In biblical days letters were conveyed and delivered by fast runners or couriers.

Job compares his life to a fast runner who reaches his destination in a short while. His days had passed away like a swift ship disappears beyond the horizon.[43]

CHAPTER TEN

The Grave

Before I go whence I shall not return, even to the land of darkness and the shadow of death: A land of darkness, as darkness itself; and of the shadow of death, without any order, and where the light is as darkness. Job 10:21-22.

---

[43]Job 10:20.

The Eastern Aramaic text reads: “Before I go from whence I shall not return, even to the land of darkness and the shadow of death, A land of loneliness and deep darkness, and of the shadow of death, without any order or time, wearisome like a deep pit.”

The reference is to death and the grave. Job speaks of the grave as a disorderly place, thick darkness, and no time. He believed that life does continue after death, but time is not relevant because it is calculated by the rotation of the stars and planets here on earth. But he also believed that people wait in the grave or *Sheol* and are inactive. This is the reason that Job speaks of loneliness in *Sheol.*

CHAPTER ELEVEN

Job’s Discourse Resented

Should thy lies make men hold their peace? and when thou mockest, shall no man make thee ashamed? Job 11:3.

The Eastern text reads: “Behold, at your words only the dead can hold their peace; for when you speak, there is no one to stop you; and when you mock, there is no one to rebuke you.”

Zophar the Naamathite was impatient to sit down and listen to Job’s lengthy discourse. Job was a sick man. His comforters had some sympathy and regard for him. When he spoke, no one could stop him and offend him, and when he spoke derisively, no one could rebuke him.

The three men had come to comfort him, but they could not tell him that he was wrong in justifying himself and claiming to be righteous.[44]

God Is Unsearchable

Canst thou by searching find out God? canst thou find out the Almighty unto perfection? It is as high as heaven; what canst thou do? deeper than hell; what canst thou know? Job 11:7-8.

The Aramaic word *sopeh* means “the boundaries thereof”; that is, “Can you find the ends or the limits of God?” Since God is the eternal Spirit and the only Creator, God has no beginning or end; and since the divine

[44]See verse 4.

presence is the pervading Spirit, above time and space, there is no place in the universe which is devoid of God.

The Eastern Aramaic text reads: "Can you understand the deep things of God? Or can you stand at the outer boundary of the Almighty? Do you know the height of the heaven? Or the depth of Sheol? How can you know?"

God Sees Evil Things

For he knoweth vain men: he seeth wickedness also; will he not then consider it? Job 11:11.

The Eastern Aramaic text reads: "For it is he [God] who knows the beginning of time; and sees wickedness, and considers it."

Zophar states that God is above time and space and knows what is to take place and also sees wickedness and considers it. (Some biblical teachers and interpreters erroneously teach that God cannot look on evil or sin. In many places, the Bible states that God saw the evil works of men.[45])

God sees and feels anything that is contrary to good. But God does not recognize evil or wickedness as a power originating from an evil force. Evil or wickedness is contrary to the nature or the essence of God, just as water is contrary to fire and evil to good. Evil actions are created by humans out of ignorance or loss of knowing that they and everyone else are children of God and one human family.

A Pure Man

For vain man would be wise, though man be born like a wild ass's colt. Job 11:12.

The Eastern Aramaic text reads: "For a pure man inspires courage, and a mighty man helps others." A man who is pure in heart sees purity and counsels people for good, but a man who is vain sees only vanity and evil. Thus, the strength of a pure man is like that of a mighty man.

The Aramaic word *ganbara,* "a mighty man," is confused with *khamara,* "an ass." This error also occurs in Genesis 49:14: "Issachar is a strong ass." It should read: "Issachar is a mighty man."

---

[45]Gen. 18:21; Judg. 3:7,12; 2 Ki. 3:1-2, 13:2; Isa. 1:16.

Toil Is Forgotten

Because thou shall forget thy misery, and remember it as waters that pass away. Job 11:16.

The Aramaic word in the text is *tedbedar,* "shall scatter or pass away." *Tedbedar* is confused with the verb *titdkhar,* "to be remembered." It should read: "Because you shall forget your misery, and you shall be led like running water."

In many Eastern lands, water dries up in the early summer months. Brooks, ponds, and rivers turn into a parched land. People who are dying of thirst often forget that once those water sources were prolific. People's toil is also forgotten and often replaced with joy.

To See Clearly

And thine age shall be clearer than the noonday; thou shalt shine forth, thou shalt be as the morning. Job 11:17.

The Aramaic word *khipra* means "pit, ditch, or mine." Job states that when a man makes his heart right and stretches his hands toward God, everything will be in his favor. Evil will flee from him, and he will be led smoothly like running water.

"The pit [or the mine] will be clearer than the noonday, and the thick darkness will be like the morning."[46] Then humans see hope and salvation ahead of them. Mines, in those days, were lighted with butter lamps and candles. At times, however, the miners worked in thick darkness.

What this saying means is that when people change their hearts and turn to God, all their difficulties disappear and they are divinely led into straight paths; for God is the light of this world, and the divine word is a lamp to the feet of those who trust in spiritual guidance.

Job's Restoration

And thou shalt be secure, because there is hope; yea, thou shalt dig about thee, and thou shalt take thy rest in safety. Also thou shalt lie down, and none shalt make thee afraid; yea, many shall make suit unto thee. But the eyes of the wicked shall

---

[46]Job 11:17, Eastern Aramaic Peshitta text, Lamsa translation.

fail, and they shall not escape, and their hope shall be as the giving up of the ghost. Job 11:18-20.

The Eastern Aramaic text reads: "Then you will have confidence because there is hope, yea, you lie down and take your rest in safety: also you shall lie down, and none shall make you afraid; yes, many shall seek to see your face. But the eyes of the wicked shall fail, and their strength shall vanish away together with the hope of their souls."

Zophar tried to comfort Job and make him change his attitude toward God. He was assuring him that finally he will be restored. Job's wealth will be returned to him, and once again he will become prominent, so much so that many men will want to come to see him as they did before. In the Near East, princes and governors are constantly surrounded by guests and noblemen. Job, one day soon, will also forget all his miseries and troubles.

CHAPTER TWELVE

Human Folly

He that is ready to slip with his feet is as a lamp despised in the thought of him that is at ease. Job 12:5.

The Eastern Aramaic text reads: "Who is ready to do away with contempt and iniquity, and to strengthen the slippery feet." The reference here is to God, clearly understood from verse 4. Job had been a laughingstock to his friends. Although he was innocent, his friends and acquaintances doubted his sincerity. God was to remove all this contempt and iniquity and strengthen the tricky feet of his accusers.

No doubt, the meaning of this verse was lost through mistranslation. Job was a Near Easterner. The book was written in the literary tongue of Aramaic, which was the lingua franca of all the people of the Near East, just as Arabic is today. Such a work as this could not be expressed in a dialect spoken by tribal people. The Hebrews, as well as the Naamathites, Temanites, and other Semitic races in southeast and southwest Arabia, used Aramaic as a literary tongue.[47]

The term "as a lamp despised" does not make sense. No one hates a lamp, but people often mock and persecute the righteous.

---

[47] 2 Ki. 18:26.

Retribution

The tabernacles of robbers prosper, and they that provoke God are secure; into whose hand God bringeth abundantly. Job 12:6.

The Eastern Aramaic text reads: "The tabernacle of robbers shall be removed, and the confidence of those who provoke God; for there is no God in their heart."

The error was caused by the resemblance of the Aramaic words *neshanon,* "to remove," and *neshamnon,* "to be fat, to prosper." The word in the King James Version, "abundantly," is emphasized in the verse, indicating that it is not found in the original text.

Prior to the rise of Islam, many Arab tribes lived by raiding and robbing. They moved their tents from one place to another in order to escape being raided by their victims. Nevertheless, sooner or later justice caught up with them, and vengeance was inflicted on them. Their tents were dismantled and taken as booty, and their sheep and cattle stolen. Just as they had plundered others, they were also plundered.

This ancient custom prevailed until World War I, when the British and the Arab governments put an end to it. Throughout his discourse, Job had been against the wicked. He could not have spoken of God as a partner of the wicked into whose hands the Divine would bring abundance of wealth.

Light out of the Shadow of Death

He discovereth deep things out of darkness, and bringeth out to light the shadow of death. Job 12:22.

The last part of the verse in the Aramaic text reads: ". . . and brings the light out of the shadow of death." No shadow can come out of light. A shadow is the absence of light. The prophet Amos says: "They have forsaken him who made Pleiades and Orion, and who turns the shadow of death into the morning."[48]

The reference here is to the times of despair when everything seemingly is hopeless. As long as there is faith there is hope, and God can change any situation. God brings joy and happiness out of dark and hopeless circumstances. Consider for a moment a seed that is buried in the dark chambers

---

[48]Amos 5:8, Eastern Aramaic Peshitta text, Lamsa translation.

of the earth, but it soon sprouts, clothed with majesty and glory.

CHAPTER THIRTEEN

Flesh in My Teeth

Wherefore do I take my flesh in my teeth, and put my life in mine hand? Job 13:14.

"Wherefore do I take my flesh in my teeth, and put my life in mine hand?" is a Semitic Near Eastern idiomatic expression that means, "Why am I so afflicted, and why is my life exposed to danger?"[49]

When people are harassed and plundered, they put their finger between their teeth, implying that all they have is what is between their teeth. Job had lost all his possessions and now was suffering from his wounds, which to his friends seemed to be incurable.

Job questioned his trials and sufferings, but he knew that whatever he did was under God's control. So he entrusted everything to God with the assurance that he would be vindicated and declared righteous.

Man's Life in God's Hand

Though he slay me, yet will I trust in him: but I will maintain mine own ways before him. Job 13:15.

The last portion of the verse in the Eastern Aramaic text reads, "because my ways are before him"; that is, "My way of life or my conduct is not hidden from him." Job trusted in God. He knew that his suffering and trials were for good.

In the end, Job was vindicated, blessed, and rewarded abundantly for his suffering and losses. Job was tested but not rejected.[50] God does not forsake the righteous nor those who put their trust in the Divine.[51]

---

[49]See verse 15.
[50]Job 8:20.
[51]Ps. 23:4, 37:24-25.

Need God's Help

Withdraw thine hand far from me: and let not thy dread make me afraid. Job 13:21.

The first part of the verse in Eastern Aramaic reads: "Do not withdraw thy help from me." Job implores God to stand by him and help him in his trial and suffering. Without God's help, the dreadful disease would terrify him.

The Aramaic term "hand" in this instance means "help or support." Without God's help Job would have been unable to bear his misfortunes.

A Human Being Wears Out

Thou puttest my feet also in the stocks, and lookest narrowly unto all my paths; thou settest a print upon the heels of my feet. And he, as a rotten thing, consumeth, as a garment that is moth-eaten. Job 13:27-28.

The Eastern Aramaic text reads: "Thou puttest my feet also in the stocks, and watchest all my ways; thou seest the imprints of my feet. Yet a man is like a worn out water skin, and a garment that is moth-eaten." Job, in answering Bildad, Eliphaz, and Zophar, says that God was hindering his coming and goings.

"Putting your feet in stocks" is an Aramaic idiom that means to be restrained. God is aware of people's goings and comings; therefore, nothing can be hidden from God. The Divine sees the imprints of people's feet. In Arabia caravans travel by means of footprints, and when these footprints are obliterated, they must travel by the stars.

It was the lack of these imprints that caused the Chaldeans to study the stars and give the world the knowledge of astronomy. In those days, footprints often were wiped away by the wind. Furthermore, Arab tribes would destroy the trails left by the camel's feet, and they would reverse their horseshoes so that their enemy could not follow them.

Job compared a human being to a worn out water skin and a moth-eaten garment. Water skins were very common in the Near East and in certain areas are still in use. Water was put in the animal skin and left hanging at the door of the tent. This was because people traveling in the desert preferred carrying water skins over earthen vessels.

Animal skin was a safe container. Old water skins and garments were thrown away. In the New Testament, Jesus of Nazareth told two of his disciples, Peter and John: "Behold, when you enter the city, you will meet a man carrying a water skin; follow him. And wherever he enters . . ."[52]

CHAPTER FOURTEEN

Born of a Woman

Man that is born of a woman is of few days, and full of trouble. Job 14:1.

"Born of a woman" is a Near Eastern idiom and refers to weaknesses that exist in human beings. Woman was used here as a contrast between those who were born of the Spirit and those who were born of the flesh. Semitic people often say, "He is born of a woman," meaning that he is weak and liable to make mistakes.

No doubt, this idiom was based on the Adam and Eve narrative. The book of Genesis states that the woman was tempted first, ate the forbidden fruit, and then gave the fruit to her husband so that he might eat of it also.

In the New Testament, Jesus used this idiomatic expression when he said, "Among them that are born of women there hath not risen one greater than John the Baptist."[53]

Clean out of the Unclean

Who can bring a clean thing out of an unclean? not one. Job 14:4.

The answer to the Aramaic saying "Who can bring a clean thing out of an unclean?" is "No one." There is no person who can produce good out of evil, or evil out of good. Jesus said: "A good tree bringeth not forth corrupt fruit; neither doth a corrupt tree bring forth good fruit."[54]

In those ancient days, just as today, some people, to justify their evil acts, claimed that good could come out of evil. But good produces good, and evil produces evil. Every tree is known by its fruits. Moreover, no spring can issue both sweet and bitter water.

---

[52]Lk. 22:10, Eastern Aramaic Peshitta text, Lamsa translation.
[53]Mt. 11:11, K.J.V.
[54]Lk. 6:43, K.J.V.

Mortal Man

But man dieth, and wasteth away: yea, man giveth up the ghost, and where is he? As the waters fail from the sea, and the flood decayeth and drieth up; So man lieth down, and riseth not: till the heavens be no more, they shall not awake, nor be raised out of their sleep. Job 14:10-12.

The reference is to mortal man—that is, the physical side of human beings—and not to the spiritual side, which is immortal and indestructible. Job was speaking of the bodies and not of the souls of people. Job himself believed that in the Spirit everyone will see God.[55]

"Till the heavens be no more" refers to eternity or endless time. A spiritual being is not subject to time and space but always was and always will be. Heaven and earth will pass away, but a human, who is the image of God, is eternal. In Job 19:26, he says, "In my flesh shall I see God."[56]

The question of immortality was a live issue then as it is today but was not well defined during the time of Job. The early Hebrews made little mention of a life hereafter. The life in this world was so hard and harsh that people thought little or nothing of life hereafter.

Transgression Sealed

My transgression is sealed up in a bag, and thou sewest up mine iniquity. Job. 14:17.

The last part of the verse in the Eastern Aramaic text reads: ". . . and thou removest from me my sins." Job says that his transgressions are sealed in a bag like an item that is covered and put away. Sealed means to be hidden, set aside. Job feels his transgressions are put away and his sins set aside.

CHAPTER FIFTEEN

Enraged

Should a wise man utter vain knowledge, and fill his belly with the east wind? Job 15:2.

---

[55]See Job 7:7, Lamsa translation.
[56]K.J.V.

"Fill his belly with the east wind" is a commonly used Near Eastern idiom, and it means "to utter supposedly great things." When an individual becomes enraged, it is said that he or she has wrath or wind in the belly, or that his belly burst with anger. False pride, likewise, is called wind. This is because the sound of the wind is meaningless, and no one knows its destination or its source.

The east wind is noted for being strong.[57] The Eastern Aramaic text reads: "Should a spiritually minded man answer with knowledge and then become enraged?"

Deceitful Riches

Because he covereth his face with his fatness, and maketh collops of fat on his flanks. Job 15:27.

The Eastern Aramaic text reads: "Because he has deceived himself with his wealth, and he places Pleiades above Aldebaran." The Aramaic word *tarbeh* (his fatness) means "his wealth or riches." Biblical authors often speak about the fat of the land, meaning the wealth or richness of the land.

"He places Pleiades above Aldebaran" means that he falsifies things and does not speak the truth. Wealth often deceives those who are carried away by it. King Solomon said: ". . . but money brings one low and causes him to go astray in all things."[58]

CHAPTER SIXTEEN

Job's Confession

And thou hast filled me with wrinkles, which is a witness against me and my leanness rising up in me beareth witness to my face. Job 16:8.

The Eastern Aramaic text reads: "Thou didst appoint me and I became a witness, but my lies have testified against me; and I spoke in his presence." The term "wrinkles" is not in the Aramaic text. Job tells Eliphaz that God had appointed him as a witness and laid a burden upon him that eats at his strength. Job confesses that he had done certain evils, and these evils were

---

[57]Ex. 14:21.

[58]Ecc. 10:19, Eastern Aramaic Peshitta text, Lamsa translation.

now against him. He was aware of his conduct and mistakes. Evidently Job must have felt that he had done something wrong to deserve such severe pain and suffering.

Horn Defiled

I have sewed sackcloth upon my skin, and defiled my horn in the dust. Job 16:15.

"Defiled my horn in the dust" is an Eastern Aramaic saying and means, "I have reduced my glory to dust" or "I have humbled myself." When a man was humbled it was said, "His horn has been broken."[59]

Horns are symbolic of triumph, excellence, royalty, and strength. "To exalt one's horn" means to give one strength and victory in battle.[60] It can also mean to prosper, become great, to become a ruler, and to be exalted.

Job's wealth and glory were gone. His skin was covered with sores. Therefore, his horn (glory) was broken and reduced to dust. "He hath cut off in his fierce anger all the horn of Israel."[61]

CHAPTER SEVENTEEN

Job Rebukes His Comforters

My days are past, my purposes are broken off, even the thoughts of my heart. They change the night into day; the light is short because of darkness.
Job 17:11-12.

The Eastern Aramaic text reads: "O you time wasters! Dawdlers! Who think about nothing! O you destroyers of the hearts of the people! You change the night into day; and you bring forth the light before the darkness is over."

Job's friends who had come to comfort him had worn him out with their arguments and accusations. These wise men were trying to show him up. They were attempting to prove to Job that his own evils had brought the calamity on him. Job answers them angrily and tells them they had not done anything good for him.

---

[59]Jer. 48:25.
[60]See 1 Sam. 2:1.
[61]Lam. 2:3, K.J.V.

They were wasters of time. He also reminds them of their shrewdness and their subtle manner of debating. They were so clever at debate that they could prove day was night and night was day.

CHAPTER EIGHTEEN

Candle an Heir

Yea, the light of the wicked shall be put out, and the spark of his fire shall not shine; The light shall be dark in his tabernacle, and his candle shall be put out with him. Job 18:5-6.

"Candle" or "lamp" is used metaphorically, meaning "an heir."[62] Darkness is symbolic of mourning. In the Near East, an heir is known as the light of the family. When he dies, during the mourning days the people sit in darkness. "Spark of his fire" means "his lifeline." His distant relatives also shall perish.

CHAPTER NINETEEN

Wicked, Not Babies or Children

Yea, young children despised me; I arose, and they spake against me. Job 19:18.

The Aramaic word *awaleh* means "the ungodly, the wicked." It has been confused with *aweleh,* meaning "babies, children, and infants." These Aramaic words are written alike, but are pronounced differently.

Job is complaining of wicked, unkind people who, when he rose to say something, spoke against him. His counselors also despised him. Job had lost everything he had. His honor and his glory were gone with his wealth. The people no longer respected him.

Little children could hardly have spoken against Job, or even known of his suffering or the loss of his wealth.

Writing on Rock and Lead

That they were graven with an iron pen and lead in the rock for ever! Job 19:24.

---

[62] 1 Ki. 15:4.

At the time of Job, much of the writing was engraved on rocks. Great events and triumphs of emperors were inscribed on stone tablets and on rocks as a memorial forever. Rock symbolized strength and endurance. Other writing materials, such as sheepskin and papyrus, soon perished. Tablets could be broken and parchment deteriorated, but rock lasted for ages. (One of the Dead Sea Scrolls was written on copper.)

Even in the 20th century one could see many Assyrian inscriptions on large rocks that were still in tact. Some of them were written in the eighth century BCE. Job wanted his wise words to be engraved with an iron pen on a lead tablet or on a rock to be preserved for posterity.

Saviour

For I know that my Redeemer liveth, and that he shall stand at the latter day upon the earth. Job 19:25.

"Redeemer" is wrongly used, because in redeeming one has to pay a price or a debt. The Aramaic noun *paroqa* is derived from *paraq,* "to save, deliver." *Paroqi* means "my Saviour."

Paroqa, "saviour," is one who saves or delivers with his strength without paying a price to anyone. For example, one who jumps into a river to save a child from drowning would not have to pay a price to anyone. The act of saving is performed out of love for another human being.

Jesus of Nazareth died willingly to save humanity from evil forces and not to redeem people by paying some sort of debt to the devil. But instead, being powerful, he destroyed the power of evil and sin. Jesus gave his life voluntarily, like a man who risks his life to save another person from drowning. He said, "I give my life of mine own."[63]

God is our Saviour because God saves humanity from sin and evil forces when one turns to the Divine.[64] God, being the Sovereign over the universe, has power to save, but God pays no ransom to anyone.

Resurrection

And though after my skin worms destroy this body, yet in my flesh shall I see God. Job 19:26.

---

[63]See Jn. 10:17-18.

[64]See Ps. 19:14 in the Lamsa translation.

The Eastern Aramaic text reads: "Although devouring worms have covered my skin and my flesh, Yet, if my eyes shall see God, then my heart also will see the light; but now my body is consumed."[65] The concept of a newer and longer life was prevalent in all ancient religions. The Assyrians, Babylonians, and Egyptians believed in the immortality of the soul and life hereafter. They supplied the dead with all the necessities of life, even with seeds and other things. The Egyptians embalmed their dead many centuries before the birth of Moses. They believed that one day the soul (*ata*) would return to the body.

Prior to the Babylonian captivity the Israelites believed in the immortality of the soul, but during the captivity and thereafter, they began to feel the need of another life in a physical body to compensate for what they had lost in this life.

"Flesh" (body) here means "a person." Even when the flesh is consumed, the Spirit, which is the image of God, shall see God.[66] According to the New Testament, the resurrection will be a spiritual one; that is to say, people will rise in a spiritual body and in the Spirit and likeness of God.[67]

The Hebrew prophet Isaiah states that the earth will cast out the dead.[68] The prophet Daniel speaks of a resurrection either to everlasting life or to everlasting condemnation.[69] According to Daniel, those who have suffered injustices will enjoy life, but the wicked will suffer for what they have done. Some Hebrew prophets taught that a day of reckoning would happen and all those who did evil would pay for their injustices.

The apostle Paul, in his letter to the Corinthians, writes: ". . . and the dead shall be raised incorruptible, and we shall be changed."[70]

CHAPTER TWENTY

The Children of the Wicked

His children shall seek to please the poor, and his hands shall restore their goods. Job 20:10.

---

[65]Job 19:26-27, Eastern Aramaic Peshitta text, Lamsa translation.
[66]See Job 7:7, Eastern Aramaic Peshitta text, Lamsa translation and Ecc. 12:7.
[67]See Ps. 17:15.
[68]Isa. 26:19.
[69]Dan. 12:2.
[70]1 Cor. 15:52.

The Eastern Aramaic text reads: "His children shall be crushed with poverty, and he shall stretch out his hands toward them." The Aramaic word *tabar* means "to break or crush." The triumph of the wicked is short, and the joy of hypocrites but for a moment.[71]

Embezzlement

He hath swallowed down riches, and he shall vomit them up again: God shall cast them out of his belly. Job 20:15.

"He hath swallowed down riches, and he shall vomit them up again" is a saying that means one has acquired riches by embezzlement, extortion, or other corrupt practices, but at last will pay for it. The Aramaic word that means "to eat" also means "to embezzle." Biblical authors write, "You have eaten the houses of widows." But in the Aramaic text the saying reads, "the riches which he had swallowed down."

"God shall cast them out of his belly" is a Near Eastern style of speech meaning that God will punish him for his unjust acts. Semites believe evil deeds will catch up with those who practice them. Near Easterners attribute everything to God. People often say, "God will bring his food forth out of his nostrils." They believed in the law of compensation; that is, he who gives alms and does good will be rewarded with good, but he who is unjust and acquires wealth by corrupt means will receive evil as his reward.

Poison of Asps and Vipers

He shall suck the poison of asps: the viper's tongue shall slay him. Job 20:16.

"The poison of asps" and "the viper's tongue" metaphorically suggest sickness and death. Near Easterners believed that wicked men, particularly extortionists and embezzlers of the poor, in due time will be afflicted with sickness or will meet a violent death because of their evil deeds.[72]

Brooks of Honey and Butter

He shall not see the rivers, the floods, the brooks of honey and butter. Job 20:17.

---

[71]See Job 12:6, Eastern Aramaic Peshitta text, Lamsa translation.
[72]Job 4:7-8.

"Brooks of honey and butter" represent prosperity and abundance. Usually, butter and honey are found on the tables of the rich. The poor seldom see them on their tables When butter and honey are plentiful, it is said, "they run like a river."

When God's kingdom reigns, everything, including honey and butter, will be as plentiful as water. Generally, the scarcity of food is due to wars, destruction, and greed. Wherever there is harmony and peace, there is prosperity and abundance.

The Wicked Perish

There shall none of his meat be left; therefore shall no man look for his goods. Job 20:21.

The Eastern Aramaic text reads: "There shall none of his posterity be spared; therefore his good will not be remembered."

Zophar the Naamathite argues that the triumph of the wicked is short, and that no matter how much they prosper and how much their excellency mounts up, in the end they shall perish and be forgotten. This is because they had oppressed the poor, committed injustices, and confiscated the property of widows.[73]

The posterity of the pious abides, and the good which they have done on earth never perishes.

With the Measure You Measure

In the fulness of his sufficiency he shall be in straits: every hand of the wicked shall come upon him. Job 20:22.

The Aramaic words *bekelalta dakil* mean, "With the measure with which he had measured he shall be recompensed." In the Near East, when a man gives short measure, he in turn is given short measure. And when he measures with a long-arm or a full-and-shaken wheat measure, he in turn is given generous measure.

Jesus said: "For with the same judgment that you judge, you will be judged, and with the same measure with which you measure, it will be

---

[73]Job 12:6, Eastern Aramaic Peshitta text, Lamsa translation.

measured to you."[74]

Zophar and his companions believed that Job's troubles were a result of Job's own evil devices. Therefore, he was to blame for his suffering. So they tried to make him confess his guilt. But Job was an upright man. Near Easterners believed that both the good and bad were rewarded accordingly. Sickness and misfortunes were attributed to evil deeds.

CHAPTER TWENTY-ONE

Descendants

How oft is the candle of the wicked put out! and how oft cometh their destruction upon them! God distributeth sorrows in his anger. Job 21:17.

"Candle" or "lamp" in Aramaic means "heir or posterity." Thus, "How oft is the candle of the wicked put out," means that the heirs of the wicked do not live long enough to inherit. People in the Near East often say: "May the Lord God bless your candle." "May your candle be burning for many generations." "God has given him a lamp." David's descendants ruled on the throne for nearly four centuries.

The prosperous and wicked who persecute the poor and oppress the needy often are left without an heir, and their possessions are inherited by the meek and those they have oppressed. Jesus of Nazareth taught that the meek are blessed and that they would inherit land or property.[75]

CHAPTER TWENTY-TWO

Clothes as a Pledge

For thou hast taken a pledge from thy brother for nought, and stripped the naked of their clothing. Job 22:6.

In the Near East, when the poor borrowed money, they might have to put up even their clothes as collateral. A poor man might give his robe, the one

---

[74]Mt. 7:2, Eastern Aramaic Peshitta text, Lamsa translation. See also Mk. 4:24 and Lk. 6:38, Eastern Aramaic text.

[75]See Mt. 5:5. Also see 1 Ki. 15:4 and the commentary on the "Lamp" in Vol. 3, *Aramaic Light on Joshua through 2 Chronicles.*

that he slept in at night. The greedy rich who took the clothes, robes, and bedclothes were generally upbraided and even condemned by pious men. ". . . hath not restored the pledge.[76]" ". . . nor take a widow's raiment to pledge."[77]

The clothes taken as a pledge from the poor were badly needed both day and night. "They drive away the ass of the fatherless, they take the widow's ox for a pledge."[78] Job or his servants had loaned money and taken pledges from the poor, as all rich people in the Near East did.

Water and Bread Shared

Thou hast not given water to the weary to drink, and thou hast withholden bread from the hungry. Job 22:7.

Pious rich men in the Near East provided water to weary travelers, strangers, and the poor. At times on a highway a large jar of water would be placed in a wall of a memorial monument for thirsty travelers to drink.

Water is still scarce in many parts of the biblical lands, and travelers and strangers often suffer thirst. This is more true in deserts and among nomad tribes who depend on wells for water. Sometimes water is found only in the tents of the rich and the sheiks. And some of them share it with the thirsty.

Bread also was shared with the hungry and with strangers. But some greedy people withheld both their bread and water from the thirsty and the hungry. When bread and water were scarce, the people ate and drank secretly so that they would not have to share it with the needy. "Stolen waters are sweet, and bread eaten in secret is pleasant."[79]

On the other hand, pious men would offer their bread and water to the hungry and the thirsty. To give water to the thirsty and bread to the needy was and is considered one of the most pious acts in biblical lands. This is because bread and water, so essential to life, are scarce.

Job, in upholding his piety, states, "If I have withheld the poor from his desire, or have defrauded the widow, or have eaten my bread alone, and the orphans did not eat of it . . . Because from my youth I was brought up in sorrows, and from my mother's womb with sighing . . . But they were

---

[76]Ezk. 18:12, K.J.V.
[77]Dt. 24:17, K.J.V.
[78]Job 24:3, Eastern Aramaic Peshitta text, Lamsa translation.
[79]Prov. 9:17, Eastern Aramaic Peshitta text, Lamsa translation.

reared upon my knees and were warmed with the fleece of my sheep . . ."[80]

Arm

Thou hast sent widows away empty, and the arms of the fatherless have been broken. Job 22:9.

"Arms of the fatherless have been broken" is an Aramaic idiom that means they have been left helpless. In Aramaic, arms are symbolic of men's strength and power, and when the arms are broken, it is symbolic of weakness and hopelessness. ". . .let it [my arm] be broken from the bone.[81] ". . .with a stretched out arm. . ."[82] ". . .by the greatness of thine arm. . .[83]

No Opportunity

Which were cut down out of time, whose foundation was overflown with a flood: Which said unto God, Depart from us: and what can the Almighty do for them? Yet he filled their houses with good things: but the counsel of the wicked is far from me. Job 22:16-18.

The Eastern Aramaic text reads: "Those who were cut down before their time, who were stopped at the crossing place of the river of life, and then did not remember who had laid down their pattern of living, who said to God, Depart from us; what can God do for us? Yet he filled their houses with good things, and the counsel of the wicked kept away from them."

Eliphaz speaks to Job of young men who died before their time. These men knew nothing of the way of God, nor did they expect God to do anything for them. This is because they did not know the pattern that their forefathers had set for them. In other words, death and misfortune in life had prevented these young men from knowing the truth of God and yet God took care of them. He filled their houses with good things and stopped the counsel of the wicked from coming near them.

There are many good people who know nothing about God or have a spiritual understanding of religion, nor do they expect anything from God.

---

[80]Job 31:16-20, Eastern Aramaic Peshitta text, Lamsa translation.
[81]Job 31:22, Eastern Aramaic Peshitta text, Lamsa translation.
[82]Jer. 32:21, Eastern Aramaic Peshitta text, Lamsa translation.
[83]Ex. 15:16, Eastern Aramaic Peshitta text, Lamsa translation.

Nevertheless, good things happen for them and evil counsel does not touch them.

The Humble

When men are cast down, then thou shalt say, There is lifting up; and he shall save the humble person. Job 22:29.

The Aramaic word *demithmakakh* means "who is humbled." The Eastern Aramaic text reads: "For it is said, He who humbles himself shall be exalted; and he who is meek shall be saved."

The meek are praised for their humility. The proud shall be humbled, but the meek shall be saved and exalted and shall inherit the earth.[84] To be meek is to be gentle, natural, and respectful of the rights, opinions, or practices of others.

The Innocent

He shall deliver the island of the innocent: and it is delivered by the pureness of thine hands. Job 22:30.

The Aramaic word *zakaiah* means "innocent, blameless, guiltless." The Eastern Aramaic text reads: "The innocent man shall be spared wherever he is, and he shall escape by the purity of his hands." "Island" is a mistranslation, probably deriving from a faulty or damaged text.

CHAPTER TWENTY-FOUR

The Wicked

Why, seeing times are not hidden from the Almighty, do they that know him not see his days? Job 24:1.

The Aramaic word *awalin,* "the ungodly, the wicked," is confused with *zabnin,* "times." The Eastern Aramaic text reads: "Why are the wicked not hidden from the presence of God, and why do those who know him never enjoy their days?"

---

[84]Mt. 5:5.

The ungodly do not hide themselves from the presence of God, because they do not recognize him as their Lord and Creator. They remove landmarks to steal land from the poor, violently seize the sheep of the weak, and keep the pledges of the widows and destitute. What Job is questioning is: "Why are the wicked allowed to live?"

Grazing Rights

Some remove the landmarks; they violently take away flocks, and feed thereof. Job 24:2.

Removing of landmarks was very common among both the settled tribal people and the nomads. In grazing regions a landmark generally was a heap of stones that could be easily moved a few hundred yards or more to either side of a boundary.

When sheep were found grazing without a permit beyond the territory of their owners, they were confiscated. This was because pasture lands and wells were rented or leased for money or sheep. Some powerful and wicked men, in order to confiscate the sheep from weak tribes, removed the landmarks and seized the sheep as a fine.[85]

The Oppressors

They are of those that rebel against the light; they know not the ways thereof, nor abide in the paths thereof. Job 24:13.

The Aramaic word *mediary*, "dwelling place, habitation," has been confused here with the Aramaic word *marodey,* "rebellious men." The difference between the letters *resh* and *daleth* is a dot placed over or under the letter. The Eastern Aramaic text reads: "They were in God's world; but they knew not his ways; nor did they walk in his paths."

These people were in God's world and yet they did not see the ways of God. They took away the bread and the clothes of the poor and forced them to reap in their fields and tread in their wine presses.[86]

---

[85]Dt. 19:14 and Isa. 5:8.

[86]See verses 9 and 10, in the Eastern Aramaic Peshitta text, Lamsa translation.

CHAPTER TWENTY-FIVE

Mortal Man

How much less man, that is a worm? and the son of man, which is a worm? Job 25:6.

This verse should read: "How much less man, who is dust, and the son of man, who is a worm!" *Rimtha* in this instance means "dust." The text uses two words: *rimtha,* "dust," and tolaa, "worm." Also, the Aramaic words *nasha,* "man," and *barnasha,* literally "son of man," are used collectively, meaning "a man, humankind, a human being."

Bildad the Shuhite argues that man cannot be justified with God, seeing that he is born of a woman (meaning weak), who had transgressed against the law. The reference is to Eve, who gave birth to a weak humanity.

CHAPTER TWENTY-SIX

The Slain Men

Dead things are formed from under the waters, and the inhabitants thereof. Job 26:5.

The Eastern Aramaic text reads: "Behold, the mighty men shall be slain, and they shall lie down quieter than still waters." "Quieter than water" is a Near Eastern Semitic idiom that means to be in complete stillness or silence.

During their lives, mighty men and men of great power had been boastful, turbulent and noisy, but in their graves they would be silenced and sleep quietly.

The Earth Floating in the Air

He stretcheth out the north over the empty place, and hangeth the earth upon nothing. Job 26:7.

Nearly 2,500 years before Copernicus and Galileo discovered that the sun was the center of our solar system, Job, through divine inspiration, declared that God, by his omniscient intelligence, had hung the earth on nothing.

The Assyrians and Chaldeans, who were noted for their studies of the stars and planets and who were responsible for the development of the calendar, which was based on the solar system, knew that the earth revolved around the sun. The Christians in Mesopotamia in the tenth century CE were warned not to believe that the sun was the center of the universe. This knowledge reached Europe during the Arab conquest of Spain between the seventh and the thirteenth centuries.

After centuries of study of our vast universe, today humankind is able to explain some parts of this complex system that for ages was beyond humanity's grasp.

We know that the revolving and rotating movements of the stars are governed by a great power that many people call God. Modern scientists may call it the immutable law created through harmony and a perfect balance between the force of gravity and centrifugal force, or the field created by the motion of the revolving planets.

Only God could have constructed such a complex system governed by an immutable and eternal law. That is why the psalmist cried out: "The heavens declare the glory of God; and the firmament shows his handiwork."[87]

The Chaldeans (Babylonians), centuries before Galileo, knew that the earth was round and floating like a ball in the air. The Babylonians prior to the departure of Abraham from Ur of Chaldea knew that the earth was a small planet revolving around the sun and that the sun was the center of our universe.

The Babylonians had developed the 12-month calendar, with 24 hours in a day and the 7-day week. They also knew about the movement of the stars and planets. And their knowledge was fairly good in comparison to our knowledge today, considering their lack of telescopes and other measuring devices that we have at our disposal.

We have made a little improvement on the calendar, but we are still guided by the findings of the past. The week is still the same, and the number of months and hours have not changed.

Being a pastoral people, the Hebrews' concept of a flat world was tribal. Job was from the land of Uz. Therefore the book was written from the point of view of Chaldean astronomy. Job, no doubt, was a descendant of Abraham, or some kin of the Israelites.

---

[87]See Ps. 19:1, Eastern Aramaic Peshitta text, Lamsa translation.

"Hangeth the earth upon nothing" of course implies that it is floating in space and not stretched out upon the water as the Hebrews thought. Mar-Isaac, bishop of Baghdad in the eighth century, warned the Christians not to believe the Chaldean doctrine that the earth revolves around the sun. He thought it was a false teaching.

This ancient astronomical knowledge was passed on by the Babylonians and Assyrians to the Persians, and the latter passed it on to the Greeks during their conquest of Asia Minor and Greece, just as the Arabs were responsible for the transmission of science from the Near East to Spain, and from there to the rest of Europe. The book of Job is the only book in the Bible that speaks of a round world.

Powerful Acts of God

He divideth the sea with his power, and by his understanding he smiteth through the proud. Job 26:12.

The reference here is to the Red Sea when the Lord caused it to go back by a strong east wind.[88] When the water over the shoals went back during the night, the sea was divided; that is, as the crossing place became dry land, the waters were suddenly divided into two bodies—the Bitter Lakes and the tip of the Gulf of the Suez. This dry passage was the crossing place of the Israelites. According to the author of Exodus, the Lord God brought the powerful east wind that divided the sea and guided the Israelites to cross at the right time.

All races and peoples in Arabia and Chaldea had heard of God's wonders in Egypt, especially those who were the descendants of Abraham.

God Did Not Form the Crooked Serpent

By his spirit he hath garnished the heavens: his hand hath formed the crooked serpent. Job 26:13.

The last part of this verse in the Eastern Aramaic text reads, "his hand slew the fleeing serpent." The Aramaic words *kitlath eedeh* means "his hand slew." The word "formed" is not correct. The Divine neither created nor formed a force that was contrary to itself. "Serpent" refers to an enemy,

---

[88]Ex. 14:21.

deception, and sometimes an evil dictator. It also means a sea monster or evil forces.

Job confesses the greatness of God. According to Job, it was God who was responsible for defeating the Egyptian army when Israel left Egypt. It was God who crushed all of Joshua's enemies when Israel entered the land of Canaan. It was God who also brought an end to all evil forces and deceptions. All armies that were retreating from conquering Israelites were as fleeing serpents.

CHAPTER TWENTY-SEVEN

A Temporary Booth

He buildeth his house as a moth, and as a booth that the keeper maketh. Job 27:18.

The Eastern Aramaic text reads: "For the wicked has built his house upon a spider's web, and like a booth he had made his shelter." "Spider's web" is used metaphorically, meaning that the foundation of the house is flimsy. This idiom is still prevalent in Near Eastern languages. A spider's web is weak and is easily destroyed by the wind and by larger insects and birds.

The term "booth" refers to the shelter that farmers and vine dressers built in vineyards and in fields where cucumbers and melons were grown. The booth was made of thin branches and covered with grass. Just as soon as the cucumbers and grapes had been gathered, the booth was deserted and finally destroyed or burned.

In the book of the prophet Jonah, the author tells us that the prophet made such a booth to protect himself from the heat.[89]

CHAPTER TWENTY-EIGHT

A Ruined Mine

The flood breaketh out from the inhabitant; even the waters forgotten of the foot: they are dried up, they are gone away from men. Job 28:4.

---

[89]Jonah 4:5.

Mistranslations have obscured the whole meaning of this verse. The Eastern Aramaic text reads: "They have inherited a ruined mine from an alien people; they are gone astray from the right path and their number has diminished from among men."

A great many people around Job were hypocrites and evildoers.[90] Job likens evildoers to miners who inherited a ruined mine from a foreign people who worshiped idols and had gone astray because of the crooked paths.

The former inhabitants of the world had gone astray from God's way of life. The present inhabitants, metaphorically, had inherited a ruined mine and the number of good men had diminished. (Note: miners are always exposed to dangers.)

Mining Difficulties

He cutteth out rivers among the rocks; and his eye seeth every precious thing. He bindeth the floods from overflowing; and the thing that is hid bringeth he forth to light. Job 28:10-11.

The Eastern Aramaic text reads: "He divides the rivers by his might; and his eye sees every precious thing. He binds up the rivers that they may not overflow, and the thing that is hid, he brings forth to light."

"Rivers" refer to underground rivers or streams that the miners divert in order to prevent the mines from being flooded. Mining gold, silver, and precious stones was dangerous in those days just as it is today. But human beings have been endowed with wisdom and understanding to divert the course of rivers and streams, not only on the ground, but also under the ground.

Where Is Wisdom Found?

Man knoweth not the price thereof; neither is it found in the land of the living. Job 28:13.

The Aramaic word *ela,* "except," has been confused with the Aramaic word *la*, "no, not, neither." The Eastern Aramaic text reads: "No man knows the treasure thereof; neither is it found except in the land of the

---

[90]See Chapter 27.

living."

Job points out that wisdom is beyond human comprehension, and it is found only in the land of the living—that is, in the spiritual realm where that which we see now as imperfect will be revealed as perfect, and where that which we see in part we will see as a whole.

Wisdom and understanding were revealed to the prophets and men of God through inspiration from the Highest. Wisdom is hidden from human eyes simply because wisdom is perfect and spiritual, and it cannot be easily revealed through impurities. When we rise in our consciousness and penetrate the terrestrial veil, then we can find wisdom and apply it through our understanding. Only God knows the source of wisdom and only God can make it manifest to people.

Wisdom Is Priceless

The topaz of Ethiopia shall not equal it, neither shall it be valued with pure gold. Job 28:19.

The Eastern Aramaic text reads: "For the price of wisdom is above everything, and nothing can equal it. The pearls of Ethiopia and the topaz cannot equal it."

Ancient Ethiopia embraced a large portion of southwestern Arabia. This region was famous for its jewels, especially pearls, which were common in southern Arabia and along the Persian Gulf. When the queen of Sheba came to see Solomon, she brought him many precious stones, pearls, and other gifts.

The present Ethiopia has no access to the Arabian Sea and the Gulf of Persia, but pearls are imported and exported by pearl merchants.

CHAPTER TWENTY-NINE

Candle of God

When his candle shined upon my head, and when by his light I walked through darkness. Job 29:3.

In many Near Eastern cities where streets were narrow, servants carried lamps or candles in front of their lords or held them high over their heads so that they might see their way and guide their footsteps safely.[91]

"His candle" refers to God's light, reverence, and glory. Job was a religious man with strong convictions and faith in God. He was guided and governed by God's laws and ordinances. He was praised by the people and called pious. But now he wondered why this evil had befallen him.

Job, during his suffering and agony, at times complained and lamented his downfall. Now the poor man was destitute. The candle of God was taken away from him. Job's glory and wealth were gone. He was so afflicted that he could not even go to the place of worship.

Wealthy

When I washed my steps with butter, and the rock poured me out rivers of oil. Job 29:6.

"When I washed my steps with butter" is a Near Eastern saying that means "when I was very wealthy and had large flocks."

Near Easterners often say, "He is bathing with butter or milk," meaning his sheep produce abundantly. This is similar to the English phrase, "He is rolling in money." In the Near East, rich men bathe with milk. In the desert lands milk is more abundant than water.

The holy land is a rocky place. The grass is very poor, but this poor land produces butter and olive oil, because olive trees and goats thrive in rocky places.

Job had lost all of his wealth and popularity, but he never lost his faith in God.

Hand on Mouth

The princes refrained talking, and laid their hand on their mouth. The nobles held their peace, and their tongue cleaved to the roof of their mouth. Job 29:9-10.

In the Near East, when a king, a prince, or a nobleman spoke, other men (even those who also were nobles and high officials) kept quiet and put their hands over their mouths as a token of respect and admiration for the speaker and for what was being said. However, common men were

---

[91]Ps. 119:105.

frightened when they spoke or answered a question in the presence of these highly social ranking men.

Even young people paid high respect to these officials and nobles. They never uttered a word in their presence and, at times, they even hid themselves when they listened to them.

Eyes to the Blind

I was eyes to the blind, and feet was I to the lame. Job 29:15.

These phrases are used metaphorically, meaning, "I gave good counsel to those who were spiritually blind and helped those who were ready to slip to walk straight."

Job was not only a wealthy man who was highly honored, but he was also a pious and wise elder whose counsel was continually sought by many people—especially the weak.

Straight like a Reed

Then I said, I shall die in my nest, and I shall multiply my days as the sand. Job 29:18.

The Aramaic word for "reed" is *kania*, and the word for "nest" is *kina*. The translators from the Aramaic (or the transcribers) confused *kania* with *kina*. The resemblance between these two words is so close that an occasional error of this kind is inevitable. The letter *yodh* (i) or (y) so closely resembles the letter *nun* (n) that at times even a native scribe who is versed in Aramaic might make a mistake. The Eastern Aramaic text reads: "Then I said, I shall become straight like a reed, I shall deliver the poor and multiply my days like the sand of the sea."

In the Near East, when a person is straightforward or honest, it is said, "He is like a reed"; that is, he is perfect in his conduct. This is because reeds grow straight. Our word for canon law is derived from the Aramaic word *kania* (reed).

Job thought he had been straight and perfect in all his ways, but he found that he was not as pious as he thought in his heart that he was. But now Job was going to change his way of life and strive to be perfect like a reed; then he was to multiply descendants and become prosperous and great again.

CHAPTER THIRTY

Job's Enemies Shamed

To dwell in the cliffs of the valleys, in caves of the earth, and in the rocks. Job 30:6.

The Eastern Aramaic text reads: "Fleeing to dwell in the cliffs of the valleys, in caves of the earth, in crevices." Job predicts the sudden fall of the wicked men who mocked him and scorned his righteousness. The day would come when, because of fear and shame, they would hide in crags and caves. Job's fortune would be restored and all who had rejoiced in his calamity would hide because of fear and shame.[92]

Job's Adversaries

Upon my right hand rise the youth: they push away my feet, and they raise up against me the ways of their destruction. Job 30:12.

The Eastern Aramaic text reads: "They rise up against my right hand, they have tripped me up; they have perplexed me through the crookedness of their ways." The word "youth" is not present in the Aramaic text.

Job complains against his adversaries and his friends who were happy over his downfall. Many of them, instead of comforting, caused more mischief for him. Others lied against him and gave him wrong counsel that confused him.

Girded up

By the great force of my disease is my garment changed: it bindeth me about as the collar of my coat. Job 30:18.

The Aramaic text reads: "I have put on my garment; and girded up myself with my robe." Job had trusted in God and therefore he was sure of his restoration. The term "disease" is due to mistranslation or defects in the text as is seen from the italics in the King James Version. "Girded up

---

[92]See verse 1.

myself with my robe" is a Near Eastern saying which means, "I am ready to start." Job was ready to begin his comeback. The Lord had revealed to him that his suffering and his trial were not in vain. Job was destined to be greater than in the former days.

Job Believes

Thou liftest me up to the wind; thou causest me to ride upon it, and dissovlest my substance. For I know that thou wilt bring me to death, and to the house appointed for all living. Job 30:22-23.

"Lifted me up to the wind" is an idiom that means "you have made me great." It is often said among Aramaic speaking people: "He is riding the clouds," meaning he is successful and honored.

God had made Job a great and wealthy man, and later on he humbled him. Nevertheless, Job believed God would bring him back from death to a place that God had appointed for the living. "O remember that the spirit is still alive; even yet my eye shall again see good."[93]

Interestingly the King James Version translates the verse as: "For I know that thou wilt bring me to death . . . " But the Eastern Aramaic text reads: "And yet I know that thou wilt bring me back from death to the meeting place for all living." Apparently, this mistake was caused by translating from one language to another.

Solitary Life

I am a brother to dragons, and a companion to owls. Job 30:29.

The Eastern Aramaic text reads, "I am become a brother to jackals, and a companion to ostriches," which means, "I have become an outcast living in desolate places." Job's fearful disease made many people shun him. Even some of his best friends and acquaintances turned their faces away from him. Job, in order to convey the thought of being deserted by his friends and relatives, describes himself as dwelling in the deserts with jackals and ostriches.

In the Near East, until recent days, men who were afflicted with an

---

[93]Job 7:7, Eastern Aramaic Peshitta text, Lamsa translation.

incurable disease were abandoned. Many of them wandered in cemeteries, fields, and forests. This is because hospitals were unknown, and incurable diseases were greatly feared.

Job Has Lost His Flesh

My skin is black upon me, and my bones are burned with heat. Job 30:30.

The Aramaic word *kepod* means "shrunk"; that is, "My skin has shrunk." Job speaks of his suffering and the loss of his flesh. "My skin has shrunk" is an idiom which means, "I have become lean." The Eastern Aramaic text reads: "My skin has shrunk upon me, and my bones are burned as with heat."

Some people maintain that Job's skin turned black as a sign of his guilt. But this is not true. Job was neither perfect nor wicked. But he was a pious and unblemished man. This is why at last he was vindicated.

CHAPTER THIRTY-ONE

Job's Purity

I made a covenant with mine eyes; why then should I think upon a maid? Job 31:1.

The Eastern Aramaic text reads: "I made a vow with my eyes that I would never lust after a virgin." Rich men in the Near East were polygamists and, in some lands, still are. They acquired young concubines whenever they wanted them. Some of them took their concubines by force. In some cases men presented their virgin daughters to kings, princes, and men of great wealth.

Job was a pious man who had lived a pure life. He had never walked in the way of the ungodly or swerved from the way of God. So he had made a vow that he would never try to entice a young women, that is, a virgin.[94]

---

[94]See verse 9-10.

Job Was a Just Man

Then let me sow, and let another eat; yea, let my offspring be rooted out. Job 31:8.

The Eastern Aramaic text reads: "But when I sowed, then I ate, and when I planted, then I cultivated and gathered the crops." In the Near East often one man sows and another reaps; one man plants and cultivates and another enjoys the fruit.

In biblical days, when the enemy occupied the land, the people gathered the grain and picked up the grapes and the fruits of the trees. Or sometimes wicked men and oppressors confiscated vineyards, orchards, and fields and gathered their produce.[95] At times, some sowed and let others reap. When teaching his disciples, Jesus of Nazareth said: "For in this case the saying is true, One sows and another reaps."[96]

Some of these corrupt and unjust practices were prevalent in many lands, especially when they were ruled by dictators and oppressors. In many regions of the modern Near East, sown fields and vineyards continue to be confiscated. Job declares that he has not confiscated sown fields by violence, but that he has worked hard for everything he has gained.

Bake Bread for Another Man

Then let my wife grind unto another, and let others bow down upon her. Job 31:10.

The Aramaic word *appey* means "to bake bread." It is very similar to *appay,* meaning "face." The Eastern Aramaic text correctly reads: "Then let my wife grind for another, and let her bake bread at another man's place." This literally means, "Let me be so destitute that there will be no wheat or flour in my house."

The wives of poor men in the Near East worked in the houses of the rich, grinding wheat and baking bread. Wheat was ground at home and the bread was baked daily. This work was done only by women, each one working in her own house preparing food for her own family.

---

[95]See Micah 6:15.

[96]Jn. 4:37, Eastern Aramaic Peshitta text, Lamsa translation.

Only poor and destitute men would permit their wives to grind or bake bread for others. They may perform other services for a stranger, but to grind or bake bread would hurt the pride of the husband. This is because when women perform such tasks, they uncover their arms and wear light garments.

Defrauding Widows

If I have withheld the poor from their desire, or have caused the eyes of the widow to fail. Job 31:16.

The phrase "have caused the eyes of the widow to fail" is an Aramaic idiom which means "have defrauded the widow." The Aramaic word *kheshakh* means "darkness." In the Near East, when a man was defrauded or deceived, it was said, "They have darkened his eyes," which means that he has failed to see the value of an article that he had bought or sold.

Until recent years, widows in biblical lands had few legal rights, and in some places they had none. Therefore, they could not transact business or manage property. These tasks were generally performed by men.

Invariably, many widows entrusted their money, property, and important business transactions to seemingly pious men, who acted on their behalf. Some of these men defrauded the widows and orphans. Job insists that he had done none of these evil acts but that he had fed them and clothed them.

Jesus said, "Woe unto you, scribes and Pharisees, hypocrites! for ye devour widows' houses, and for a pretense make long prayer: therefore ye shall receive the greater damnation."[97] "Devoured" means "embezzled."

Job upholds his integrity and piety. Although he was rich and looked upon as a prince, Job respected the poor and the widows.

Job's Hospitality

If his loins have not blessed me, and if he were not warmed with the fleece of my sheep. Job 31:20.

The first part of the Eastern Aramaic text reads: "But they were reared upon my knees . . ." The translator evidently misunderstood these words.

---

[97]Mt. 23:14, K.J.V.

Job implies that not only had he fed and clothed the poor and the needy but also that some of them grew up in his house and he had raised them. "Reared on my knees" is an Aramaic idiom which means, "I took care of them from the time of their birth."

It was not unusual to see poor workers and their wives and children living in some of the houses of rich employers or landlords. One could see workers' and employers' children playing together. Job was a wealthy landlord and had hundreds of male and female servants who tended his flocks and herds, some of whom were born and raised in his own house.

Sun Worship

If I beheld the sun when it shined, or the moon walking in brightness. Job 31:26.

The first part of the Aramaic text reads: "If I have adored the sun when it shone . . ." Because of its warmth and light, the sun was sometimes worshiped as a god. Sun worshipers rose up early in the morning and bowed to the sun as it rose. The Parsees of the Near East (Zoroastrian religious sect), or the sun worshipers in the modern world practice obeisance to the sun as it appears on the horizon. They also worship fire and keep it in their temples. The moon was also worshiped as a deity.

Moses warned the Israelites against bowing to the sun and the moon. He said: "And lest you lift up your eyes to heaven, and when you see the sun and the moon, and the stars and all the host of heaven, should go astray and worship them and serve those things which the Lord your God has provided for all the peoples under heaven."[98]

Job could not have helped seeing the sun and the moon, but he did not revere them or worship them as deities.[99]

Good Luck

And my heart hath been secretly enticed, or my mouth hath kissed my hand. Job 31:27.

"My mouth has kissed my hand" is a Near Eastern way of speaking about

---

[98]Dt. 4:19, Eastern Aramaic Peshitta text, Lamsa translation.

[99]2 Ki. 17:16.

cheating in business. When merchants made large, unexpected profits, they kissed the backs of their hands as a token of good luck.

Job tries to prove that he had lived uprightly and that he had done no evil to anyone. In other words, Job never consented to wrongdoing. He never "kissed the back of his hand."

Job Was Benevolent

Did I fear a great multitude, or did the contempt of families terrify me, that I kept silence, and went not out of the door? Job 31:34.

The Eastern Aramaic text reads: "If I have trampled upon the rights of the others (but on the contrary, it is the multitude of families which has ruined me. Nor have I turned away anyone at the door; or engaged in gossip) let the provocations of God lay me low!"

Job had done everything he thought was righteous in the eyes of God and pious men. He had kept all the ordinances of the law and done what God commanded him to do. Now he sums up some of his good deeds and also insists that he had done no evil. He had not engaged in gossip nor turned the poor from his gate empty-handed. On the contrary, he had spent much of his wealth in helping many destitute families.

Job Demands God's Answer

Oh that one would hear me! Behold, my desire is, that the Almighty would answer me and that mine adversary had written a book. Surely I would take it upon my shoulder, and bind it as a crown to me. I would declare unto him the number of my steps; as a prince would I go near unto him. Job 31:35-37.

The Eastern Aramaic text reads: "O that one would hear me! If God is present, let him answer me, and let him write the sentence in a book. Surely I would take it upon my shoulder, and make it a crown to me. I would declare to him the number of my steps; as a prince I would go near to him."

The term "that mine adversary had written a book" is incorrect in the King James Version. In the Aramaic text Job says: "Let God write a sentence in a book." That is, let God declare him righteous or evil. Job would accept this sentence gladly upon his shoulders and wear it as a crown.

Job is utterly disgusted with vain gossip. Some were upholding his integrity and honesty, and others condemned him. Job wants God to decide the case, and then he would accept the divine verdict. Now if Job is wrong, let God sentence him and write in a book so that all future generations could read God's judgment.

When men were sentenced in biblical days, the sentence and the nature of the crime were recorded on a scroll. Jesus of Nazareth was accused of committing a crime because he had made himself a king. The sign on the cross above his head read: "This is Jesus the King of the Jews."[100]

"Declaring the number of his steps" is an idiom that means "I will confess to God all my goings and comings," or "Everything I have ever done is never hidden from God.

CHAPTER THIRTY-TWO

Young Respect the Old

Now Elihu had waited till Job had spoken, because they were elder than he. Job 32:4.

According to Near Eastern etiquette, a younger man must remain silent until all the elders who are present have spoken.

Generally, the Elders were the governing body that directed the affairs of a tribe, town, or city. They sat in council with princes and kings. The older a man was, the more his wisdom and knowledge were respected. This is why the younger men had to keep silent and wait; in some cases, they never had a chance to express their opinions. When the elders were through speaking and were tired, the younger men could speak and give counsel.[101]

Impatient

Behold, my belly is as wine which hath no vent; it is ready to burst like new bottles. I will speak, that I may be refreshed: I will open my lips and answer. Job 32:19-20.

Elihu could no longer hold his peace. He had waited too long to let the

[100]Mt. 27:37.
[101]See verse 16.

elders share their wisdom with one another. But now he had to speak out and admonish Job. He could no longer restrain himself.

"My belly is as wine which has no vent" is a Near Eastern idiom that means, "I cannot keep silent any more." Near Easterners, when they are restrained from speaking or have some secret to impart, say, "My belly is bursting," expressing, "I can no longer restrain myself; I must speak now."

New wine that was stored in goatskins without an opening for fermentation to escape causes the skins to burst.[102] "Bottles" should read "skins." In the Near East, new wine used to be transported in new goatskins.

CHAPTER THIRTY-THREE

God Speaks Once

For God speaketh once, yea twice, yet man perceiveth it not. In a dream, in a vision of the night, when deep sleep falleth upon men, in slumberings upon the bed. Job 33:14-15.

The first part of the Aramaic text reads: "For God speaks once; he does not speak a second time." The reference here was to visions or revelations, which, as a general rule, came once only. But some of the visions were repeated, which signified that the event would come soon. For example, Pharaoh saw two visions that had similar meanings—that is, the vision of the cows and the ears of wheat.[103] God also spoke in visions and dreams to the Hebrew patriarchs ("And God appeared unto Abraham and said . . .") and to the prophets. At times a second vision would explain another.

A large portion of the Scriptures is based on the visions that men of God saw during the night. The rest were written from experiences and occurrences in the daily life of the people.

The Bible reader must discriminate between a vision and a story based on an actual daily occurrence. Throughout the Bible, God spoke in visions and dreams. God spoke to Noah, Abraham, Isaiah, Jeremiah, and other patriarchs in visions, and, in later days, to Jesus and his apostles.

God speaks to human beings during the silent hours of the night when the

---

[102]For additional information about new wine in old skins, see Mt. 9:17, Mk. 2:22, and Lk. 5:37, Eastern Aramaic Peshitta text, Lamsa translation.

[103]Gen. 41:1-7.

mind is at rest. This is because during the night, the mind does not record events but instead records spiritual messages. We know that one's sense of time is based on events that take place during the day. Thus, if someone were to sleep for just a full 24 hours or for a year, he or she would not be able to tell the difference when awakened. In the realm of the Spirit there is neither time nor space. Things that may happen a hundred years hence may be seen as happening now.

Prophets and men of God rose high in their meditations and contemplations in order to be on the spiritual beam and see the things that would happen below them. They went into deserts and lonely places to contemplate so that they could detach their minds from earthly things and thus commune with the living God and look into the realm of the Spirit, which contains the pattern of the earthly realm. It was believed that this was how Daniel foresaw the rise and fall of many empires and kingdoms, from the fifth century BCE to CE 10.

Mary, the mother of Jesus, saw a vision; Joseph, his father, was warned through visions; Peter and Paul were guided by visions. Some visions were revealed in symbols because symbols could be remembered more easily; for example, Pharaoh would recall seeing the seven cows and seven ears of wheat. Then there were the highly symbolic visions that Isaiah, Ezekiel, and Daniel saw.

Some visions came to men as they fell into a trance, yet their eyes were open.[104] Peter was in a trance when he saw a great sheet let down from heaven by its four corners.[105]

Spiritual Admonitions

That he may withdraw man from his purpose and hide pride from man. He keepeth back his soul from the pit, and his life from perishing by the sword.
Job 33:17-18.

The Eastern Aramaic text from verse 14 through verse 18 reads: "For God speaks once; he does not speak a second time; In a dream, in a vision of the night, when deep sleep falls upon men, while slumbering upon the bed; then he opens the ears of men, and humbles them according to their rebelliousness. That he may cause man to depart from his evil doings, and

---

[104]Num. 24:4.
[105]Acts 10:10-16, 11:5.

remove pride from him; He spares his soul from corruption, and his life from perdition."[106]

Not all visions were relevant to future events, such as wars and catastrophes. Some of the revelations were spiritual guidance through which the divine exhorted and admonished. God also reproved people who were bent on doing evil deeds and some who had done evil. For example, when David had Uriah the Hittite, his most faithful general, killed deliberately on the battlefield, he was sentenced by God through the king's personal court prophet, Nathan. Job tells that God communes with people in dreams and visions and admonishes them in matters that were difficult and trying for them.

God constantly speaks. People do not hear the divine voice simply because they are not attuned to spiritual matters. An inner voice needs an inner ear. When one is in a psychic state or an ecstatic trance, when the Spirit of the Lord is upon him or her, both the inner eyes and ears can open and that which is unseen or is far off becomes clear and manifest.

When human beings become wealthy, prominent, and hold high offices, it is easy for them to become proud and make themselves inaccessible. They feel it is beneath them to speak with those of a lower social status. Interestingly, many judges and kings of Israel were humble and approachable. Many men and women came to them seeking justice.

If the rulers of the world and statesmen were familiar with the practical use of psychic phenomena, many dangerous problems that often result in wars, death, cruelty, and greed would be overcome. Spiritual forces would take over and direct them in the right way. But in order to do this, one has to dispense with human pride, fear of tomorrow, greed, and worldly personal ambitions. This is what Job refers to.

Cancer

His flesh is consumed away, that it cannot be seen: and his bones that were not seen stick out. Job 33:21.

The Eastern Aramaic text reads: "His flesh is wasted away because of his fear, so that a greater part of his bones can be seen." "His flesh is wasted away" signifies that the man was suffering from cancer. Job's affliction

---

[106]Job 33:14-18, Eastern Aramaic Peshitta text, Lamsa translation.

was skin cancer and not boils. The Aramaic word *shookhna* means "cancer."[107] *Shookhna* also means "heat." Heat splits the atom and melts elements. "But the day of the Lord will come as a thief in the night, when the heavens shall suddenly pass away and the elements shall separate as they burn, and the earth also and the things that are in it shall not be found. Now since all these things are to be dissolved . . ."[108] The heat of the cancer destroys the flesh and causes it to fall apart.

Some cancer can be created by fear. When an individual fears that a particular disease is going to come upon him or her, that person paralyzes the healing forces that are operating in the body all the time. These healing forces in humans are constantly repairing the damages that occur in the body. But when doubt and fear operate and dominate a person's mind, the body is left defenseless.

Job was always afraid of this dreadful disease. "For the thing which I greatly feared is come upon me, and that which I was afraid of has befallen me."[109]Job was an extremely wealthy man, and he was always aware of the fact that some of his wealth was acquired unjustly by his shrewd servants. He knew that the law of compensation would catch up with him.

Unhealed hatred, envy, and injustices can cause a person to become sick, and diseases will manifest themselves in the body. When people become angry, they lose their mental and emotional balance and become like a car that is careening out of control.

Healing of Cancer

If there be a messenger with him, an interpreter, one among a thousand, to shew unto man his uprightness: Then he is gracious unto him, and saith, Deliver him from going down to the pit: I have found a ransom. His flesh shall be fresher than a child's: he shall return to the days of his youth. Job 33:23-25.

The Eastern Aramaic text reads: "If a man have an angel to whom one would listen once in a thousand times, the angel would show him the way of uprightness. And be gracious to him and say, Deliver this man lest he go down to corruption; he has found salvation: Then his flesh will change to that of his childhood; and he shall return to the days of his youth."

---

[107]See Job 2:7, Lamsa translation.

[108]2 Pet. 3:10-11, Eastern Aramaic Peshitta text, Lamsa translation.

[109]Job 3:25, Eastern Aramaic Peshitta text, Lamsa translation.

Job was the wisest man of his day. He was the first man to tell that the earth was not stretched out flat on water but is a globe that hangs in the air.[110] The book of Job is filled with knowledge and understanding.

Certainly, Job knew something about the human body, diseases, and the fear of sicknesses. He knew that one who sows seeds of evil will reap evil, and one who scatters seeds of good will gather good. Job, as a great philosopher, knew that God was not the author of evil but that humans brought evil on themselves.

The remedies that Job prescribes for the healing of cancer are these: To do away with fear so that the healing forces would be free to operate; to repent by erasing every thought of evil from one's mind and heart.

If humans would accept only one out of a thousand of God's counsels, it would be enough to completely renew one's body, regain strength, and the flesh would be like that of a child. A child is free from fear of disease, want, and death. Today, many in the field of medical science realize that fears and wrong thinking are also responsible for hampering the healing processes. When one changes the way of thinking, the body will also change.

CHAPTER THIRTY-FOUR

God Not a Partner of Evil

Therefore hearken unto me, ye men of understanding: far be it from God, that he should do wickedness; and from the Almighty, that he should commit iniquity. Job 34:10.

Elihu, like Eliphaz, blames Job for his misfortune and vindicates God. Job has declared himself righteous and seemingly has accused God of having taken his righteousness from him and caused him to suffer. Moreover, Elihu accuses Job of being a companion of the workers of iniquity, of having walked with wicked men, and of having said that it profits man nothing that he should delight himself with God.[111]

Again, Elihu, like Eliphaz, believes in the law of compensation, that

[110] Job 26:7.

[111] See verse 37.

every man is rewarded according to his works.[112] He maintains that God does not pervert judgment. Moreover, Elihu believes that Job is receiving only what is due him and that his illness and trials are the result of some evil deeds that he has done.

God Sees All and Knows All

For his eyes are upon the ways of man, and he seeth all his goings. Job 34:21.

Since in the invisible realm of the Spirit there is no darkness, man's ways and deeds cannot be hidden from God, who knows all and sees all. Moreover, God cannot be blamed for humanity's difficulties and mishaps, which are the result of wrong actions and thinking, nor can God reward anyone with that which he does not possess.

Nothing happens without God's knowledge. Not even a sparrow or a hair falls without the divine being aware of it. When evil is done, God knows it and sees it, because anything evil is contrary to the divine nature.[113]

CHAPTER THIRTY-SIX

God's Eyes on the Righteous

He withdraweth not his eyes from the righteous: but with kings are they on the throne; yea, he doth establish them for ever, and they are exalted. Job 36:7.

The righteous are constantly before the eyes of God, who sees them and watches over them. God does not forsake the righteous or those who trust in the divine. The Lord knows the way of the righteous[114] and upholds the righteous.[115] "I have not seen the righteous forsaken."[116]

Jesus of Nazareth, a true, righteous prophet and sinless man of God, was not forsaken by God at Calvary. He was spared by God all through his life so that on the cross, he might confirm the joyful message that heralded a

---

[112]See verse 11.
[113]See verses 24-25.
[114]Ps. 1:6.
[115]Ps. 37:17.
[116]Ps. 37:25, K. J. V.

new way by which to conquer the world—the way of meekness and gentleness, the way of forgiveness. It was a way that makes people free and worthy to be called the children of their heavenly Father.

The Righteous Are Delivered

Desire not the night, when people are cut off in their place. Job 36:20.

The Eastern Aramaic text reads: "He shall deliver you from those who drive you away in the night, and give peoples for your sake, and the nations for your life." The verse refers to oppressors who strike during the dark hours of the night and carry away both people and plunder. The Lord sustains those who trust in the divine ways. See the above commentary on Job 36:7, "God's Eyes on the Righteous."

God's Dwelling Place

Also can any understand the spreadings of the clouds, or the noise of his tabernacle? Behold, he spreadeth his light upon it, and covereth the bottom of the sea. Job 36:29-30.

In biblical days clouds were considered as the tabernacle or the dwelling place of God. This was because clouds were higher than the highest thing on earth and, in biblical terminology, they were symbolic of glory, honor, and majesty.[117] The Lord called to Moses out of the cloud which had covered the top of Mount Sinai.[118] "And the Lord descended in the cloud."[119] Jesus ascended into heaven in a cloud.[120]

The Aramaic text reads: ". . . out of the greatness of his tabernacle." In this verse, "light" means lightning that lightens even the bottom of the sea.

God Cares for the Just and the Unjust

The noise thereof showeth concerning it, the cattle also concerning the vapor. Job 36:33.

---

[117]Ps. 36:5.
[118]Ex. 24:15-18.
[119]Ex. 34:5.
[120]Acts 1:9.

The Eastern Aramaic text reads: "He shows his possessions [or substance] to his friends, and to the wicked also." The Aramaic word *kinyaney,* "his possessions or wealth," also means "cattle." The meaning of this word is determined by the context. The Aramaic word *awaleh* has been wrongly rendered "vapor."

What Elihu means is that God is merciful to all his children—to the good and to the bad. God's blessings are shared with the good and the wicked, just as a human father shares his prosperity with both his obedient and disobedient children. Jesus said: "So that you may become sons of your Father who is in heaven, who causes his sun to shine upon the good and the bad, and who pours down his rain upon the just and the unjust."[121]

God is patient with the wicked, just as a loving father is patient with his disobedient children. God knows that some of the wicked will see the light and turn from their evil. For example, in the gospel of Luke we are told that the thief who was crucified with Jesus repented while he was dying on the cross. Also Saul, who became the apostle Paul, changed from a persecutor of the Jewish followers of Jesus to a man of God, and Francis of Assisi from a sinner to a saint.[122]

CHAPTER THIRTY-SEVEN

Equinox

How thy garments are warm, when he quieteth the earth by the south wind? Job 37:17.

The reference is to the equinox. December is the coldest month of the year in the northern hemisphere, and the sun is then farthest southward. But after December 22, the rays of the sun begin to grow gradually warmer. Near Easterners wear woolen robes, which conduct the heat of the sun's rays. One can feel the warmth of the sun in one's robe.

The Zoroastrians celebrate the day when the light prevails against darkness and heat over cold. March 22 is called *Nowruz,* "the new day." The year begins with the returning of the sun to the halfway point in the spring, the vernal equinox. The date of Christmas coincides with the

---

[121]Mt. 5:45, Eastern Aramaic Peshitta text, Lamsa translation.

[122]See verse 10.

ancient Roman holiday celebrating the returning of the sun from its southward trend, the winter solstice.

Man's Knowledge Limited

Hast thou with him spread out the sky, which is strong, and as a molten looking-glass? Job 37:18.

The last portion of this verse differs in the Aramaic Bible; the words "looking glass" are not there. The Aramaic words *lamsamakho akhda* mean "to support it together." The root of these words is *samak,* "to support, lean upon, rely on." It should read: "Were you with him when he spread out the great sky, helping him hold it up?"

Elihu is trying to convince Job that man cannot grasp the wonders of God or make himself equivalent to him in wisdom, power, and majesty. Man is a creature and not a creator and does not know all the secrets of the complex universe.

Gold Gleams out of the North

Fair weather cometh out of the north: with God is terrible majesty. Job 37:22.

The Aramaic word *dahba*, pronounced *dahwah*, means "gold." The Eastern Aramaic text reads: "Golden gleams come out of the north; and light shines from God," that is, out of the northern regions come golden gleams and the light of truth and understanding from God.

In biblical days, most of the gold came from Tarshish, Assyria, and other lands north of Canaan.[123] There is no mention of gold mines in the land of Canaan or Israel. Some gold came from Ethiopia.

Gold symbolizes purity, truth, and light. Metaphorically, gold means understanding and enlightenment. This is because through the light of God we are able to see gleams of truth.

---

[123]Gen. 2:11.

CHAPTER THIRTY-EIGHT

Earth with End

Whereupon are the foundations thereof fastened? or who laid the corner stone thereof. Job 38:6.

The Aramaic word *ebreh* means "the ends thereof." The Aramaic word for "foundations thereof" is *shatisaw*. The author speaks of the limits of the earth. Job, like all other men, wondered about the earth's outer ends and the vastness of the universe. This question was never answered by the ancient savants. Even today most of the universe is a mystery to human beings.

Not until Columbus crossed the Atlantic Ocean did people accept the earth as being round. In those ancient days our earth was supposed to be flat, and the Atlantic Ocean was looked upon as the end of the world. But as human knowledge grew, the concept of the earth and the universe grew also and still continues to grow.

Job believed the earth was hanging in the air. "He stretches out the north from the empty place, and hangs the earth upon nothing."[124] But the size and the limits of the globe were a great mystery to Job.

Star's Song

When the morning stars sang together, and all the sons of God shouted for joy? Job 38:7.

"Stars sang" is an Aramaic idiom meaning that the stars radiated abundant light. When describing harmony and beauty, Semites describe them in poetic and figurative speech. Stars were likened to human beings, singing and guiding people traveling in the deserts. Stars are very brilliant in the Arabian desert, and as they appear close to the earth on the horizon, they seem almost to beckon one.

It is often said that nature sings, meaning that nature is harmonious. Then again, people speak of stars as walking before men, which in Aramaic speech means men are following in the direction of the stars. All the

---

[124]Job 26:7. Eastern Aramaic Peshitta text, Lamsa translation.

dwellers of the desert travel by the means of the stars.[125]

In those days, stars were associated with the birth of kings and great men, and they shared in their victories. This is why the pagans worshiped the stars. "There shall come a Star out of Jacob."[126] The star means a king, hence, the Messiah or the greatly anticipated Anointed One of God.

When the sons of God (good men) live in peace and harmony, all nature shares in their joy. According to the writers of Hebrew Scripture, all nature declares the glory of God and sings praises to his name. Nature's songs and praises are conveyed in music, beauty, and harmony, and not in words.

CHAPTER THIRTY-NINE

Wild Goats

Their young ones are in good liking, they grow up with corn; they go forth, and return not unto them. Job 39:4.

The word "corn" is not correct. The wild goats do not feed on corn. It should read: "They bring up their young ones, until they grow up and are weaned." When the young wild goats are grown up and able to take care of themselves, they are weaned and let go on their own.

CHAPTER FORTY

Behemoth Protects Helpless Animals

Surely the mountains bring him forth food, where all the beasts of the field play. Job 40:20.

The Eastern Aramaic text reads: "He roams about the mountains, and all the wild beasts of the field lie down under his protection." The reference is to the behemoth (hippopotamus) which, in those days, was difficult to catch.[127] The hippopotamus fights lions, tigers, and large snakes. Wherever the hippopotamus is, the other beasts of the field graze in peace.

---

[125]Mt. 2:2.
[126]Num. 24:17.
[127]See verses 15-19.

Not Afraid of Rivers

Behold, he drinketh up a river, and hasteth not: he trusteth that he can draw up Jordan into his mouth. Job 40:23.

As stated in the above comment, Behemoth is another name for hippopotamus. The Eastern Aramaic text reads: "Behold, if he plunges into the river, he is not afraid; he is confident, though the Jordan reaches to his mouth."

The hippopotamus is a land and water animal, and it might have flourished in the marshes of the Jordan when the Hebrew patriarchs lived in Canaan. But today, there are none to be found in the Jordan Valley. The writer of the book of Job might have seen the huge animal somewhere else or even heard of it from travelers. The Jordan was the largest river in Canaan and was well-known to the people.

When guns were unknown, a hippopotamus was hard to catch. Spears, arrows, and nets had no effect on it. The animal's skin was too tough for arrows and spears, and its body too large and powerful to be dragged into a net. In those early days, therefore, a hippopotamus was a great wonder. But today, in the face of modern weapons, he is as helpless as any other animal.

CHAPTER FORTY-ONE

Limitation of Human Knowledge

Will he make a Covenant with thee? wilt thou take him for a servant for ever? Job 41:4.

The Eastern Aramaic text reads: "Will he make a covenant with you? Or will you count him as a servant for ever?" According to the text, the Lord God speaks of the strength of the hippopotamus and the impossibility of it being trained by humans like a bird that is trained.

Yet, this large animal is one of the smallest of God's wonders that humankind cannot understand or overcome. God revealed to Job how little human beings know about the things that are around them, and how many things are beyond their comprehension.

CHAPTER FORTY-TWO

Job Was Aided

And the Lord turned the captivity of Job, when he prayed for his friends: also the Lord gave Job twice as much as he had before. Then came there unto him all his brethren, and all his sisters, and all they that had been of his acquaintance before and did eat bread with him in his house: and they bemoaned him and comforted him over all the evil that the Lord had brought upon him: every man also gave him a piece of money, and every one an earring of gold. So the Lord blessed the latter end of Job more than his beginning: for he had fourteen thousand sheep, and six thousand camels, and a thousand yoke of oxen, and a thousand she asses.
Job 42:10-12.

According to the storyteller, Job's fortune was restored Although Job wavered at times and questioned God's wisdom and blamed the Lord for his affliction, he did not curse God nor desert God. Despite his great pain and wound, he remained loyal to God and, therefore, God reimbursed Job. The Lord gave him double of everything he had lost.

This new wealth did not fall from heaven. The Lord God touched the hearts of all the people who knew him. People brought him gifts of sheep, camels, donkeys, gold, silver, and women. Near Easterners are noted for their rendering of help to others during times of disasters, especially when the victims are princes and men of wealth and prominence. Also, the Aramaic text reads "and every man also gave him a ewe" and not "every man also gave him a piece of money."

God is not the author of material things. Heaven does not contain animals, gold, or silver. All the gifts and blessings that are received come through human channels. God moves on the hearts of the givers and the receivers.

At times, when a family is plundered and has lost their sheep, the members of the tribe come to their rescue, and in a few hours they have the same number of sheep. This generous act insures the future of the family and tribe. Jesus said, "Give and it will be given to you; good measure shaken down and running over they will pour into your robe. For with the measure that you measure, it will be measured to you."[128]

---

[128]Lk. 6:38, Eastern Aramaic Peshitta text, Lamsa translation.

The Day, the End, the Glory

And he called the name of the first, Jemima; and the name of the second, Kezia; and the name of the third, Keren-happuch. Job 42:14.

In the Near East, most of the names of men and women are significant of events which took place when the person was born. Nearly all biblical names have meanings. *Emama* (Jemima) means "day, midday, noontide." When his daughter *Emama* was born, Job was living in a new and bright day. The days of his suffering, poverty, and humiliation were past, just as night flees before the dawn. *Kesoaa* (Kezia) is derived from the Aramaic *kesa* or Hebrew *kaseh*, "the end." The name of this second child signifies the end of Job's trials, tribulations, and misfortunes. Job has come through his trials and sufferings victoriously.

Karna-pokh (Keren-happuch) means, "My glory (horn) has returned to me." The horn is symbolic of strength and glory. Job's glory and his power were lost during his trials and afflictions, but now his fortunes had returned. Job was once more healthy and wealthy and had a better understanding of God. The Lord had given him more sons and daughters, his neighbors had given him gold and silver, and his substance had increased abundantly.

INTRODUCTION TO THE PSALMS

No book in Holy Scripture has received such worldwide use as the book of Psalms. Indeed, this sacred portion of Scripture has been an integral part of the prayer books of Jewish and all Christian denominations and is highly revered. For centuries, many people have turned to the Psalms for devotion, inspiration, and consolation.

The Aramaic word for psalm is *mazmora,* which is cognate with the Hebrew *mizor.* Its Semitic root is *zamar,* "to sing praises, to chant, to talk with tones, to play on a stringed instrument." The Hebrew word for the book of Psalms is *tehillim*, "songs of praise." Our English term "psalms" comes from the Greek word *psalmoi,* "songs of praise," by way of Latin *psalmorum.* Today, as in the past, the Psalms function among Jews and Christians as a hymnal for worship and prayer book for devotion.

In the ancient Near East, shepherds sometimes sang these psalms and later poets put them to their lips and gave praise to the God of Israel. Temple singers glorified God with these psalms in the midst of the worshipers. Some psalms represent the prayers of Israel for deliverance from oppressors. Others were songs of joy when Israelites triumphed over their enemies. They all came through divine inspiration and, in the course of time, became the inspired songs, praises, and fervent prayers of Israel.

The Twenty-third Psalm, for instance, a Psalm of David, is revered and read by millions of people of many races. This psalm is a praise and prayer wherein the Creator of the universe is portrayed as a loving shepherd, who cares for his flocks day and night, and the people as sheep, who need direction, protection, and guidance.

Furthermore, the book of Psalms, like the books of the Prophets, contains messianic prophecies. And according to Christian interpretation of the psalms, the psalmists foresaw the rejection and the suffering of the Messiah and his moral victory over death and *Sheol.*

It was also believed that a large portion of the psalms was composed by King David and later written by the court scribes. This was based on an ancient and pervasive tradition that existed during biblical times. Some psalms were composed during David's early youth when he wandered on the hills of Judah and in the desert feeding sheep.[1]

---

[1]However, modern biblical scholars dispute this ancient notion on the basis of linguistic and contextual evidence.

Indeed, David, like many Near Eastern shepherds, was a poet-musician who spent many of his lonely hours singing, playing the harp or lyre, and composing songs. During these times in the solitude of the hills and valleys, David saw that the heavens declare the glory of God and the works of the divine hand are revealed in the firmament. Later, he played music before King Saul. The psalms of David were continually sung, sometimes by the shepherds and then by the new poets and by the temple singers.

Many of the psalms were composed during the reign of King Hezekiah, some during the exile in Babylon, and others at the time of the Maccabees when Israel was harassed by her enemies all around.

The first inspired folk song was the Song of Moses when the Israelites crossed the Red Sea and Pharaoh's army was destroyed. Miriam, his sister, and many women with timbrels, danced when this song was sung. The Song of Deborah was composed by her when King Nabin was defeated by Barak. Then we have the inspired Lamentations of Jeremiah, which is a wailing song composed when Jerusalem and the holy temple were destroyed by the Chaldean army.

The book of Psalms is divided into five *sepreh*, "books," and each book is divided into several *holalies*, "praises and hallelujahs." Some of the praises were accompanied by musical instruments, such as a psalter, guitar, and lyre, but most of them were sung without instruments. They were also songs that were used during battle.

PSALM ONE

Counsel of Sinners

Blessed is the man that walketh not in the counsel of the ungodly, nor standeth in the way of sinners, nor sitteth in the seat of the scornful. Ps. 1:1.

The Eastern Aramaic text reads: "Blessed is the man who walks not in the way [*urha*] of the ungodly, nor abides by the counsel [*reyana*] of sinners; nor sits in the company of mockers." TheAramaic word *reyana* means "counsel, decision." That is, when sinners plot to do evil, he does not agree with them, nor does he participate in their evil deeds.

At times, we cannot help but find ourselves in the company of those who might wish to do evil, but we should not agree with them when we see that they are conspiring against their neighbors or plotting to commit crimes against the weak and the poor.

PSALM TWO

Revolt of Kings

The kings of the earth set themselves, and the rulers take counsel together, against the Lord, and against his anointed. Ps. 2:2.

The word "set" is not present in the Aramaic text. The Aramaic word *qam* has many meanings—such as, "to stand up, rise up, conspire, revolt, halt." In this passage it means "to conspire." The first part of the verse in Aramaic reads: "The kings of the earth and the rulers have conspired and have taken counsel together . . ."

There are several interpretations of this psalm. One interpretation is that this is a messianic psalm that foretold the rejection and the suffering of Jesus of Nazareth, who became known as the Anointed, that is, the Christ.

The messianic kingdom, with its new laws and moral principles, was opposed by the princes and the kings of this world, because Jesus, as the anointed of God, tried to cut off their bands and remove their harsh yoke from the people.[2] They revolted because they did not want to come under the bonds of the Spirit and the easy yoke of God. But his dominion, at last, reached to the ends of the earth.[3]

Spiritual Sonship

I will declare the decree: the Lord hath said unto me, Thou art my Son; this day have I begotten thee. Ps. 2:7.

The first part of the verse in the Aramaic text reads: "To declare my promise [or covenant] . . ." The reference is to the divine promises that were made by God to Abraham and David.

"Begotten" is a figure of speech and should not be taken literally. God is the Eternal Spirit and neither begets nor is begotten. "Begotten" in this verse means "to be made manifest." According to the gospel of John, the Messiah/Christ (the Anointed) always existed in the mind of God from the

---

[2]See Ps. 2:3.

[3]See also Ps. 2:8-9, and the Lamsa translation of Lk. 1:32-33, Rev. 2:27.

very beginning. "The Word [Christ] was in the beginning, and that very Word was with God, and God was that Word."[4]

Messiah/Christ is the eternal promise of God that became manifested in the fullness of time. God, before time, knew humanity would go astray from the true path of life; therefore, the Messiah was the preordained promise of God to bring humankind back on the good path of life.[5]

The word "son" in Aramaic means an image or likeness of the father but is often used metaphorically to mean "love." Near Easterners who love and trust one another call each other "my son." This is because a good son occupies the highest place in the heart of his father. God called Solomon "my son." The term son is applied also to members of the same faith.

God is Spirit and the Messiah/Christ is God's spiritual and eternal son, who is the heir to the kingdom. God made manifest divine love to humanity through the Messiah, the true expression of God on earth.

Spiritual Kingdom

Ask of me, and I shall give thee the heathen for thine inheritance, and the uttermost parts of the earth for thy possession. Ps. 2:8.

The messianic kingdom was to have dominion throughout the world. But it was to be a spiritual kingdom that would embrace all nations and peoples. This universal kingdom was envisioned by the Hebrew prophets, who hailed the Messiah as an Everlasting King. Both the Messiah and his eternal kingdom can only be understood spiritually. The prophet Daniel calls it the stone not cut by human hand, which in due time would defeat and transform the realms of the Gentiles and establish the reign of justice and peace.

Rod of Iron

Thou shalt break them with a rod of iron; thou shalt dash them in pieces like a potter's vessel. Ps. 2:9.

The first part of the verse in Aramaic reads: "You shall shepherd them with a rod of iron . . ." The Aramaic verb *tra* means "to discipline, instruct,

---

[4]Jn. 1:1, Eastern Aramaic Peshitta text, Lamsa translation.
[5]See 1 Pet. 1:20.

guide, shepherd." Shepherds carry a wooden rod, which is generally a branch, to direct the sheep to the right path. When the sheep scatter, the shepherd taps them gently with the rod.

The Gentiles were to be disciplined with an iron rod, denoting a very strict discipline. This is because many tribal people were lawless, and it would be difficult to discipline them

When King Solomon died, his son Rehoboam told the people that his rule would be harsher than that of his father, and the taxation would be much higher.[6] The Gentiles' rule would be broken like a potter breaks malformed and damaged vessels.

The Gentiles had harassed and persecuted the Israelites. Israel was expecting a complete deliverance from them. The Messiah was to fulfill this prophecy, but he would do it through meekness and loving kindness, which were contrary to most kingdoms and their way of dominion.

Kiss the Son

Kiss the Son, lest he be angry, and ye perish from the way, when his wrath is kindled but a little. Blessed are all they that put their trust in him. Ps. 2:12.

"Kiss" in this instance means "to do obeisance." Near Easterners kissed the hands of noblemen, princes, and holy men, and bowed to them as a token of homage. During a gathering for worship, people would bow and kiss sacred objects as a token of reverence to the holy place where God's name was invoked and prayers were offered. A kiss was also a sign of approval.

"The Son" refers to the Messiah. The people are admonished to acknowledge him, do homage to him, and put their trust in him, so that they may not go astray from God's way and bring wrath upon themselves from their wrongdoings.

PSALM FOUR

Comforted Me

Hear me when I call, O God of my righteousness: thou hast enlarged me when I was in distress; have mercy upon me, and hear my prayer. Ps. 4:1.

---

[6] 1 Ki. 12:14.

The Eastern Aramaic text reads: "When I have called thee, thou hast answered me, O my God and Savior of my righteousness; thou hast comforted me when I was in distress; have mercy upon me and hear my prayer."

The Aramaic word *beaolsan* means "distress," that is, mental pain or pressures of danger. The Aramaic *arwaht li* means, "Thou hast comforted me," or relieved me of the anxieties, troubles, and dangers of this life.

The Psalmist believed that God's help and guidance were always ready for those who sought divine help with a sincere heart. He knew this because he already had some experience with God when his prayers had been answered before.

Anger Without a Cause

Stand in awe, and sin not: commune with your own heart upon your bed, and be still. Selah. Ps. 4:4.

The Aramaic word *regaz* means "be angry." This phrase should read: "Be angry and yet sin not." Sin in this instance refers to a crime. Men who become angry at one another might strike with a dagger or sword. Anger, when greatly agitated, cannot be easily repressed or controlled; but by meditation and examination of one's own heart, agreement can be reached with an adversary and solutions be found to a problem. Often, anger is provoked by misunderstanding and may actually have no basis in reason.

Hasty wrath may lead to murder. In other words, anger is the trigger of quarrels and violence. Jesus said, "But I say to you that whoever becomes angry with his brother for no reason is guilty before the court."[7]

Sacrifice of Righteousness

Offer the sacrifices of righteousness, and put your trust in the Lord. Ps. 4:5.

"The sacrifices of righteousness" refers to acts of mercy and justice. Hebrew prophets condemned animal sacrifices because some of the people who offered them defrauded the widows, oppressed the poor, and took bribes. The sacrifices were supposed to absolve the guilty. But, "The sacrifices of the wicked are an abomination to the Lord; but the prayer of

[7]Mt. 5:22, Eastern Aramaic Peshitta text, Lamsa translation.

the upright is his delight."[8]

The psalmist exhorts the people to offer sacrifices of righteousness rather than the sacrifice of animals. Pagan ceremonies delighted in wickedness, immorality, and human sacrifices. But the God of Israel shunned all false worship and the works of iniquity.

The Hebrew prophet Isaiah condemned the multitude of sacrifices. He says, "Of what purpose is the multitude of your sacrifices to me? says the Lord; I am full of the burnt offerings of rams, and the fat of fed beasts; and I do not delight in the blood of bullocks, or of lambs, or of he-goats . . . I do not eat that which is obtained wrongfully, and taken by force."[9]

PSALM SIX

A Concept of Death

For in death there is no remembrance of thee: in the grave who shall give thee thanks? Ps. 6:5.

The early Hebrews, like other Semitic races, had little knowledge of immortality. Most people believed that death was the end completely. According to the belief of the Israelites, *Sheol* was a place underground and far away from the jurisdiction of the living God. It was also believed that in *Sheol* there was no remembrance of God.[10]

This concept changed from time to time. Some teachers of religion believed that *Sheol* was a place for the departed who were waiting for the resurrection and the great day of judgment This particular concept was crystalized by the prophet Daniel, who stated that there would be a resurrection of the dead, the separation of the righteous and the wicked, and a day of reckoning.

Sheol was so dreaded that people believed no one could be freed from it. But Jesus of Nazareth told Peter that the gates of *Sheol* would not prevail against his congregation of followers and disciples.[11] According to the epistle of first Peter, Jesus spent three days in *Sheol* preaching to the souls

---

[8]Prov. 15:8, Eastern Aramaic Peshitta text, Lamsa translation.
[9]Isa. 1:11-13. See also Jer. 6:20.
[10]See also Ps. 115:17.
[11]See Mt. 16:18, Lamsa translation.

of the departed.[12] Paul in his epistle wrote: "O death, where is your sting? O *Sheol,* where is your victory?"[13]

The concept of death and life is different today and is far superior to the naive and rudimentary knowledge of the people in the past. Life and death are one. Death is not an annihilation but a transformation from the physical form of life into a totally spiritual one.

Weeping Bitterly

I am weary with my groaning; all the night make I my bed to swim; I water my couch with my tears. Ps. 6:6.

The Eastern Aramaic text reads: "I am weary with my groaning; and every night I water my bed and wash my mattress with my tears." "I water my bed and wash my mattress with my tears" is an Aramaic idiom that means, "I was so sorrowful that I wept all night." The Aramaic word *arsi* means "mattress." These sayings are still used today and are never taken literally. Semites often say, "Rivers of water poured out of my eyes."

This psalm was probably composed by David when he was in distress because of his sin. He had done away with Uriah, one of his most faithful soldiers.[14] King David wept vehemently and repented for his sin, and the Lord forgave him.[15]

PSALM SEVEN

God Is a Just Judge

God judgeth the righteous, and God is angry with the wicked every day. Ps. 7:11.

The Eastern Aramaic text reads: "God is a righteous judge; yea he is not angry every day." The translators confused *la*, "not," for *leh,* "him or his." The Aramaic word for "judge" is *diana*, and the word for "judgment" is *dina*. Both words are written alike but pronounced differently.

The Psalmist compares God with an earthly judge who at times becomes

---

[12]See 1 Pet. 3:1, Lamsa translation.

[13]1 Cor. 15:55, Eastern Aramaic Peshitta text, Lamsa translation.

[14]2 Sam. 11:15-17.

[15]Isa. 25:8 refers to God's power to forgive.

very angry. This is more true of Near Eastern judges in the ancient world, who were not paid for their services but were allowed to exact all they could get from those who came before them seeking justice. The judges' facial expressions were always serious. Their anger was to frighten the disputants and thus exact more money and bribes from them.

"The Lord is merciful and gracious, slow to anger and plenteous in mercy."[16] According to the belief system of the times, God will judge the wicked but not the righteous. Only those who have broken the law are tried before an earthly judge. God is often portrayed in Scripture as angry, happy, sorry, and jealous simply because men have all these attributes. In other words, God is pictured as a king, an angry judge, and a warrior. Interestingly, the word "wicked" is not in the original text, as is indicated in the King James Version by printing it in italics.

PSALM EIGHT

Sucklings

Out of the mouth of babes and sucklings hast thou ordained strength because of thine enemies, that thou mightest still the enemy and the avenger. Ps. 8:2.

"Sucklings" is used allegorically to mean "unlearned." In the Near East, ignorant and illiterate men are frequently called sucklings or babes. People often say: "You are still a child [or a babe]; you have no understanding."

However, little children are innocent and more ready to accept life. Jesus thanked God for the simple men and women who accepted his teaching. "I thank thee, O my Father, Lord of heaven and earth, because thou hast hidden these things from the wise and the men of understanding, and hast revealed them to children."[17]

The truth is often hidden from those who depend on human reason alone but is revealed to those who, like little children, are willing to learn and are pure in heart. The Hebrews were humble and trying to seek God's truth and way. They were a pastoral people whom God called out of other races to praise God's name and proclaim it throughout the world. Not one of Jesus' disciples was highly educated. Matthew was the only one who could read

---

[16]Ps. 103:8, Eastern Aramaic Peshitta text, Lamsa translation.

[17]Mt. 11:25, Eastern Aramaic Peshitta text, Lamsa translation. See Lk. 10:21 also.

and write; the others were uneducated peasants and fishermen who were looked upon by the scribes and learned almost as outcasts.

It was out of the mouths of these men, whose minds were virgin, that the good news of God's sovereign presence and counsel was to be preached and demonstrated. It was through them that the things that were hidden from the wise and the prudent would be revealed so that learned men could not say they were the founders of the kingdom of God. The glory and honor were given to God.

Son of Man

What is man, that thou art mindful of him? and the son of man, that thou visitest him? Ps. 8:4.

In the book of Genesis the Aramaic word for "man" is *nasha.* It derives from *naphsha,* "soul, life, breath." This is because God breathed into Adam's nostrils the breathe of life, and *Adam,* meaning "red soil," became a living being. However, the Aramaic word that is used in the text of the psalm is *gawra,* which also means "man."

"Son of man," *barnasha,* is used frequently in some books of the Bible. It denotes man's origin—made from the earth, hence vulnerable.[18] This term was used to distinguish between a mortal man and immortal spirits and angels and to point out that a human being is a frail creature.

Ninety times the prophet Ezekiel is called "son of man,"[19] meaning a human being. Jesus often referred to himself as the son of man. This is because he was human and continually demonstrating humility and gentleness. Daniel, in his apocalyptic book, saw a resemblance "like the Son of man," which means "someone who looked like a human being."[20]

PSALM NINE

God Does Not Forsake the Righteous

And they that know thy name will put their trust in thee: for thou, Lord, hast not forsaken them that seek thee. Ps. 9:10.

---

[18]Job 25:6. The terms "dust and worm" in this verse implies earthliness.
[19]In Aramaic *bar nasha* and in Hebrew *ben Adam* — "son of man."
[20]Dan. 7:13.

Generally, Near Easterners never think of God as forsaking them. They may forsake God, but they know that God never forsakes them. During times of trouble and trial, they always call on God. And when God is slow in answering them, they often ask for death and curse the day in which they were born. "When the poor and needy seek water, and there is none . . . I the God of Israel will not forsake them."[21] God never forsakes those who trust in the divine and defend the cause of truth and justice.

A Lawgiver

Put them in fear, O Lord: that the nations may know themselves to be but men. Selah. Ps. 9:20.

The Eastern Aramaic text reads: "Appoint for them a lawgiver, that the Gentiles may know themselves to be but men." Israel had the law and Holy Scripture that had become like a lamp to their feet and a light to their path. But the Gentiles had no law or moral code equal to that of the Israelites. Such words as mercy, loving kindness, and compassion were alien to their ears. They were like sheep without a shepherd.

The law of and ordinances of Moses had made the Israelites a strong and united people. The Gentiles needed a lawgiver like Moses to show them right and wrong in the lands where they governed. Among these tribal peoples, justice was trampled on, and they plundered one another.

The Gentile kings and emperors were gods of the state, and they thought themselves to be superior to other states. But a lawgiver was to teach them that they were only men and equal to other races. The Arabs were kindred of the Israelites. They were the descendants of Lot, Ishmael, and Esau, but they and the Israelites were continually fighting each other.

Muslims believe that the lawgiver was Muhammad. His teaching, in the sixth century CE, became a light not only to the Arab people but to millions of people in Indonesia, Malaya, India, and many other places in Asia. Prior to this event, tribal Arab people worshiped many gods.

According to the prophet Isaiah, the Messiah was to be the light of the Gentiles. The teachings of Jesus of Nazareth, who became known as the Messiah/Christ, are based on the word of God, the Hebrew Scriptures.

---

[21]Isa. 41:17, Eastern Aramaic Peshitta text, Lamsa translation.

PSALM TEN

Lift up Thine Hand

Arise, O Lord; O God, lift up thine hand: forget not the humble. Ps. 10:12.

The Eastern Aramaic text reads: "Arise, O Lord, O my God, lift up thine hand; forget not the afflicted." "Lift up thine hand" is a Semitic saying that means "fight." When the people speak of a coward, they say, "He cannot lift up his hand."

Near Easterners, when quarreling, raise their hands as an expression of their threat. Semites often say, "He has lifted up his hand or stretched forth his hand against him."[22]

Paul says that he wishes men would lift up their hands in prayer and not in anger.[23] The psalmist implores God to fight against the wicked, avenge the poor, and not forget the humble and meek of the land.[24]

PSALM TWELVE

Double Heart

They speak vanity every one with his neighbor: with flattering lips and with a double heart do they speak. Ps. 12:2.

"Double heart" is an Aramaic idiom that means hypocritical or insincere. In American idiomatic English one would say "two-faced." In those days the heart was considered the seat of one's faculties. The term *reyana,* "mind," was rarely used during biblical times. The ancients believed that life was supposed to be in the blood, and blood passes through the heart. Therefore, double heart also means a double minded person who says one thing but really means something else. One cannot trust what they say.

"But the Lord looketh on the heart."[25] "A man's heart deviseth his

---

[22]See Lk. 22:53.
[23]1 Tim. 2:8.
[24]See verses 13-18.
[25]1 Sam. 16:7, K.J.V.

way."[26] "Not of double heart"[27] means "sincere, unequivocal, determined."

Ancient Punishment

The Lord shall cut off all flattering lips, and the tongue that speaketh proud things: Who have said, With our tongue will we prevail; our lips are our own: who is lord over us? Ps. 12:3-4.

"Cut off the lips" is a Near Eastern saying still in common use. The phrase means that God will silence the speech of deceptive men and of those who magnify themselves and utter proud things against God. In the Near East, the lips, tongues, ears, and noses of culprits and blasphemers were cut off. This form of punishment was prevalent until the 1950s.

PSALM FOURTEEN

Devour People

Have all the workers of iniquity no knowledge? who eat up my people as they eat bread, and call not upon the Lord. Ps. 14:4.

Those who "eat up" or "devour my people" refers to those who oppress and exploit the people. Near Easterners who are misgoverned, heavily taxed, and oppressed say, "we have been eaten." Also, when money or other property is embezzled, they say, "They have eaten the money."

Jesus of Nazareth said: "Woe to you, scribes and Pharisees, hypocrites! for ye devour [Aramaic *akhliton,* you eat] widows' houses, and for a pretense make long prayer."[28] The poor and the needy were oppressed and exploited by those in power, who never even remembered the name of God.

PSALM FIFTEEN

Charging Interest

He that putteth not out his money to usury, nor taketh reward against the

---

[26]Prov. 16:9, K.J.V.
[27]1 Chron. 12:33, K.J.V.
[28]Mt. 23:14, K.J.V.

innocent. He that doeth these things shall never be moved. Ps. 15:5.

Israel was admonished by Moses not to charge interest for any money loaned to fellow Israelites. Those who obeyed this law and loaned money without interest would be permanently established.

Although the Israelites were not to charge interest to their own people, they could charge all the interest they so desired on loans to the Gentiles. They were also admonished not to sell meat from animals that had died a natural death, but they could sell it to Gentiles.[29]

At that time, the law was written when people were polytheistic; each race adhered to the laws and ordinances of its own god and rendered help to its own people, but not to the Israelites or other tribal people.

PSALM SIXTEEN

Cup of Goodness

The Lord is the portion of mine inheritance and of my cup: thou maintainest my lot. The lines are fallen unto me in pleasant places; yea, I have a goodly heritage. Ps. 16:5-6.

"Cup" is often used metaphorically, signifying trials and uncertainties. In the Near East, when a man wanted to do away with his enemies or rivals, he invited them to a banquet and poisoned their cups. The fearful and doubtful guests had to drink from it.

There are also references in the New Testament to the metaphor of the cup. For example, Jesus referred to his arrest at the garden as the "cup." "The cup which my Father hath given me, shall I not drink it?"[30] Then again, he said, "Let this cup pass from me: nevertheless not as I will, but as thou wilt."[31]

However, the cup of which the psalmist speaks in this verse is the cup of goodness. The Lord's cup is the portion of his goodness and his *loving-kindness* to those who trust in him and walk in his way. The psalmist is mindful of God's deliverance of Israel from her enemies and the portion of the land that fell to Israelites in good places. The land of Israel served as a

---

[29]See Dt. 14:20-21.
[30]Jn. 18:11, K.J.V.
[31]Mt. 26:39, K.J.V.

bridge between Egypt and the Fertile Crescent.

Intuition

I will bless the Lord, who hath given me counsel: my reins also instruct me in the right seasons. Ps. 16:7.

The last section of this verse in the Eastern Aramaic text reads: ". . . my intuition also guides me during the night." A literal translation of this verse from Aramaic would read, "He corrected my kidneys"; that is, He gave me intuition to find my true way.

In biblical days, the heart was considered the center of human reason. Kidneys and liver were also considered in the same way. God's guidance comes in dreams, visions, and through intuition. Many of these old terms of speech have become obsolete. Today no one believes that the heart is the seat of human reason. (However, according to the latest scientific findings the heart contains about 30 to 40 percent neurons.)

Hope

Therefore my heart is glad, and my glory rejoiceth: my flesh also shall rest in hope. Ps. 16:9.

The Aramaic word *sbra,* "hope," derives from *sbar,* "to hope, trust, expect, be confident." It should not be confused with *sbara*, "imagination, illusion, uncertain thought." *Sbra* as used by the psalmist means an expectation of something that will surely happen.

Sbarta or *swarta,* "gospel," comes form the same root, *sbar,* meaning "to proclaim good tidings, preaching full of hope, joyful message, joyful expectation." When hope is assured, good tidings are proclaimed or preached.

Sheol Is Not Hell

For thou wilt not leave my soul in hell: neither wilt thou suffer thine Holy One to see corruption. Ps. 16:10.

New Testament writers usually interpreted this verse as a messianic psalm. The reference is to the Messiah, whose soul was not to be left in

Sheol. According to the New Testament, the body of Jesus, who became known as the Messiah/Christ, did not see corruption because he arose from death and ascended into heaven.[32]

Sheol was supposed to be a dark and dreary place under the earth where all human souls were held regardless of their good or bad deeds on earth. However, this Semitic term does not mean "hell" but rather a place of inactivity where people lived a quasi-life and were in waiting. Hell as a burning place is misunderstood. The gospel writers used this term to describe mental torment and regret and not a literal place. There is a great difference in meaning between the terms *Sheol* (Old Testament) and *Gehenna dnoora,* "hell fire" (New Testament). Hell fire was unknown to the Hebrew prophets.

The psalmist declared that *Sheol* was under God's dominion. He writes: "If I ascend into heaven, thou art there; if I descend into Sheol, behold thou art there also."[33]

PSALM SEVENTEEN

Shadow of the Wings

Keep me as the apple of the eye; hide me under the shadow of thy wings. Ps. 17:8.

Hebrew prophets and poets used figurative speech to convey spiritual ideas, basic faith, and truth to unlearned listeners. "Wings" in Aramaic are symbolic of protection and speed. During times of danger, cold, and heat, little birds take refuge under their mother's wings, which offer protection from the early morning cold and the heat of the day. Also, when the little ones are menaced by birds of prey, they gather under the mother's wings.

The psalmist describes God metaphorically as a bird that is constantly mindful of its brood, ever ready to offer them a shelter when they are in danger. God's counsel and truth offer an everlasting protection to those who are weary and in danger. In Psalm 91:4 we read: "He shall cover thee with his feathers, and under his wings shalt thou trust: his truth shall be thy shield and buckler."[34]

---

[32]Acts 2:27.

[33]See Ps. 139:8, Eastern Aramaic Peshitta text, Lamsa translation.

[34]K.J.V.

Possessions of the Wicked

From men which are thy hand, O Lord, from men of the world, which have their portion in this life, and whose belly thou fillest with thy hid treasure: they are full of children, and leave the rest of their substance to their babes. Ps. 17:14.

The Eastern Aramaic text reads: "From the dead that die by thy hand, O Lord; and from the dead of the grave, divide their possessions among the living; fill their belly with thy treasure, so that their children are satisfied and have a portion remaining for their own children." In the ancient days, plagues and catastrophes were attributed to the wrath of God; this is the reason it reads "from the dead that die by thy hand, O Lord . . ."

The psalmist implores God to divide the possessions of the wicked who were slain among the righteous who were living, so they might have plenty to leave some to their children, who may, in turn, leave to their children.

PSALM EIGHTEEN

Rock—Protection

The Lord is my rock, and my fortress, and my deliverer; my God, my strength, in whom I will trust; my buckler, and the horn of my salvation, and my high tower. Ps. 18:2.

The Aramaic word *takipa* means "the strong one, strength." The reference is to God, whose strength never fails. At times "rock" is used figuratively, meaning "strength and protection." In Psalm 31:3, God is called *Beth-gosa,* "the house of refuge." The Aramaic word has been rendered "fortress" instead of "refuge." In the Near East, during severe storms and whirlwinds, the shepherds take refuge under rocks.[35]

Floods of Troubles

The sorrows of death compassed me, and the floods of ungodly men made me afraid. Ps. 18:4.

The word translated as "floods" in the King James Version signifies

---

[35]Ps. 18:31; Isa. 17:10.

difficulties and troubles. When speaking of difficult problems and troubles, Near Easterners often depict themselves as surrounded with rushing floods of water or in the bottom of the sea.

David offers thanks to God, who had delivered him from his enemies, and for God's goodness to him when he was surrounded with difficulties. The Eastern Aramaic text reads: "For the pains of death surrounded me, and the rush of ungodly men has confused me."

Thick Darkness

He made darkness his secret place; his pavilion round about him were dark waters and thick clouds of the skies. Ps. 18:11.

When the Lord descended upon Mount Sinai in fire, the smoke of the mountain ascended as the smoke of a furnace.[36] "Darkness" in this verse is symbolic of God's secret place. No one was to see the divine face. That is why God dwelt in darkness. Also, not being able to see God, no one could make an image of the Lord God. They saw God's glory and heard the divine voice, but no one beheld the face of God.[37]

The glory of God was revealed in a cloud upon Mount Sinai. In Semitic languages "cloud" is symbolic of glory, protection, and omnipresence: "Clouds and darkness are round about him."[38] ". . . who makest the clouds his chariot."[39] According to the New Testament writers, Jesus of Nazareth as Messiah is to come in the clouds of heaven.[40]

Shun the Crooked

With the pure thou wilt show thyself pure; and with the froward thou wilt show thyself froward. Ps. 18:26.

The Eastern Aramaic text reads: "With the clean thou shalt be clean: and from the crooked thou shalt turn aside." The Aramaic word used at the end

---

[36]See Ex. 19:18 and Dt. 4:11.
[37]Dt. 4:15-16.
[38]Ps. 97:2. K.J.V.
[39]Ps. 104:3, K.J.V.
[40]Mt. 24:30, Mk. 13:26.

of the verse is *tithpatal* and not *tithaakam.*[41]

Patal has many meanings, such as "twist, awry, crooked, forward, shifty, perverse." Colloquially, it means "to shift to one side, to get out of the way, to turn aside." The psalmist declares that God turns aside from the crooked.

Candle, God's Light

For thou wilt light my candle: the Lord my God will enlighten my darkness. Ps. 18:28.

"Candle" symbolizes light, truth, and understanding. It is also used metaphorically to mean "an heir." Light is symbolic of enlightenment, and darkness is symbolic of ignorance.

The true religion of Israel was the light of God that enlightened the dark paths of Israel. As long as this lamp—that is the candle—was burning, the people were happy, prosperous, secure, and full of hope. At times, however, the light of God was temporarily put out by unjust and iniquitous priests, kings, and princes.

This psalm was composed and sung by David as a thanksgiving to God for all the goodness and favors he had received during his life. The king implores the Lord to lighten his darkness, remove the dark spots in his life, and grant that his heirs will sit upon the throne of Israel and reign with justice and righteousness.

A Leader Among the Gentiles

Thou hast delivered me from the strivings of the people; and thou hast made me the head of the heathen: a people whom I have not known shall serve me. Ps. 18:43.

The last section of the verse in the Eastern Aramaic text reads: ". . . and thou wilt make me the leader of the Gentiles; a people whom I have not known shall serve me." This verse is interpreted as a messianic psalm. It is also understood and recited by and on behalf of a Davidic king.

The Messiah was to be ruler of the Gentiles. Their kingdoms were to become the kingdom of the Messiah and the Lord God.[42] This psalm reveals that the time will come when the Gentiles would acknowledge the

---

[41]See 2 Sam. 22:27.
[42]See Ps. 22:27-28.

God of Israel. Many Hebrew prophets predicted the conversion of the Gentiles to the knowledge of God.

Spiritually speaking, the movement that grew out of the work and mission of Jesus of Nazareth has untied many nations of the world. The Bible and its Semitic culture has exerted a tremendous influence on the lives of millions of people. Hebrew laws and ordinances have been adopted by many nations.[43]

PSALM NINETEEN

Knowledge Revealed

The heavens declare the glory of God: and the firmament sheweth his handywork. Day unto day uttereth speech, and night unto night sheweth knowledge. There is not speech nor language, where their voice is not heard. Their line is gone out through all the earth and their words to the end of the world. In them hath he set a tabernacle for the sun. Ps. 19:1-4.

Verse 4 of this psalm in the Eastern Aramaic text reads: "Their good news has gone out through all the earth, and their words to the end of the world. He has set his tabernacle in the sun among them."

"He has set his tabernacle in the sun among them" means that God's light embraces the entire universe. God does not hide anything from his creations. Every day brings news and discoveries. Every night reveals God's glory and might through the billions of stars. All these ideas are couched in metaphoric expressions.

Bridegroom Coming out

Which is as a bridegroom coming out of his chamber, and rejoiceth as a strong man to run a race. Ps. 19:5.

Wedding feasts in the East lasted from three to seven days, according to the social standing of the bridegroom and the bride.[44] During the festivities both the bridegroom and the bride remained in the house, surrounded by men and women who danced, ate, drank, and celebrated. As the houses

---

[43]See Dt. 18:15-18.

[44]See Judg. 14:12.

were small, some people could not get in, especially the poor, for only those who brought food as gifts could enter and leave freely.

All who had been unable to enter the house waited outside to have a glimpse of the bridegroom when he was ready to come out and walk a distance to refresh himself. In some regions in the Near East, toilets were unknown. The bride went out when it was dark, accompanied by her bridesmaids.

The people rejoiced when they saw the bridegroom dressed in his wedding garments and ornaments. However, the bride was usually covered with a large and long veil.

Instruction to Young Men

The law of the Lord is perfect, converting the soul: the testimony of the Lord is sure, making wise the simple. Ps. 19:7.

The Aramaic word *yalodeh,* "simple," also means "children, youths." Interestingly, *yalodeh* may also imply "not intelligent." It depends on the context of the sentence. Near Eastern children are taught the law and are required by their teachers to recite it aloud. The law of Moses and the ten commandments were among the first subjects taught to the Hebrew children. "Hear, O Israel: the Lord our God is one Lord."[45]

The law of the Lord is simple; it is perfect and free from ambiguities and qualifying clauses that would obscure the truth and pervert justice.

Reverence of the Lord

The fear of the Lord is clean, enduring for ever: the judgments of the Lord are true and righteous altogether. Ps. 19:9.

The word translated as "fear" in the King James Version in hundreds of passages of Scripture should read "reverence," that is, "the reverence of the Lord." Near Easterners, when entering into the presence of a king, a prince, or a nobleman, stood in awe as a token of reverence to him because he was the representative of a race or nation. Ministers and high state dignitaries dropped to their knees when they paid their respects to the king.

The word "clean" here means "sincere," that is, without any political or

[45]Dt. 6:4; Mk. 12:29.

selfish motive. The homage paid to princes and kings is often insincere, motivated by selfish desire for favors and political advantages. But the Ruler of the universe is just, and God's decrees are righteous. What God wants from humanity is a pure and sincere heart. Human beings are to love and be devoted to truth, justice, kindness, and relate to their neighbors in genuine care, righteousness, and compassion.

PSALM TWENTY-TWO

Destiny

My God, my God, why hast thou forsaken me? why art thou so far from helping me, and from the words of my roaring? Ps. 22:1.

The Aramaic word *shabak* means "to keep, leave, forgive, allow, desert." One has to know how the word is used in order to know its true meaning. The Aramaic-speaking people often say: "*Leave* me bread." "They have killed the men but *left* the women." "*Forgive* them." "*Allow* them to do it." The word is *shabak* in all these instances.

The Aramaic word for "forsake" is *taaa*, which has only one meaning. Another word is *nesha*. Joseph called the name of his firstborn *Manasheh* from *nesha,* "to forsake, forget."[46] God had never forsaken the Israelites; they had forsaken God.

The Hebrew writers used Aramaic and Hebrew indiscriminately. Aramaic was spoken by the early Hebrews, the Jewish exiles, and was the vernacular of the Jews during the time of Jesus and for many centuries afterwards. It is still used today by Assyrians, Chaldeans and many other Semitic groups of people.

The Hebrew Scriptures used the word *azabatani* which, as in Aramaic, means "to leave," that is, "to let me leave." Near Easterners never think of God as deserting them but are impatient when their prayers are not granted immediately. In times of persecution, oppression, and grief, they ask God to take them away. They wonder why they are allowed to live. At times, they say, "O God, take me away. I am not better than my father." Like Elijah, Job sought death but never thought God had forsaken him.[47]

---

[46]Gen. 41:51.

[47]Job 3:1-8.

Jeremiah cursed the day he was born.[48] The psalmist is weary of life because God has not granted his prayers. He has been pursued by his enemies and is now discovered.

This verse should read: "My God, my God, why hast thou let me live? and yet thou hast delayed my salvation from me, because of the words of my folly."

Trusting in the Lord

He trusted on the Lord that he would deliver him: let him deliver him, seeing he delighted in him. Ps. 22:8.

This is a reference to the Messiah, the one ordained by the Lord God. The Messiah was to trust in the Lord to help carry out his difficult mission. He was to conquer the world by the Spirit of the Lord, rather than by the arm of man and the weapons of war.

Jesus of Nazareth fulfilled this mission by trusting in the Lord. His faith in God never wavered, not even during his trial or when he was suffering on the cross. Even when he was dying, he said, "Father, into thy hands I commit my spirit."[49] The priests and scribes who stood near the cross said: "He trusted in God; let him deliver him now, if God will have him: for he said, I am the Son of God."[50]

God never forsakes those who trust in God and those who may die for the divine mission and cause. Jesus, on the cross, according to the Aramaic text, cried, "My God, my God, for this I was spared [or kept]!"[51] which means, "This was my destiny." In other words, Jesus suffered and died as a man, and God was with him, but the Christ which was a part of him did not suffer nor was buried.

All other versions read: "Why hast thou forsaken me?" This saying is contrary to all Scriptures, for God forsakes no one. God as a loving Father even seeks those who have gone astray, always mindful of his children, and always with those who devote their lives to the spreading of the divine word.[52] Jesus, as a devout Semite, a Torah teacher and man of God, would

---

[48]Jer. 20:14-18.

[49]See Lk. 23:46, Lamsa translation.

[50]Mt. 27:43.

[51]Mt. 27:46, Eastern Aramaic Peshitta text, Lamsa translation.

[52]1 Pet. 1:19-20.

never have felt that God had forsaken him.[53]

Vicious Men

For dogs have compassed me: the assembly of the wicked have inclosed me: they pierced my hands and my feet. Ps. 22:16.

The word translated as "dogs" in the King James Version was used metaphorically, meaning "vicious men or oppressors." Verse 20 of the Eastern Aramaic text reads: "Deliver my soul from the sword, my only one from the hand of the vicious [dogs]." In the Near East the shepherd dogs are very vicious. They fight for the sheep against wolves and bears. They attack strangers who dare to approach the flock.

Wicked, vicious men and gossip mongers are often called dogs. In his epistle to the Philippians, Paul exhorts the Christians to beware of dogs, that is, to beware of vicious men, those who assassinate others by means of destructive gossip.[54] Western commentators who do not understand the metaphor believe that Near Easterners hate dogs. Dogs are loved by the shepherds and by sheep-owners, but the dogs stay with the sheep. They are not kept in houses or domesticated as dogs are in the West.

Immortality

All they that be fat upon earth shall eat and worship: all they that go down to the dust shall bow before him: and none can keep alive his own soul. Ps. 22:29.

The Hebrews, as well as neighboring peoples in Canaan, Assyria, and Egypt, had some glimpse of immortality. The prophets of Israel believed man's spirit is eternal and indestructible and that there would be a resurrection for the good as well as for the bad, so that they might receive their rewards. But the concept of resurrection and life eternal was not crystallized until the time of the captivity. Daniel was the greatest advocate of the resurrection regardless of whether the people were good or evil.

The psalmist believed in immortality. The Eastern Aramaic text reads: "All they that are hungry [for truth] upon earth shall eat and worship before the Lord; all they that are buried shall kneel before him; my soul is alive to

---

[53]See Jn. 16:32.
[54]Phil. 3:2.

him." Also, a passage in the book of Job reads: "O remember that the spirit is still alive; even yet my eye shall again see good."[55]

"Fat" is a mistranslation in the King James Version. The Aramaic word *kapneh* means "the hungry." The Aramaic word for "fat" is *patmeh*. The error might have been due to the confusion of these two words or to defects in the manuscript. No Hebrew psalmist would have used the word fat in this verse. The term fat is often used in referring to wealthy, wicked men who confiscate the property of the poor. "Hungry" does not always mean hunger for food; it can also mean hunger for justice and truth. "Blessed are those who hunger and thirst for justice, for they shall be well satisfied."[56]

Posterity

A seed shall serve him; it shall be accounted to the Lord for a generation. Ps. 22:30.

This is a messianic psalm. "Seed" here means posterity. The reference is to the generations to come who would serve the Messiah/Christ and declare his wonders and righteousness to generations of those yet to be born.

PSALM TWENTY-THREE

God as Chief Shepherd

The Lord is my shepherd; I shall not want. He maketh me to lie down in green pastures: he leadeth me beside the still waters. He restoreth my soul: he leadeth me in the paths of righteousness for his name's sake. Ps. 23:1-3.

The Eastern Aramaic Peshitta text reads: "The Lord shepherds me and I lack nothing at all! And upon pastures of strength he makes me dwell. He guides me by restful waters and has restored my life; And upon paths of justice he leads me because of his reputation."

The Hebrew text does read: "the Lord is my shepherd." But in the Aramaic text the noun "shepherd" becomes an action verb, "shepherds." The Aramaic text puts God in the act of shepherding. *Raa* is the Aramaic verbal root, and it not only means "to shepherd" but also "to feed, tend,

---

[55]Job 7:7. Eastern Aramaic Peshitta text, Lamsa translation.
[56]Mt. 5:6, Eastern Aramaic Peshitta text, Lamsa translation.

herd, keep, pastor, nourish." Metaphorically it signifies "to rule, lead, guide, and govern." Near Easterners believed that God sees after them exactly as a skilled chief shepherd cares for his sheep.

In the Near East the greatest was the chief shepherd. All other shepherds answered to him. He was the overseer for all the flocks under his care and occupied a very important position in the community. For endless generations, sheep raising had been the highest occupation in the holy land, Arabia, and Mesopotamia until the arrival of Western technology in these countries. A skilled shepherd is vital because without an adept shepherd, the sheep will scatter and become the prey of thieves and every kind of vicious beast. He treats all the flocks with equal care and concern and makes sure that they lack nothing at all. He heals and dresses the sick and wounded animals and is willing to give his life for the sheep.

Shepherds continually search for rich, fertile grazing areas where water is ample and grass is plentiful. They especially look for such places near mountains because it is usually cool and shaded. It is also a place where the entire camp may enjoy the richness of the land. "Green pastures" symbolize harmony, security, strength, peace, and abundance.

Sheep enjoy pastures that are fertile where they do not have to go far and can lie down and eat. This almost effortless form of grazing makes them fatter and more content. When they are well cared for and satisfied, they produce better wool and by-products.

"Restful waters" refers to sweet, clear, and slow running water. When water moves too swiftly, the sheep cannot drink. At times, a shepherd will build small nooks near the edges of a fast moving stream to make it easier for his flocks to drink. Also, sheep will not drink still, stagnant water. Their shepherd always tests the water before they drink.

In ancient Near Eastern lands, water was scarce and very precious. Biblical writers symbolized truth by referring to it as living water. For them, truth was as precious as water.

The chief shepherd knows all the safe pathways upon which to guide his flocks. He must be careful not to take shortcuts through rocky and treacherous paths, so his sheep don't fall and break their legs. He also will not lead them through vineyards or wheatfields because landowners might seize and kill them. After all, the chief shepherd must maintain his name sake—that is, his reputation as a skilled and careful shepherd. If he leads the sheep to bad places and his flocks suffer loss, his reputation is ruined.

Rod and Staff

Yea, though I walk through the valley of the shadow of death, I will fear no evil; for thou art with me; thy rod and thy staff they comfort me. Ps. 23:4.

"The valleys of the shadows of death" are winding paths between mountains where dark shadows may obscure many perils for the travelers. Bandits and thieves usually hide in dens and caves. Leading sheep through these valleys is an extremely tense and dangerous experience.

It is often said in the Near East that a person may be "under the shadow of death." This signifies that the individual's life is in danger. He could be killed at any moment. Only God's presence, which biblical authors have symbolized as light, can brighten one's path, dispelling fears and shadows. Those who are under the guidance of God fear no evildoer or calamity.

"Your rod and your staff have comforted me" refers to discipline and protection. Near Eastern shepherds carry rods and staffs. They use their rods to direct the sheep, and the staffs become weapons to protect them from wild animals, snakes, and thieves.

Generally, a shepherd who has been appointed to care for the lambs of the various flocks carries a tender rod (branch of a tree or from a bush) and gently taps the lambs on their backs while guiding them. Sheep feel comforted by the guiding rods and protecting staffs of their shepherds. Figuratively, the rod and the staff represent spiritual discipline and true teaching that protect from anything that may be false or harmful.

Treatment of Enemies

Thou preparest a table before me in the presence of mine enemies: thou anointest my head with oil; my cup runneth over. Ps. 23:5.

Near Easterners are more generous in entertaining their enemies than their friends. They believe friends are always friends, but enemies must be won by means of hospitality, gifts, and favors. "If you meet your enemy's ox or his ass going astray, you shall surely bring it back to him again."[57]

Tales of hospitality and lavish entertainments are handed down from one generation to another. When an enemy is entertained, the host will make sure to place piles of bread and dishes of diverse foods before him to

---

[57]Ex. 23:4, Eastern Aramaic Peshitta text, Lamsa translation.

convince him that the host loves and honors him. But if the bread and other foods are not abundant, the guest will rejoice to see that his host is too poor to entertain him lavishly. The guest also believes that his host is an enemy.

Some men, when entertaining their enemies, borrow dishes, bread, and other food just to embarrass them and heap coals of fire upon their heads. "If your enemy be hungry, give him bread to eat; and if he be thirsty, give him water to drink; for when you shall do these things for him, you will heap coals of fire upon his head, and the Lord will reward you."[58]

Good deeds and kindness destroy enmity and bring enduring reconciliation. Acts speak louder and are more powerful than words. Jesus said, "Let your light so shine before men that they may see your good works and glorify your Father in heaven."[59]

"Thou anointest my head with oil" and "my cup runneth over" refer to prosperity. Near Easterners often use butter, olive oil, and wine for medicine as well as for food. They anoint their heads with olive oil and also use it on chapped hands and feet. These items are very expensive; therefore, the people consider themselves living a life of luxury when they have them.

When butter and olive oil are scarce, they are used sparingly, mostly for food and emergency medicine only. The Hebrew text reads" "My cup runneth over." My translation of this verse from the Aramaic text is somewhat different: "My cup gives joy like pure wine."[60] The cup that gives great joy represents more than ample supply of food and drink. The bounteous table, the anointing oil, and the cup that enlivens one represent great happiness, wealth, and health.

PSALM TWENTY-FOUR

An Ancient Belief

For he hath founded it upon the seas, and established it upon the floods. Ps. 24:2.

The Hebrews, like other wandering tribal people and small nations, believed that the earth was stretched out upon the waters. In those early

---

[58]Prov. 25:21-22, Eastern Aramaic Peshitta text, Lamsa translation.

[59]Mt. 5:16, Eastern Aramaic Peshitta text, Lamsa translation.

[60]Eastern Aramaic Peshitta text, Errico.

days people seldom traveled far away from their own lands, nor did they communicate with distant nations. In some instances they saw only as far as the horizon, and what they saw appeared to be flat and surrounded by the great seas and oceans.

The small races and nations who lived in semidesert lands tending their sheep and cattle had no time to study astronomy; neither would they care whether the earth was flat or round. Their main concern was grass and water for their flocks and herds.

Astronomical and geographical research was conducted by the Assyrian, Babylonian, and Egyptian savants, who wanted to solve their agricultural problems. It was they who were responsible for our calendars and the division of time into months, weeks, and hours. It was they who invented alphabets to record time and events. Most of the astronomical, geographical, and other scientific knowledge that tribal people possessed was borrowed from the great nations around them.

Job states that the earth hangs in the sky.[61] The Assyrians and Babylonians who gave us our calendars must have known that the earth was round and that it was not the center of the universe. But Near Eastern tribes were content with what they had. They built no roads and did not invent anything; they lived a simple life close to nature.

Hill of the Lord

Who shall ascend into the hill of the Lord? or who shall stand in his holy place? Ps. 24:3.

"Hill of the Lord" refers to Mount Zion. Jerusalem is built upon Mount Zion, and the temple was built upon Mount Moriah where Abraham had been commanded in a vision to go and sacrifice his son Isaac.[62]

Every year thousands of people ascended the "hill of God" from Jericho, Hebron, Bethlehem, Philistia, and other regions in the lowlands to worship in the temple of God. All pious men and women brought their offerings to the temple of God in Jerusalem, which the Lord God had selected for his dwelling place. Interestingly, hills and mountains are symbolic of strength and trust. Trusting in the living God is as firm as a mountain.

---

[61]Job 26:7.
[62]Gen. 22:2.

PSALM TWENTY-FIVE

Only Son

Turn thee unto me, and have mercy upon me; for I am desolate and afflicted. Ps. 25:16.

The last part of this verse in the Eastern Aramaic text reads: ". . . for I am the only son and destitute." David was a poet and musician. In seeking God's mercy and loving kindness, he compares God to a father who has only one son. The reference is to Israel, which was the only state that worshiped the living God, the Creator. Gentiles worshiped images.

In the Near East when a father has only one son, he does everything for him. In biblical days, Israel was called God's son. This is because it was believed that God took care of the nation.

PSALM TWENTY-SIX

Wash My Hands in Innocence

I will wash mine hands in innocency: so will I compass thine altar, O Lord. Ps. 26:6.

"I will wash mine hands in innocency" means, "I will repent of my sins." In Aramaic it is often said, "I have washed my hands of him," meaning, "I have nothing to do with him," or "I am absolved of any guilt."

The hand is the agent of one's thinking and symbolic of power and action. One has to put away worldly power and repent of evil in order to come close to the altar of the Lord. In the New Testament we read that Pilate washed his hands of guilt when he let Jesus be crucified.

An Even Place

My foot standeth in an even place: in the congregations will I bless the Lord. Ps. 26:12.

"My foot standeth in an even place" means, "I shall stand firm," or "I shall not slip or stumble." The foot is used here because the Semitic term for religion is "way." "The way of the Lord" and the term "walking" are used to mean "good conduct" and "walking in the right way."

PSALM TWENTY-NINE

Gift Offering

Give unto the Lord, O ye mighty, give unto the Lord glory and strength. Give unto the Lord the glory due unto his name; worship the Lord in the beauty of holiness. Ps. 29:1-2.

The Eastern Aramaic text reads: "Bring unto the Lord the offspring of rams; bring unto the Lord glory and honour . . . worship the Lord in the court of his holy temple." When the Israelites visited holy shrines and holy men, they brought offerings with them—the choicest of their sheep, rams, and lambs.

Then again, after the victories by which they were delivered from their oppressors, they proffered thanks offerings to God and rejoiced over their triumph. They danced, ate, and drank on that day as a token of rejoicing.

It is said that this psalm was sung after the defeat of the Assyrian army and the deliverance of Jerusalem from the hand of the King of Assyria. The king exhorts the people to bring lambs, sheep, and rams to the temple of the Lord as a thanks offering for their salvation. Israel had been saved once more. Apparently, the song was composed by David but sung by Hezekiah.

Thunder

The voice of the Lord maketh the hinds to calve, and discovereth the forests: and in his temple doth every one speak of his glory. Ps. 29:9.

The Eastern Aramaic text reads: "The voice of the Lord makes the hinds to tremble [to be disturbed], and uproots the forests." Thunder was known as the voice of the Lord because it was a sound of nature. The Hebrews attributed all natural phenomena to the might of God, who knows all and controls all.

Thunder and lightning are still feared in the Near East, especially in the flat, desert lands where one cannot find protection. Cedars and other trees are often broken by lightning, and cattle and sheep are killed.[63]

---

[63]See verses 5-8.

The people believed that the voice of the Lord and the divine rebuke of the Assyrian king broke the army, which resembled a great forest and had besieged Jerusalem.

God Controls Floods

The Lord sitteth upon the flood; yea, the Lord sitteth King for ever. Ps. 29:10.

The Aramaic word *aphekh* means "he causes it to go backward, he stops it, he controls it." "Sitteth upon the flood" might have been used metaphorically to mean that he crushes enemy armies.

Floods cause considerable damage in biblical lands. Sometimes it does not rain for two or three years, but when it does rain, it turns into a deluge, destroying the fields, washing away the soil, and drowning people and animals in the path of violent torrents.

The Lord God turned away the Assyrian invasion that had swept away many kingdoms and people before it. According to the biblical writer, God controlled the power of the Assyrian army and caused it to suffer a severe defeat.

PSALM THIRTY

Out of Sheol

O Lord, thou hast brought up my soul from the grave: thou hast kept me alive, that I should not go down to the pit. Ps. 30:3.

This psalm was ascribed to Hezekiah, king of Judah, when he was very ill. The king was sick unto death, and the prophet Isaiah came to see him and told him to set his house in order for he was to die at any time.[64] But Hezekiah prayed, and he was healed.[65]

The Eastern Aramaic text reads: "Thou hast brought up my soul from Sheol; thou hast saved me that I should not join those who go down to the pit [grave]."

The king's recovery was a great miracle, wrought by means of earnest prayer. Sheol was a terrifying place, supposedly beyond the jurisdiction of

---

[64]2 Ki. 20:1.

[65]Isa. 38:1-6.

God. The dead were cut off from the living and imprisoned in the depths of the earth. Both Sheol and death were feared in those days because few were aware of the resurrection. Jesus of Nazareth, through his death on the cross and his resurrection, destroyed the power of Sheol.

Rebuke for Good

For his anger endureth but a moment; in his favor is life: weeping may endure for a night, but joy cometh in the morning. Ps. 30:5.

The Eastern Aramaic text reads: " For there is rebuke in his anger and life in his good will; weeping may last for a night, but joy comes in the morning."

According to the authorized version of Scripture, Psalm 7: 11 teaches that God is angry with the wicked every day.[66] But according to the Aramaic text, God is declared a righteous judge and is not angry every day.[67]

Near Eastern judges were usually angry, especially when some of the disputants did not bring any gifts. Judges were not paid a salary but lived off of the gifts or bribes that people brought them. Near Easterners had the habit of cursing these kinds of judges. These men were also feared and hated by the people because their evil works had created a chasm between them and the public.

The psalmist, in 7:11, compares the Lord God, the great and merciful judge, with human judges. The Lord is the father of humankind and, therefore, loves and cares for everyone. But in this psalm and according to the people's belief, there was a rebuke in God's anger because it disciplined the people for good. Weeping endures but a short time, but joy comes suddenly.

PSALM THIRTY-ONE

David Is Tranquil

And hast not shut me up into the hand of the enemy: thou hast set my feet in a large room. Ps. 31:8.

---

[66]K.J.V.

[67]See Ps. 7:11, Eastern Aramaic Peshitta text, Lamsa translation.

"Thou hast set my feet in a large room" means, "Thou hast comforted me and established my feet in tranquility"; that is, "My enemies have not captured me or besieged me." Also, the first part of the verse in the Aramaic text reads: "And thou hast not surrendered me into the hand of my enemies."

David, in his early life, was constantly harassed and pursued by his enemy, Saul. But now King David was free and the ruler over a large kingdom that extended from Israel to the River Euphrates and from the border of Egypt to Lebanon.

Forgotten Forever

I am forgotten as a dead man out of mind: I am like a broken vessel. Ps. 31:12.

The last part of the verse in the Eastern Aramaic text reads: ". . . I am like something given up for lost." *Mana* in Aramaic means "vessel, dish, thing, something." Nomad people often borrowed copper vessels and dishes from one another and might forget to return them or might lose them during raids in which their camps were plundered.

This psalm is a supplication of the Israelites when they were oppressed by their enemies. It could have been sung after the people had returned from Babylon, or during the time of King Hezekiah when Judah and Jerusalem were pressed by the Assyrian army. Judah was seemingly lost and hopeless and did not know where to turn.

God's Protection

Oh how great is thy goodness, which thou hast laid up for them that fear thee; which thou hast wrought for them that trust in thee before the sons of men! Ps. 31:19.

"Before the sons of men" means "against the opposition of worldly men." Those who revere their God and obey his commandments are often persecuted by those who deny him and do evil in God's presence.

But God protects those who worship and remain loyal to him. They are kept in God's secret place where no one can touch their souls. "Thou shall hide them in the secret [fortress] of thy presence from the pride of man."[68]

---

[68]See verse 20.

PSALM THIRTY-TWO

Blot out Sins

Blessed is he whose transgression is forgiven, whose sin is covered. Blessed is the man unto whom the Lord imputeth not iniquity, and in whose spirit there is no guile. Ps. 32:1-2.

The Aramaic word *kasah,* "cover," means "effaced" or "obliterated" so that God can no longer see them. "Covered" does not convey the correct idea. One can cover or hide one's sins, but they are still there. Moreover, sins can be covered from men but not from God. The Aramaic text of verse one reads: "Blessed is he whose transgression is forgiven and whose sin is blotted out."

The Hebrew *kippur,* "atonement," means to eradicate the sin and blot out iniquity by means of self-denials, prayers, and offerings. *Kipper* means to deny oneself pleasures or to afflict oneself. All this was done to blot out the sins, not to cover them.[69] In Nehemiah, we read: "And forgive not their offenses, and let not their sins be blotted out from before thee."[70] When sins are forgiven, then they are blotted out for good.

Heavy Discipline

When I kept silence my bones waxed old through my roaring all the day long. For day and night thy hand was heavy upon me: my moisture is turned into the drought of summer. Selah. Ps. 32:3-4.

The Eastern Aramaic text reads: "Because I suffered in silence all the day long, my bones waxed old during my deep slumber. For day and night thy hand was heavy upon me; intense pain developed in my heart great enough to kill me."

The psalmist has been so chastised that he feels weakness in his body. This is because the Lord God had tried to correct him from evil ways. God's admonition seemed to be too heavy upon him.

It was either King David or one of the kings of Judah who portrays himself as the state in deep trouble. The problem that the king was facing

---

[69]Prov. 17:9.

[70]Neh. 4:5, Eastern Aramaic Peshitta text, Lamsa translation.

was worrying him and taxing his vital energy.

PSALM THIRTY-FOUR

The Wicked Rich

O fear the Lord, ye his saints; for there is no want to them that fear him. The young lions do lack, and suffer hunger: but they that seek the Lord shall not want any good thing. Ps. 34:9-10.

The Eastern Aramaic text reads: "The rich have become poor and suffer hunger; they that seek the Lord shall not lack any good thing." The reference is to the wicked rich whose fortune changed suddenly. The wealthy may be rich today but tomorrow may become poor. But those who seek the Lord are protected, guided, and blessed with abundance.

Most wealth in those days was acquired by confiscation of property, murder, plundering, and other wicked ways. The wealth of the wicked rich is temporary, and what they had done to others would be done to them.

Hardships

Many are the afflictions of the righteous: but the Lord delivereth him out of them all. Ps. 34:19.

The Aramaic word *bishatheh,* "afflictions," also means "hardships" or "evils." Near Easterners believe a righteous man is subjected to many hardships in this life; that is, the wicked make life harder and harsher for the righteous. Semites often say, "It is hard to be a follower of justice and truth among wicked men." The righteous have a longer way to go and many difficulties ahead, but the Lord delivers them from all their tribulations.

PSALM THIRTY-FIVE

Lions

Lord, how long wilt thou look on? rescue my soul from their destructions, my darling from the lions. Ps. 35:17.

"Lions" is used metaphorically to mean oppressors. In the Near East, dictators and oppressors are often spoken of as lions, leopards, and wild beasts. In the book of Amos they are called "kine" or cows. "Hear this word, ye kine of Bashan . . . which oppress the poor, which crush the needy, which say to their masters, Bring, and let us drink."[71]

The Aramaic word *ykhidoth* means "the only child." Dr. Lamsa believed this psalm was composed by King David, but according to the Near Eastern text, it was sung during the time of Jeremiah when he was accused by false prophets and thrown into prison.[72] However that might have been, Jeremiah was a lone prophet and might have been the only child.

Jeremiah was known as a rebel prophet because he did not agree with the false court prophets who had misled Zedekiah, the king of Judah, by their dangerous foreign policy. His oppressors were called lions because they wanted to do away with him. The prophet barely escaped death at the hands of many false court prophets and princes who were opposed to his policy. On the other hand, Jeremiah was the only prophet during his time who spoke for God and predicted the fall of Jerusalem.

Winking with the Eyes

Let not them that are mine enemies wrongfully rejoice over me: neither let them wink with the eye that hate me without a cause. Ps. 35:19.

The last portion of the verse in the Eastern Aramaic text reads, ". . . they wink with their eyes but they do not salute," which means that they do not say, "Peace be unto you."

Near Easterners, when meeting, generally salute one another by saying, "Peace be to you." If one of them is working or carrying a burden, the other says, "My God grant you strength." Enemies, however, do not salute, but wink with their eyes or nod their heads as a gesture of hatred.

PSALM THIRTY-SIX

The Wicked Fear Not God

The transgression of the wicked saith within my heart, that there is no fear of God before his eyes. Ps. 36:1.

---

[71]Amos 4:1, K.J.V.
[72]See verses 11, 26.

The Eastern Aramaic text reads: "The unjust conceives wickedness within his heart, for there is no fear of God before his eyes." The error in the King James Version is caused by the confusion in the possessive case or the genitive: *libi* (my heart) and *libeh* (his heart).

A wicked person conceives evil in his heart because there is no reverence of God. He is so wicked that he does not know what righteousness is.

Sin, a Habit

For he flattereth himself in his own eyes, until his iniquity be found to be hateful. Ps. 36:2.

The Eastern Aramaic text reads: "He is unwilling to see his sins forgiven, or to hate them." The psalmist is saying that a wicked person is so inured to his evil that he does not distinguish between good or bad, nor does he care to correct his ways.

Fatness and Spiritual River

They shall be abundantly satisfied with the fatness of thy house; and thou shalt make them drink of the river of thy pleasures. Ps. 36:8.

"The fatness of thy house" and "the river of thy pleasures" are metaphors referring to truth and spiritual understanding that meet all human desires." "River" also means rain which causes the earth to produce food.[73]

Thousands of fat bullocks, he-goats, and lambs were slain in the courtyard of the temple to be offered to God. On such occasions fat meat and wine were abundant, and the people ate and were happy. But after the feast, the people were once more hungry for meat and thirsty for water, which was scarce in the Holy City. "There is a river, the streams whereof shall make glad the city of God, the holy place of the tabernacles of the most High."[74]

Just as water gives life in a dry place, and the shadow of a tree revives the weary in a dry land, so is the truth and the Spirit of God to those who are hungry and thirsty for justice and spiritual understanding of life. "A

---

[73]Ps. 65:9.

[74]Ps. 46:4, K.J.V.

pure river of water of life . . ."[75]

Water is symbolic of light and enlightenment. A river means "truth," that is, the teaching of God that relieves all thirsty souls. God's pleasure is goodness and loving kindness, the observance of his commandments and statutes. "River" also means "abundance."[76]

God's religion is the River of Life, which satisfies all those who are hungry and thirsty for justice and truth. It is like water on parched ground.

PSALM THIRTY-SEVEN

Righteous Not Forsaken

Commit thy way unto the Lord; trust also in him; and he shall bring it to pass. Ps. 37:5.

In many portions of the Scriptures we read that God never forsakes the righteous. All righteous people who call upon the Lord are heard, and the Lord delivers them out of all their troubles.[77] According to the belief of the people, God never allows the righteous to be in lack.[78]

Scripture teaches that the Lord hears the prayers and the supplications of the righteous who have put their trust in God and taken refuge under the divine wings. "The Lord is far from the wicked: but he heareth the prayer of the righteous."[79] "Blessed is the man that trusteth in him."[80]

God forsakes no one. He did not forsake Jesus on the cross. When Jesus cried out on the cross in Aramaic, he said, "My God, my God, for this I was kept;" that is, "this was my destiny." Jesus had predicted his crucifixion and death, and the prophecies had to be fulfilled. He never questioned God, his father.[81]

---

[75]Rev. 22:1, K.J.V.

[76]Isa. 66:12.

[77]Ps. 34:17.

[78]Ps. 55:22.

[79]Prov. 15:29.

[80]Ps. 34:8.

[81]See Mt. 27:46, Aramaic Peshitta text, Lamsa translation.

Wicked Rich

But the wicked shall perish, and the enemies of the Lord shall be as the fat of lambs: they shall consume; into smoke shall they consume away. Ps. 37:20.

The Eastern Aramaic text reads: ". . . the rich who are enemies of the Lord." The reference is to the rich oppressors who had defrauded the laborers, oppressed the poor, and taken bribes from the widows. "Behold, the wage of the labourers who have reaped your fields, that which you have fraudulently kept back, cries; and the cry of the reapers has already entered into the ears of the Lord of sabaoth [hosts]."[82] The wicked rich also oppressed the widows and the fatherless. Both the wicked and the wealthy oppressors are to be consumed and will vanish like smoke.

In the Near East the rich were tax exempt and still are in most of the backward regions. They are also allowed to levy taxes on the poor and to confiscate the property of the weak.[83] "A little that a righteous man has is better than the great riches of the wicked."[84]

PSALM THIRTY-NINE

Dumbness—Confusion

I was dumb, I opened not my mouth; because thou didst it. Ps. 39:9.

"Dumb" refers to affliction, bewilderment, or confusion. "I was dumb" means, "I did not know what to do or say." On such occasions Near Easterners remain silent.

When David was oppressed by King Saul, he did not complain, hoping the king would change his mind toward him. In those ancient days, afflictions and injustices were often blamed on God because the Lord had permitted them to be inflicted by the wicked upon the just. This was the belief system of that time in Israel's history.

---

[82]James 5:4, Eastern Aramaic Peshitta text, Lamsa translation.

[83]See Prov. 22:7; Mt. 19:23; Mk. 10:25; Lk. 18:25.

[84]Ps. 37:16, Eastern Aramaic Peshitta text, Lamsa translation.

PSALM FORTY

A Prophecy Concerning Messiah

Then said I, Lo, I come: in the volume of the book it is written of me. Ps. 40:7.

Debresh katebeh means "in the beginning of the Scriptures," that is, the book of Genesis. A great Deliverer was promised by God to save humankind. Many of the Hebrew prophets envisioned his coming and the establishment of a new and universal kingdom, a reign of righteousness, peace, and justice. This concept runs throughout Scripture like a golden thread in a brocade. The Messiah, God's anointed, was to execute justice not only in Judea but also throughout the world.

In the gospel of John, Jesus is reported as saying: "Examine the scriptures; in them you trust that you have eternal life; and even they testify concerning me."[85] The Messiah, the Anointed One, was the only hope for humanity. Everything else had been tried, but had failed to save human beings and to restore their dormant divinity.

PSALM FORTY-ONE

Looking after the Poor

Blessed is he that considereth the poor: the Lord will deliver him in time of trouble. Ps. 41:1.

The Aramaic word *khaar* is derived from *khar,* "to look at, behold, regard." But in this case it means "to look after," that is, to help them when they are in distress.

In the Near East, until recent days, the poor were subjected to hard labor, forced to carry burdens, and were heavily taxed; they were discriminated against and their properties often confiscated unjustly. The Mosaic law admonished the people to return the mantle of a poor man, which he had given as a pledge. "And if the man is poor, you shall not sleep with his mantle. But you shall return to him his mantle again when the sun goes down, that he may sleep in his own mantle, and bless you; and it shall be

---

[85]Jn. 5:39, Eastern Aramaic Peshitta text, Lamsa translation. See also Jer. 23:5; Heb. 10:7.

righteousness to you before the Lord your God."[86] "But he saves their lives from the sword, and the poor from the hand of the mighty."[87]

The Lord Heals

The Lord will strengthen him upon the bed of languishing: thou wilt make all his bed in his sickness. Ps. 41:3.

The text has not been translated clearly. The Eastern Aramaic text reads: "The Lord will strengthen him upon his sick bed; he will wholly recover from his illness." God does not bring sickness on people. God is a healer of all wounds, mental and physical.

PSALM FORTY-TWO

Bread of Tears

My tears have been my meat day and night, while they continually say unto me, Where is thy God? Ps. 42:3.

The Eastern Aramaic text uses the term "bread" instead of "meat." "My tears have been my bread" is a Near Eastern idiom, meaning "I have been sad continually, and tears ran down my cheeks while I was eating." Then again, when people suffer and are afflicted, they say, "I have been eating my bread with the tears of my eyes." None of these expressions are taken literally or are misunderstood. Semites realize that no one will deliberately eat his tears while at a meal, but they have often seen men in deep sadness weeping while eating and drinking. "Thou feedest them with the bread of tears."[88]

Poetic Language

Deep calleth unto Deep at the noise of thy waterspouts, all thy waves and thy billows are gone over me. Ps. 42:7.

---

[86]Dt. 24:12-13, Eastern Aramaic Peshitta text, Lamsa translation.
[87]Job 5:15, Eastern Aramaic Peshitta text, Lamsa translation.
[88]Ps. 80:5, K.J.V.

This phrase of the psalm is written in poetic imagery. It expresses great difficulties and challenges that people may experience. Turbulent waters are symbolic of troubles, agitation, and sorrows. Another example of this kind of poetic language is when the prophet Jonah, in his vision, was thrown into the sea because he was unwilling to go to Nineveh. The sea represented his troubled heart over his mission, and the fish that swallowed him symbolized his dilemma. "For thou had cast me into the deep, in the midst of the sea; and the flood compassed me about; all thy billows and thy waves have passed over me."[89]

PSALM FORTY-FOUR

Marked for Slaughter

Thou hast given us like sheep appointed for meat; and hast scattered us among the heathen. Ps. 44:11.

In the Near East, one could see small flocks of lambs, rams, goats, and older sheep grazing near a city or town. Generally, they would be sold by the owners to sheep merchants to be resold to butchers.

Refrigeration was unknown in Near Eastern lands, and sheep and goats were killed from day to day. The butchers counted and marked the sheep that were to be slaughtered. At times these sheep were separated from the flock and brought near the city wall to be slaughtered early in the morning.

The psalmist compares the Israelites to sheep that were marked to be slaughtered for food. This was one of the darkest periods in Israel's history. Many Israelites were killed by the Gentiles, and others were taken captive.

According to the Eastern Aramaic text, this psalm was composed and sung during the time of the Maccabees when thousands of Jews were butchered by the Syrians and were compelled by Antiochus to sacrifice to idols. All the Jews who refused to comply with the king's decree were slain.

Second Punishment

Though thou hast sore broken us in the place of dragons, and covered us with the shadow of death. Ps. 44:19.

---

[89]Jonah 2:3, Eastern Aramaic Peshitta text, Lamsa translation.

The Eastern Aramaic text reads: "For thou hast humbled us a second time in the land." The reference is to the second defeat, this time by the Greeks. The first was when they were defeated by the Chaldeans and taken captive to Babylon. And now the Jews were compelled by Antiochus to sacrifice to idols.

The Aramaic word *tinyana,* "a second time," has been confused in the King James Version with the Aramaic word *tanina*, "a dragon." These two words are written alike but pronounced differently.

This psalm was written after the Jews had returned from Babylon, built the second temple, and established the second Jewish commonwealth. After the fall of the Persian empire, the Syrians and other surrounding nations started to oppress the Jews. The period under Antiochus was one of the darkest periods in Jewish history. The holy temple was desecrated, and Jewish women were violated and put to death.

God Never Sleeps

Yea, for thy sake are we killed all the day long; we are counted as sheep for the slaughter. Awake, why sleepest thou, O Lord? Arise, cast us not off forever. Ps. 44:22-23.

The psalmist describes Israel's difficulties and harassments from the hands of their enemies. People were suffering because of their religion. Many men and women were persecuted and some were killed. They were like sheep that were marked for the daily slaughter. In the Near East, sheep that were brought to the city for slaughter were marked.

The psalmist complains to God for having allowed such tragedies to befall his people. In his appeal to God, he called upon the Lord to wake up. In this hour of depression, he feels that God has neglected his people. In another psalm, it is written that God never sleeps nor slumbers. "He will not allow your foot to be moved; he who keeps you will not slumber. Behold, he who keeps Israel will neither slumber nor sleep."[90]

When writing poetic speech, one can say things that cannot be said in prose. This is why so many of the psalms seem contradictory. God is not a person who needs sleep or needs to be awakened.

---

[90]Ps. 121:3-4, Eastern Aramaic Peshitta text, Lamsa translation.

PSALM FORTY-SIX

There Is a River

There is a river, the streams whereof shall make glad the city of God, the holy place of the tabernacles of the Most High. Ps. 46:4.

The word "river" is used metaphorically to mean truth, teaching, or the light of God. In the book of the Revelation, the author speaks of "a pure river of water of life"[91] that is present in the holy city. The water is symbolic of spiritual enlightenment. But there is no river in Jerusalem. The little brook of Kidron dries up in the early summer, and one can hardly see a trickle of water in the valley. Interestingly, when biblical authors speak of one having a great thirst, it symbolizes the lack of enlightenment. In the gospel of John, Jesus refers to "rivers of living water,"[92] meaning abundant enlightenment.

Israel looked upon God's truth that was flowing like a river in Jerusalem as a place of refuge and strength in the time of trouble. The Jewish state was established on God's promises to Israel and to the world. God's truth and justice was to leaven the Gentile world; the river of God, the true teaching, issued from Jerusalem, the city of peace that God had chosen.[93]

Jerusalem was the center of true worship. The branches of the river, "the streams thereof," were other places that had been enlightened by God's truth from Jerusalem.

The true teaching of God as revealed by the Hebrew prophets was the greatest bulwark around Jerusalem. Though the Israelites suffered hardships and were taken captive, they never lost faith in their God. Jerusalem rested on a solid foundation, the Rock of Ages, the truth that issued from Jerusalem and brought light and understanding to the Gentile world.[94]

---

[91]Rev. 22:1.

[92]See Jn. 7:38.

[93]Ps. 1:3, 65:9.

[94]See the commentary on Ezekiel 47:1-6.

PSALM FORTY-NINE

Song of Riddles

I will incline mine ear to a parable: I will open my dark saying upon the harp. Ps. 49:4.

Near Eastern poets and musicians played love songs, melodies, and lamentations on harps and other musical instruments. Parables, proverbs, and dark sayings were also sung and played on musical instruments.

The dark sayings were songs that contained riddles and were not easily understood by those who lacked poetic sense. The singer uses metaphors and similes, saying one thing but meaning something else. For example, if the singer uses the term "a beautiful garden," he really means "a beautiful woman." When he speaks of a woman's breasts, he uses the term "pomegranates."

The End of the Wicked

Nevertheless man being in honor abideth not: he is like the beasts that perish. Ps. 49:12.

The Eastern Aramaic text reads: "Nevertheless, such a man is not sustained by his honour; his end will be as the beasts, and he will perish." The psalmist speaks of wicked men and not of men in general. In verse 9, the psalmist says, "Do good for ever and you shall live for ever, and not see corruption." But both the wise and the fools will perish and their graves shall be their only habitation.

The Demented

This their way is their folly: yet their posterity approve their sayings. Selah. Ps. 49:13.

The latter part of this verse should read: ". . . in the end, demented, they will graze like cattle." The Aramaic words *bepomhon neraon* mean, "they will graze like cattle." People often say, "they eat grass," meaning that they are void of knowledge, like cattle.

We are told that Nebuchadnezzar ate grass like an ox, which means that he lost his mind.[95]

PSALM FIFTY

God of Gods

The mighty God, even the Lord, hath spoken, and called the earth from the rising of the sun unto the going down thereof. Ps. 50:1.

The Eastern Aramaic text reads: "The God of gods, the Lord . . ." The Hebrews, like other races in Canaan and Syria, believed in many gods. At times they looked upon the God of Israel as the greatest among all gods, since the gods of Gentiles were made of wood, silver, and gold. In other words, they believed in pagan deities, but they took for granted the superiority of their own God. Nevertheless, during some periods they forsook their God and went astray after pagan gods and images which had become a snare to them.[96]

But the idea of the one and only God, the Living God of Israel, always persisted and was constantly preached by the prophets. These words in the psalm were aimed at those who believed in pagan gods.

Fire

Our God shall come, and shall not keep silence: a fire shall devour before him, and it shall be very tempestuous round about him. Ps. 50:3.

In those ancient days, fire was considered the most powerful thing in the world. This is because fire was the first discovery that man had made in his progress; fire consumed forests, burned dwellings, and melted iron and brass.

God often appeared in fire, symbolizing light, power, and purity. All metals are purified by fire. God appeared to Moses in the burning bush.[97] The Israelites were led by a pillar of fire.[98] God spoke to Moses and the elders of Israel on Mount Sinai out of the midst of fire, and the people

---

[95]Dan. 4:32-33. See also the commentary on Daniel 4:32.
[96]See verse 22.
[97]Ex. 3:2.
[98]Ex.13:21.

heard the voice but did not see God.[99] God's words were as strong as fire and the divine messengers (angels) were as a flaming fire.

Fire was, and still is, worshiped by the Parsees in India, who are a remnant of the ancient Iranian religion, the Zoroastrians or fire worshipers. Fire is often used to symbolize God's vengeance, for instance, when wicked cities were destroyed.[100] In Aramaic, fire is symbolic of anger. Near Easterners often say, "Fire issued from his face," which means, "His anger blazed like fire."

God Needs No Animal Sacrifices

These things hast thou done, and I kept silence; thou thoughtest that I was altogether such a one as thyself: but I will reprove thee, and set them in order before thine eyes. Ps. 50:21.

The Eastern Aramaic text reads: ". . . you thought that I was wicked like you; but I will reprove you, and correct these sins before your eyes."

The Israelites are reproved for trusting in ceremonies and animal sacrifices instead of remembering to obey God's commandments and to be merciful and just with the poor and needy.

God desired not animal sacrifices but the sacrifices of thanksgiving for the blessings they had been given and for the good they had done in God's name. The Lord was not in need of meat offerings. All animals and birds belonged to him. What God wanted was justice and peace.[101]

PSALM FIFTY-ONE

Formed in Iniquity

Behold, I was shapen in iniquity; and in sin did my mother conceive me. Ps. 51:5.

According to the Hebrew terminology, everything was sinful when compared with God, the Holy One of Israel. Perfection and goodness were to be attained only by the observance of God's law and the ordinances.

---

[99]Dt. 4:12.

[100]See Gen. 19:24; Dt. 32:22.

[101]See Isa. 1:11; Jer. 7:22-23; Hos. 6:6; Micah 6:8.

"Who can bring a clean thing out of an unclean? no one."[102] All those who are born of women were considered sinners. According to biblical writers, humans, through sin and disobedience, had fallen from the grace of God. Therefore, they were to cleanse themselves of their sins by means of baptism in order to become a new creation.[103]

According to the Mosaic law, women were pronounced unclean for forty days when they gave birth to children, after which they were sanctified. Also, firstborn males had to be redeemed and sanctified.

The psalmist speaks collectively. The reference in this verse refers to all Israel. The people who were captive in Babylon confessed their sins and asked for mercy and forgiveness.

These people were in captivity because of the sins of their fathers. The idea of being shaped or formed in sin refers to the fact that the people had been rebellious and unwilling to repent and return to God.The psalmist uses poetic and metaphoric language.

Humbled

Make me to hear joy and gladness; that the bones which thou hast broken may rejoice. Ps. 51:8.

The Eastern Aramaic text reads: "Satisfy me with thy joy and gladness, that my broken spirit may rejoice." The term "broken spirit" is used figuratively, meaning humbleness or humility. In the Near East, when people were sad or worried, it was said their spirit was broken, which means their pride had been hurt. The Aramaic word *ruha*, "spirit," also means "pride, wind, rheumatism." But in this verse it means "pride."

This psalm was sung by the people who were in Babylon. They confessed their sins and iniquities and asked forgiveness. They had been humbled in the land of their captivity, and now they asked God to grant them joy and gladness and to create a new heart in them.

God Desires Meekness

The sacrifices of God are a broken spirit: a broken and a contrite heart, O God, thou wilt not despise. Ps. 51:17.

---

[102]Job 14:4, Eastern Aramaic Peshitta text, Lamsa translation.

[103]See verse 7.

"Broken spirit" or "poor in spirit" means humbleness, humility. "A broken and contrite heart" refers to the people's grief over the loss of spiritual values. When a man's pride is lost, he becomes humble and gentle. Jesus said, "Blessed are the humble, for theirs is the kingdom of heaven."[104]

According to Scripture, God was not pleased with animal sacrifices. What God required of the Israelites was to be humble, just, and merciful. "I will take no bullock out of thy house, nor he goats of thy fold. For every beast of the forest is mine, and the cattle upon a thousand hills."[105]

PSALM FIFTY-TWO

Green Olive Tree

But I am like a green olive tree in the house of God; I trust in the mercy of God for ever and ever. Ps. 52:8.

"But I am like a green olive tree in the house of God" means "I conducted myself well and I am worthy to be in the house of God." An olive tree is symbolic of joy, peace, and tranquility. The temple was lighted with pure olive oil. Kings, princes, prophets, and priests were anointed with olive oil.

When kings made peace with one another, they usually met with olive branches in their hands. When the dove that Noah had dispatched from the ark returned, it came with an olive branch in its beak. This signified that the rain had stopped and the time had come to leave the ark. Roman emperors wore a wreath made of olive branches and laurel leaves upon their heads.

PSALM FIFTY-THREE

Scattered Bones

There were they in great fear, where no fear was: for God hath scattered the bones of him that encampeth against thee: thou hast put them to shame, because God hath despised them. Ps. 53:5.

"Scattered the bones" is a Near Eastern idiom that means "he has

---

[104]Mt. 5:3, Eastern Aramaic Peshitta text, Lamsa translation.

[105]Ps. 50:9-10, K.J.V. See also Micah 6:6-8.

destroyed them or broken their power." Near Easterners often say, "I will break up your bones," or "I will crush your bones."

The reference is to the enemies of the Israelites who sought to destroy them. In biblical days the carcasses of the slain were left in the field. The flesh was eaten by wild animals and birds of prey, and the bones were scattered in the fields.[106]

PSALM FIFTY-SIX

Recording Tears

Thou tellest my wanderings: put thou my tears into thy bottle: are they not in thy book? Ps. 56:8.

The Eastern Aramaic text reads: "O God, I have declared my faith unto thee; record thou my tears before thee in thy book."

When mourning over their dead, Near Easterners weep bitterly, agonizing over their loss and, at times, even cut themselves and beat their faces and chests. The Aramaic text may be translated as: "Record [or place] my tears before thee in thy book."

Clothes and other articles worn by the deceased are often kept as a memorial. In those days, tears poured out over dear ones were put into small alabaster vessels as a reminder of mourning and grief. The Israelites wanted their tears to be recorded in God's book as a memorial of their suffering and repentance. ". . . and the Lord God will wipe away tears from off all faces."[107] The psalmist reminds God of the hardships the Israelites had suffered from the nations surrounding them. The people beseeched God for rest and peace.

PSALM FIFTY-SEVEN

Deliverance

My soul is among lions; and I lie even among them that are set on fire, even the sons of men, whose teeth are spears and arrows, and their tongue a sharp sword. Ps. 57:4.

---

[106]Ezk. 37:1-2.

[107]See Isa. 25:8 and Rev. 7:17.

The Eastern Aramaic text reads: "He has delivered my life from the vicious as I slept in fear, and from the sons of men, whose teeth are spears and arrows, and their tongues sharp swords."

The author of the psalm describes the evil words of his oppressors. He compares their words to spears and arrows. Wounds caused by sharp and piercing words are deeper than wounds caused by spears and arrows. The Lord had delivered the psalmist from evil men and their vicious gossip.

PSALM FIFTY-EIGHT

Scurrilous Gossip

Their poison is like the poison of a serpent: they are like the deaf adder that stoppeth her ear. Ps. 58:4.

"Poison of asps" is a Near Eastern idiom frequently used in both vernacular and literary Aramaic speech. Lies, accusations, and defamation of character are often called poison because of their evil effects. These wicked gossipers never stop to reason but, like serpents, strike unawares.

The Jews, during the time of the Maccabees, suffered many persecutions at the hands of the surrounding pagan nations, who lied and connived against them and sought their destruction.

Melt like Wax

As a snail which melteth, let every one of them pass away: like the untimely birth of a woman, that they may not see the sun. Ps. 58:8.

The Aramaic word for "wax" is *shoaa*, and the word for "snail" is *sheda,* which also means "a demon." Snails, clams, and oysters were called *shedeh* and were considered unclean. Neither Christians, Jews, nor Muslims ate them.

The Eastern Aramaic text reads *shoaa*, "wax." Therefore, the text reads differently. "Like the wax that melts, and drips before the fire, let them be destroyed." That is, "Let the wicked melt and pass away like the wax on the candle which burns and drips before the fire." Then the verse continues: "Fire has fallen from heaven and they did not see; the light of truth [sun] has been given and they did not understand."

Wax is often used in the Bible as a means of illustration. "As smoke is driven away, so let them vanish; as wax melts before the fire, so let the wicked perish at the presence of God."[108] Micah uses the same analogy—"like wax before the fire."[109] But "snail" has never been used as such an analogy; no one would say, "The wicked will pass away like a snail."

The word "woman" in the King James Version is due to the confusion between the Hebrew word *aish,* "fire," and *esha,* "woman."

Difficulties Increased

Before your pots can feel the thorns, he shall take them away as with a whirlwind, both living, and in his wrath. Ps. 58:9.

The Eastern Aramaic text reads: "Let their thorns be increased, and fear of wrath shake them violently." A thorn or brier is used metaphorically to mean snares, difficulties, grievances, sorrows or afflictions.

"He has been a thorn in my flesh" means, "He has caused me to suffer.[110]" "And there shall be no more a pricking brier unto the house of Israel, nor any grieving thorn of all that are round about them." Moreover, when Easterners curse a place they say, "Let thorns grow in you." "Thorns shall come up in her palaces."[111]

The psalm, according to the Eastern text, was composed concerning the snares that the Gentiles had laid in the way of the Maccabees. But, like other psalms, it could be applied to any similar situation.

PSALM SIXTY

A Great Tragedy

O God, thou hast cast us off, thou hast scattered us, thou hast been displeased; O turn thyself to us again. Thou has made the earth to tremble; thou hast broken it: heal the breaches thereof; for it shaketh. Ps. 60:1-2.

This psalm was composed during the period of the Maccabees when the Jews were harassed and persecuted by the Syrian kingdom. The people felt

---

[108]Ps. 68:2, Eastern Aramaic Peshitta text, Lamsa translation.
[109]Micah 1:4.
[110]See 2 Cor. 12:7 and Prov. 26:9.
[111]Isa. 34:13.

that they were forsaken and cast off by their God.

The second verse is written poetically. The great catastrophes which had befallen their people had made them tremble. This is because this period was a time of tense persecution and upheaval in the history of Israel. The Jews were forced to eat swine meat, work on the Sabbath day, and the temple was polluted by the soldiers. Many other abominations (unclean acts) were committed against the people by the Gentile armies. When a great tragedy takes place, Near Easterners say, "the earth shook," because of the impact of evil.

Washpot—Servitude

Moab is my washpot; over Edom will I cast out my shoe: Philistia, triumph thou because of me. Ps. 60:8.

"Moab is my washpot" is an Aramaic idiom that means "Moab is my lowest servant (or slave)." In the Near East, washpots were not very clean and were used for washing feet, clothes, and, at times, as toilet vessels. The psalmist looks upon Moab as the dirt under his feet.

"Over Edom will I cast out my shoe" is another Eastern idiom, meaning "Edom will pay tribute to me or serve me." In the Near East shoes were considered unclean. When men entered a house they took off their shoes, and servants removed the shoes of rich men and high government officials. Edom was to be reduced to servitude.

This psalm contains the hope of Israel for restoration and freedom from their oppressors. The Jews sincerely repented and then sought mercy from their God. During their dark hour, the Jews at last turned to God for help. Only God could defeat their strong enemies around them. The last section of the verse in Aramaic reads: ". . . over Philistia will I triumph."

PSALM SIXTY-ONE

Rock of Comfort

From the end of the earth will I cry unto thee, when my heart is overwhelmed: lead me to the rock that is higher than I. For thou hast been a shelter for me, and a strong tower from the enemy. Ps. 61:2-3.

The Eastern Aramaic text reads: ". . . for thou hast led me upon a rock and hast comforted me." The Lord has answered the prayer of the people. This psalm might have been sung at the time when the Persian kings had granted the exiles permission to rebuild the temple.

"Rock" is used metaphorically, meaning "assurance, strength, protection." "God is my rock" in Aramaic means, "God is my protection" or "the truth on which my faith rests." During storms and hurricanes people take refuge in caves and under rocks. "I will put you in a cave of the rock."[112] "He is the Rock," meaning strength.[113]

PSALM SIXTY-SIX

Gifts to the Temple

I will go into thy house with burnt offerings: I will pay thee my vows. Ps. 66:13.

Whenever the Israelites went to the temple they took gifts with them as thanks offerings to the Lord. They never went empty-handed. Even when they visited prophets and men of God, they took gifts consisting of bread, honey, parched wheat, fruits, and other things.

The gift offerings and animal sacrifices were eaten by the priests, the Levites, and worshipers. In those days there were no restaurants or hotels. People brought animal and cereal offerings to the holy places.[114]

When men and women made a vow to the Lord, they brought a free-will offering to God when it was fulfilled.[115]

PSALM SIXTY-SEVEN

God's Way

That thy way may be known upon earth, thy saving health among all nations. Ps. 67:2.

The Aramaic word *aorhakh,* "thy way," also means "thy religion." Aramaic speaking people today still ask: "What is your way?" meaning

---

[112]Ex. 33:22, Lamsa translation.
[113]Dt. 32:4. See also Mt. 7:24.
[114]1 Sam. 1:4; 2:13-17, Lamsa translation.
[115]Dt. 23:21-23.

"What is your religion?" Another term for "religion" is *dina,* "right judgment, justice, balance." This is why the term religion does not appear in the Bible; the word "way" has been used throughout the Sacred Book. Literally, it means path or road.

God's way is truth, justice, peace, and understanding. It leads people into the paths of righteousness and, finally, into the kingdom of God. When God's way, or religion, is known and practiced in all nations, the full reign of God will be hastened.

PSALM SIXTY-EIGHT

Divide the Spoil

Kings of armies did flee apace: and she that tarried at home divided the spoil. Ps. 68:12.

In the Near East when an army was defeated, the soldiers of the victorious army and the citizens plundered the camp of the enemy and divided the spoil. This ancient custom prevailed until recent years.

The last section of the verse in Aramaic reads: ". . . and the household of God shall divide the spoil."According to the Eastern text, this psalm was sung by David when he was bringing up the Ark of God from the house of the Hittite and while he was dancing. David had defeated the Philistines and broken their oppressive yoke from the necks of his people. But the words of this psalm were also used by Moses and Joshua when they related the wonders of God in their days. This psalm is a war song. It was recited before the army charged against the enemy.[116]

Sleep among the Thorns

Though ye have lain among the pots, yet shall ye be as the wings of a dove covered with silver, and her feathers with yellow gold. Ps. 68:13.

The first part of the verse reads differently in the Eastern Aramaic text: "Though you sleep among thorns, yet shall you be protected . . ." The word "thorns" is used metaphorically, meaning "grievances" and "tribulations." When Near Eastern people are oppressed and heavily taxed, they say, "We

---

[116]See verse 1.

live in thorns," or "He has been a thorn to me."

Some of the birds' nests are made of thorns and grass but are inlaid with soft and warm feathers. The psalmist portrays the Israelites as living in thorns, and God's mercy and protection are as the feathers of doves that protect the young in the nest.

Israel was harassed from all sides. The Philistines, the Moabites, the Ammonites, and the Arameans (Syrians) were all like thorns. At times the Israelites were subjugated by their enemies; yet they were protected by their God, who gave them grace in the eyes of the foreign rulers. This is because during these periods the people repented and turned to God and forsook their errant ways. In God there is no want, no need, no fear. When God is with a people or a nation, who can be against it?

Hills Leap

Why leap ye, ye high hills? this is the hill which God desireth to dwell in; yea, the Lord will dwell in it for ever. Ps. 68:16.

The Eastern Aramaic text reads: "What do you want, O you mountains of Bashan? This is the ridge which God desires to dwell in; yea, the Lord will dwell in it forever."

The term "mountain" is used figuratively, meaning "the people who dwell in the mountain." The reference is to the mountains of Bashan, which were ruled by the vicious dictators who oppressed the people.

Division of Spoils

Thou hast ascended on high, thou hast led captivity captive: thou hast received gifts for men; yea, for the rebellious also, that the Lord God might dwell among them. Ps. 68:18.

The Eastern Aramaic text reads: "Thou hast ascended on high, thou hast carried away captives; thou hast blessed men with gifts; but rebellious men shall not dwell before the presence of God."

During raids rebellious men who had disagreed with the council received no portion of the spoil that was divided among the warriors after their victories.

According to the psalmist, God would not bestow gifts on the men who had transgressed and rebelled against the commandments and the divine plan. The error in the King James Version is due no doubt to mistranslation. Israel had numerous enemies, and David's reign was fraught with many dangers and rebellions.[117]

Depths of the Sea

The Lord said, I will bring again from Bashan, I will bring my people again from the depths of the sea. Ps. 68:22.

"Depths of the sea" is an Aramaic saying which means "far-off lands." In those days the people thought the sea could not be measured and that its depth was endless. This expression also means "out of difficult situations." The Eastern Aramaic text reads "cliffs" instead of "Bashan."

Bashan was on the frontier of Syria and, therefore, the first land to be occupied by the invading armies that came from Mesopotamia and Persia. During these invasions, many people took refuge in cliffs and caves.[118]

The Lord God of Israel had assured the people that he would protect them and gather them, no matter where they had been taken or where they had been hiding.

A Great Slaughter

That thy foot may be dipped in the blood of thine enemies, and the tongue of thy dogs in the same. Ps. 68:23.

When Near Easterners describe a great slaughter they say, "The blood was high to the knee." In the ancient days wars were fought with swords and spears at close range in the streets, in fortresses, and in the battlefields. Blood sometimes flowed like streams of water.

Most dogs in the Near East were not fed and had no owners. They roamed around and ate anything they could get. They licked blood and ate dead bodies in the field. When the chariot in which King Ahab was slain was washed, the dogs licked up the blood.[119]

---

[117]See verse 21.

[118]Isa. 2:21; Jer. 49:16.

[119]1 Ki. 22:38.

Fountain of Israel

Bless ye God in the congregations, even the Lord, from the fountain of Israel. Ps. 68:26.

"Fountain" refers to true teaching and the life-giving religion of Israel. Water is symbolic of light and truth; therefore, a "fountain" means "everlasting truth and light that never runs out." The fountain or truth of God issued from the hills of Judea, which irrigated the entire Gentile world.[120]

PSALM SIXTY-NINE

Zeal Has Eaten Me up

For the zeal of thine house hath eaten me up; and the reproaches of them that reproached thee are fallen upon me. Ps. 69:9.

"Eaten me up" is a Near Eastern idiom that means "has made me courageous, has moved or provoked me, or has forced me to act." Jesus' disciples remembered this psalm when their master said, "The zeal of thine house hath eaten me up!"[121] Psalm 119:139 reads: "My zeal hath consumed me." Zeal for good works, justice, righteousness, and freedom makes people so courageous that at times they are even willing to die for God's way of life. [122]

Vinegar

They gave me also gall for my meat; and in my thirst they gave me vinegar to drink. Ps. 69:21.

Oppressed people were fed with bitter herbs (gall) and were given vinegar to drink instead of water. In those days, prisoners were not fed or even given water.

In the New Testament we read that when Jesus was on the cross, he

---

[120]Ezk. 47:1-3.

[121]Jn. 2:17.

[122]See Ps. 119:139.

became thirsty and cried out but they gave him vinegar. Wine and vinegar were more abundant than water.[123]

During times of droughts, not only sheep and cattle died because of the lack of water, but people also perished. On such occasions water is so scarce that it is often stolen from those who have the precious element. The author of the book of Proverbs writes that "stolen water is sweet."[124]

Table as a Snare

Let their table become a snare before them: and that which should have been for their welfare, let it become a trap. Ps. 69:22.

When a man planned some kind of conspiracy, he would prepare a lavish table with abundant varieties of food and drink and invite the prospective conspirators into his house. In those days tables generally were made of skins and cloth and were spread on the floor before the guests. This custom remained until World War I. After eating and drinking, the host would open the subject, reveal his devices, and seek agreement from the guests at his table. Generally, the well fed and drunken guests would agree to almost anything that the host proposed.

At times these plots and conspiracies were soon discovered and the culprits severely punished. In these cases the table was called a snare, because the shrewd host had enticed the guests by means of food and wine. The reference in the psalm is to the table of the enemies of the Jews, who were constantly conniving against them.

PSALM SEVENTY-ONE

Oral Praises

My mouth shall show forth thy righteousness and thy salvation all the day; for I know not the numbers thereof. Ps. 71:15.

The Aramaic word *saprotha* may mean "the office of a learned scribe, the learning of grammar, or a scribe learned in law." The last section of the psalm in the Eastern Aramaic text reads: ". . . for I cannot read." Near

---

[123]Mt. 27:48.
[124]Prov. 9:17.

Eastern priests, deacons, and singers generally sing from a book. The unlearned offer oral praises and thanksgiving that are different from those composed by the poets and song writers.

The psalmist says that he praises the Lord aloud because he is uninstructed or unlearned and thus unable to praise God by reading the scriptural praises in the temple. In the modern Near East, many illiterate Semites know the prayers by heart, and they pray and praise God aloud.

PSALM SEVENTY-TWO

Mountains

The mountains shall bring peace to the people, and the little hills, by righteousness. Ps. 72:3.

Metaphorically, the term "mountains" can mean a kingdom or state. Judah was a mountainous country. The phrase "the mountains shall bring peace to the people" means nature will share in making matters pleasant for God's people. Such comments are not taken literally. Interestingly, mountains in Aramaic are also symbolic of insurmountable problems and challenges, but not in the case of this psalm.

The Islands

They that dwell in the wilderness shall bow before him; and his enemies shall lick the dust. Ps. 72:9.

The Eastern Aramaic text reads: "They that dwell on the islands shall bow before him . . ." The psalmist refers to the large islands beyond the Mediterranean—Britain and Ireland. These islands were known to both the Israelites and the Arameans. The latter, being a great naval power, had colonies and mines in these islands.[125] The inhabitants of these islands resisted invasion, and many of them remained independent for many centuries.

The psalm points to the Messiah/Christ, the King of kings. All kings of the earth were to bow before him. Today all the lords of the islands kneel

---

[125]Isa. 23:1-3.

before the King of kings and offer prayer to him.[126]

Messianic Kingdom

There shall be a handful of corn in the earth upon the top of the mountains; the fruit thereof shall shake like Lebanon: and they of the city shall flourish like grass of the earth. Ps. 72:16.

The first part of the verse in the Eastern Aramaic text reads: "He shall multiply like wheat upon the earth; his seed [offspring] shall spring up on the mountain tops, as on Lebanon . . ." The reference is to the remnant of Israel and the establishment of the messianic reign throughout the world.[127]

According to the Eastern text, this prophecy is about King Solomon and the blessings which the Lord had bestowed upon Israel. The peaceful reign of Solomon symbolized the messianic kingdom. Solomon's kingdom extended from the great sea to the River Euphrates only, but today the messianic kingdom embraces the entire world.

A Marginal Note

The prayers of David the son of Jesse are ended. Ps. 72:20.

Verse 20 in the King James Version is a marginal note inserted into the text by a scribe. Similar insertions are to be found at the beginning and the end of other portions of the Scriptures.

These insertions, or marginal notes, were made to facilitate the reading of the lesson. For example: "Thus far is the judgment of Moab" at the end of chapter 48 of Jeremiah. "The prophecy concerning the fall of Babylon, which Isaiah the son of Amoz saw."[128] "The prophecy concerning the fall of Moab."[129] "The prophecy concerning the fall of Damascus."[130] Isaiah did not write or dictate any of these phrases.

This verse proves beyond a doubt that the Peshitta has nothing to do with the Masoretic text from which other translations were made, nor with the

---

[126]See verses 10-15.

[127]See verses 7-11.

[128]Isa. 13:1, Lamsa translation.

[129]Isa. 15:1, Lamsa translation.

[130]Isa. 17:1, Lamsa translation.

Greek text, but that it is a copy of the original Hebrew, as many leading scholars in the Near East have stated.

If the Peshitta had been transcribed from the Masoretic text or translated from the Septuagint, verse 20 would have been included. The copyist would not have omitted it, but this verse is not included in the original Peshitta, and verse 19 ends with "Amen and amen," which means that it is the end of the psalm.

PSALM SEVENTY-THREE

Blemish

Their eyes stand out with fatness: they have more than heart could wish. Ps. 73:7.

The Aramaic word *tarba* means "fat or grease." The Eastern Aramaic text reads: "Their iniquity comes through like grease; they do according to the evil dictates of the heart."

The evil works of the wicked come through like grease on a garment. Fat is also symbolic of wealth. In biblical days the wealthy classes oppressed the poor, robbed widows, and misused the power that they had gained by evil ways. Their wickedness could not be hidden from the eyes of the people. It remained on them as a spot on a garment. This is also true of good works, which shine like costly jewels that one may wear.

The Proud Ungodly

They set their mouth against the heavens, and their tongue walketh through the earth. Ps. 73:9.

"They set their mouth against the heavens" means that they boast and blaspheme against God. Riches acquired unjustly cover their eyes, and human pride encompasses them.

"Their tongue walketh through the earth" means that they gossiped and bragged about their wealth and power. These were the ungodly who for a time prospered and were powerful but sooner or later were uprooted and their place was remembered no more. These ungodly men prospered by means of violence and believed that there was no judgment; nor were they aware of the presence of God in human affairs.

Abundance after Captivity

Therefore his people return hither: and waters of a full cup are wrung out to them. Ps. 73:10.

The Eastern Aramaic text reads: "Therefore will my people return hither, and they shall have everything in abundance."

The reference is to the people who had returned from captivity. Now they are praising God, who had been gracious to them while they were still in captivity and given them favor in the eyes of pagan kings and princes who had helped them on their way. Some of the people had doubted the prophecies concerning the restoration and thought that God was not aware of what was taking place. But now the people were to have abundance of prosperity and their enemies were to be confounded and ashamed.

Riches Acquired Unjustly

Surely thou didst set them in slippery places: thou castedst them down into destruction. Ps. 73:18.

The Eastern Aramaic text reads: "Thou didst appoint their portion according to their deceitfulness; thou didst cast them down when they exalted themselves."

In Hebrew thinking, nothing could be done or could take place without God's knowledge and permission. Hence, since the ungodly prospered and became powerful, God must have allowed them to have riches and power so that they might later slip and destroy themselves. Though riches are a great temptation to those who acquire them unjustly and use them wrongly, they can be a blessing to the pious.

God never causes anyone to go astray or to slip. Irresponsibility and evil doings bring about one's downfall; one reaps what one sows. God had endowed humanity with a free will and the power to choose good or evil.

PSALM SEVENTY-FOUR

Enemies of God

Lift up thy feet unto the perpetual desolations; even all that the enemy hath done wickedly in the sanctuary. Ps. 74:3.

The Eastern Aramaic text reads: "Exalt thy servants over all those who are carried away by power; all those who oppress are enemies of thy sanctuary."

The psalmist exhorts God to exalt Israel over her enemies; that is, let Israel be victorious in battle. He also tells the Lord God that all those who oppress Israel are God's enemies and should be defeated. It was believed that Israel and God were fighting for a common cause.

Destruction of the Second Temple

A man was famous according as he had lifted up axes upon the thick trees. Ps. 74:5.

The Eastern Aramaic text is totally different from other versions. It reads: "Thou knowest this as the exalted one who sits on high; they have hewn down the doors with axes as they would cut the trees of the forest."

The complaint here is against the severe treatment of the Jews and the destruction of the second temple by Antiochus Epiphanes during the Maccabean period. The temple doors were cut down with axes and hammers, just as one would cut down a tree in the forest. They also defiled the holy sanctuary. The pagans had no regard for the house of God, which they profaned.[131] The Jews were also oppressed, and many of them were taken captive. Others were forced to eat swine meat. The psalm is a prayer for relief and an appeal to God, reminding the Lord of the covenant and mercies of the past.

Carved Work

But now they break down the carved work thereof at once with axes and hammers. Ps. 74:6.

When the holy sanctuary was entered by the pagan armies the doors were broken with axes and hammers, and all the work of the craftsmen was destroyed. The entire sanctuary was ransacked and burned. There were many wreaths of chain work on the capitals of the temple pillars. All the woodwork of brass, silver, and gold was destroyed.

Temples, with their fabulous gold and silver treasures, were a great

---

[131]See verse 6.

temptation to pagan rulers. When Herod's Temple (the third temple) was destroyed by Titus in AD 69, millions of dollars in gold coins, gold bars, and much silver and other costly articles were taken away to Rome.

The Heads of the Dragons

Thou didst divide the sea by thy strength: thou brakest the heads of the dragons in the waters. Thou brakest the heads of leviathan in pieces, and gavest him to be meat to the people inhabiting the wilderness. Ps. 74:13-14.

When describing great dictators and oppressors, the Hebrew prophets and poets often used figurative speech and metaphors such as dragons and sea monsters.[132] The reference is to Pharaoh and his army. When the Israelites crossed to the other side of the Gulf of Suez, the Egyptian army was drowned in the channel (the crossing place).

The Israelites and the Bedouins in the desert plundered what was left of the Egyptian camp and took the garments and weapons of Pharaoh's warriors which were strewn along the seaside.

PSALM SEVENTY-FIVE

Wine and Dregs

For in the hand of the Lord there is a cup, and the wine is red; it is full of mixture; and he poureth out of the same: but the dregs thereof, all the wicked of the earth shall wring them out, and drink them. Ps. 75:8.

The first section of this verse in the Eastern Aramaic text reads: "For in the hand of the Lord there is a cup, full of a mixture of the dregs of wine." In the Near East, red wine is generally preferred over white. When princes, governors, and noblemen are entertained, the host serves red wine. Red wine can easily be mixed with poison or hashhash (a kind of drug) without being detected by the guests.

Mixing of poison with wine is very common in many lands and has been practiced since biblical days. Delilah, no doubt, tempered the wine with hashhash and gave it to Samson before he fell asleep upon her knees.[133]

---

[132]Rev. 12:3.
[133]Judg. 16:19.

Wine and dregs are used metaphorically. The wine and the cup are symbolic of God's wrath, fury, and vengeance, which were to be poured out against the wicked.[134] "For thus says the Lord of hosts, the God of Israel, to me: Take the wine cup of this fury from my hand, and make all the nations to whom I send you drink it." The nations who had been drunk with power were to face destruction. They were to drink from the cup which now was in the hand of the Lord.[135]

The Second Affliction

All the horns of the wicked also will I cut off; but the horns of the righteous shall be exalted. Ps. 75:10.

The Aramaic word *tinyana* means "a second time," that is, a second visitation or a second punishment. The reference is to the second captivity.

The Babylonian captivity was the second affliction of Israel. The ten tribes had been taken captive to Assyria in 722 BCE. Now Judah was captive in Babylon. And because of oppression, the people became reconciled to their God and, therefore, were mindful of God's wonders in the ancient days.

PSALM SEVENTY-SEVEN

Waters Were Afraid

The waters saw thee, O God, the waters saw thee; they were afraid: the depths also were troubled. Ps. 77:16.

The psalmist refers to the crossing of the Red Sea.[136] According to Scripture, the lord caused the sea to go back all night by a strong east wind. The statement that the waters "were afraid" is used poetically. The wind also brought a heavy rain, accompanied by thunder and lightning, which lighted the earth. The depths of the sea were also disturbed by the strong wind and the torrents of rain. Nature itself shared in the great victory over the Egyptian army.

---

[134]Job 21:20.
[135]Jer. 51:7.
[136]Ex. 14:21-22.

The psalmist describes God's mighty power not only over the Egyptian army but also over the forces of nature. In other words, God made nature be on the side of the Israelites and against the Egyptians. We may state it this way: Moses was so divinely guided that nature was on his side. He and his people arrived at the crossing place at the right time, when the forces of nature were favorable to them. The Egyptians, not being divinely guided, came at the wrong time, when the forces of nature were against them.

The gospel writer also recorded a time when Jesus rebuked the strong wind and stilled the storm. Nature is on the side of those who are with God.

Thy Way in the Sea

Thy way is in the sea, and thy path in the great waters, and thy footsteps are not known. Ps. 77:19.

In desert lands, tribal movements and armed forces are traced by the imprints of their horses and camels. But God's ways and footsteps are hidden from physical sight and can only be discerned spiritually.

"Thy way is in the sea" is a Near Eastern idiom which means, "No one knows your way or can see the imprints of your footsteps." That is to say, "Your ways are unpredictable." Ships leave no imprints on the surface of the sea, and birds leave no tracks in the air, nor can their paths be seen. Such are the hidden ways of God and his footsteps through time.[137] But one can hear God's small voice in the sea, on the land, and in the air.

Job says, "Touching the Almighty, we cannot find him out." God's ways are hidden from the eyes of men; they are not like men's ways. At times we fail to understand God's plans and purposes simply because we judge them by our human standards.

Just as God cannot be seen with the eyes of the flesh, the ways of the Lord can only be understood and discerned spiritually. ". . . for there shall no man see me, and live."[138]

---

[137]Hab. 3:15.
[138]Ex. 33:20.

PSALM SEVENTY-EIGHT

One Generation Teaches the Other

Give ear, O my people, to my law; incline your ears to the words of my mouth. I will open my mouth in a parable: I will utter dark sayings of old: Which we have heard and known, and our fathers have told us. We will not hide them from their children, shewing to the generation to come, the praises of the Lord, and his strength, and his wonderful works that he has done. Ps. 78:1-4.

One of the Mosaic ordinances was to always remember goodness, loving kindness, miracles, and wonders of God in the days of their forefathers. The Israelites were admonished to relate these events poetically from one generation to another.

The retelling of God's wonders served as a lesson to all generations of the people of Israel. Even today, the Jews share their knowledge of the ancient days with the new generation. No generation is deprived of God's mercies and loving kindness to their race.

Water Standing as a Heap

He divided the sea, and caused them to pass through; and he made the waters to stand as a heap. Ps. 78:13.

The last phrase of the verse in the Eastern Aramaic text reads: ". . . he made the waters to stand as in skins." In desert lands during wars, water is carried in skins on the backs of donkeys, mules, and camels and piled up at the camp.

The strong east wind caused the water of the Gulf of Suez to go back.[139] The waters piled up in a heap because of the force of the east wind. But when the wind ceased, the water returned to its place. Powerful winds often drive water backward and cause it to pile up; during severe storms the wind often dries up smaller bodies of water.

When the Israelites crossed the tip of the Gulf of Suez, the water stood up in a heap as though it were in sheepskins. And when the Egyptians tried to pursue them, the wind ceased and the waters rushed back, drowning all the Egyptians.

---

[139]Ex. 14:21.

God has power over all forces of nature, which the divine has ordained. When one is in harmony with God, all the forces of nature are on one's side. Moses and his people were guided to cross at the right time, when the forces of nature were on their side.

Water Miraculously Provided

He clave the rocks in the wilderness, and gave them drink as out of the great depths. He brought streams also out of the rock, and caused waters to run down like rivers. Ps. 78:15-16.

The Aramaic word *tera* means, "to cleave, make a breach, pierce, cut, split." The reference is to the wandering of the Israelites in the wilderness where water is scarce and hard to find. Moses was guided by God to find hidden wells.[140] He also was divinely led to dig wells in rocky places and, at times, to bore the flint rocks in search of water.

Moses trusted in God and therefore overcame all the desert difficulties. What was hidden from the eyes of the people was divinely revealed to him. When the psalmist says that God "caused waters to run down like rivers," he means that the water came out abundantly. When rocky places are bored, the water sometimes gushes out because of geological formations.

The miracle is that Moses, through spiritual guidance, was able to supply his thirsty people with water in a dry land. When humans are divinely guided, what is impossible becomes possible.

Quail

He caused an east wind to blow in the heaven: and by his power he brought in the south wind. He rained flesh also upon them as dust, and feathered fowls like as the sand of the sea. And he let it fall in the midst of their camp, round about their habitations. Ps. 78:26-28.

Large flocks of quail that migrate from Europe to the Arabian desert were caught between two strong winds and fell to the ground exhausted. When the quail cross the Mediterranean Sea, they are sometimes exhausted and fall helpless on the beaches and nearby land. Thousands of them may drown in the sea.

---

[140]Num. 21:16.

The fact that the winds brought the quail at a time when the Israelites were craving meat was a miracle. All acts of God are miracles and wonders in the eyes of men.[141]

God Was Not Jealous

For they provoked him to anger with their high places, and moved him to jealousy with their graven images. Ps. 78:58.

The Eastern Aramaic text reads: "For they provoked him to anger by sacrificing on high places, and made him indignant with their graven images." The Aramaic words for "jealousy" and "indignant" are identical.

God could not have been jealous of images made of wood, stone, silver, and gold. There was nothing in these idol-gods made by men to make anyone jealous. The writer portrays God as being indignant because the people had broken the commandments and were worshiping false deities that the Lord had warned their fathers not to worship. Some of the people also offered their children as burnt offerings to these pagan idols. This is the reason the author reveals God as being angry.

The worship of images was forbidden because images were made by men and sold for a profit, but humans were created by God in the divine image and likeness.

PSALM EIGHTY

Bread of Tears

Thou feedest them with the bread of tears; and givest them tears to drink in great measure. Ps. 80:5.

"Bread of tears" means oppression, high taxation, and persecution. In the Near East when people are harassed, highly taxed, and misruled, they weep and groan under their heavy burdens. They sow, but others reap; they plant, but others eat the fruit of their trees.

One can hear people say, "This is the bread of tears." This is because they weep when they see their children hungry and crying for bread. When

---

[141]Ex. 16:13. See Errico and Lamsa, *Aramaic Light on Exodus through Deuteronomy,* "Quail," pp. 41-42.

the fathers and mothers eat and are aware of the lack of bread, tears run over their cheeks and mingle with the bread.

Vine out of Egypt

Thou hast brought a vine out of Egypt: thou hast cast out the heathen, and planted it. Thou preparedst room before it, and didst cause it to take deep root, and it filled the land. The hills were covered with the shadow of it, and the boughs thereof were like the goodly cedars. She sent out her boughs unto the sea, and her branches unto the river. Ps. 80:8-11.

"Vine" is symbolic of Israel. Hebrew prophets and poets used poetic terms of speech, parables, metaphors, and allegories when describing important events. "My well-beloved hath a vineyard in a very fruitful hill."[142]

At the outset, God took Abraham from Ur of Chaldea and brought him to Canaan. When he was uprooted from there, he was planted in Egypt. After four centuries God took the Israelites out of Egypt and planted them in the land of Canaan. Most of the other races throughout Canaan were cast out in order to make room for Israel because she was the vine of God.

"Vine" is also symbolic of teaching. Teaching spreads like the branches of a vine. And just as the vine branches must abide with the vine, so the disciples and followers of a teacher or prophet of religion must abide in his words in order to receive guidance and understanding. Jesus, when instructing his disciples, said, "I am the vine, ye are the branches."[143]

When the hedges were broken down, the wild beasts trampled on God's vine (Israel) and broke its branches; that is, when God's commandments were transgressed and the way forgotten, pagan doctrines and practices destroyed the fences around the vineyard of God. The true religion was the only defense that Israel had against the strong nations around her.

The Boar

The boar out of the wood doth waste it, and the wild beast of the field doth devour it. Ps. 80:13.

---

[142]Isa. 5:1.

[143]Jn. 15:5, K.J.V.

Nearly all vineyards in the Near East are fenced or hedged to protect the vines from sheep, goats, and wild animals. In some of the vineyards men keep constant watch, especially during the night. Bears, boars, and other wild animals might sneak in and destroy the plants.

The boar and wild beasts here are used symbolically, meaning false prophets who had introduced pagan teachings into the Jewish religion, and pagan enemies who sought the destruction of Israel.

PSALM EIGHTY-TWO

Judging Angels

God standeth in the congregation of the mighty; he judgeth among the gods. Ps. 82:1.

The Eastern Aramaic text uses the word "angels" instead of the two words "mighty" and "gods." Angels are spirits and are used as God's messengers. The term "angel" also means God's counsel.

In biblical days, the Hebrew concept of God was different from what was revealed later. The Hebrews believed in many gods, but their God was greater than other gods. Nevertheless, during the time of Abraham, the Hebrews believed that their God was the only God, and the Gentile gods were nothing.

During the period of Theocracy, the Israelites lost their pure concept of God. When they lost battles, they blamed it on their God, thus giving credence to the Gentile gods who were fighting against them and causing them to lose the war.

The God of Israel is not only the God of the Hebrews but the God of the universe. God is judge not only over kings, princes, and judges of this world but also over the heavenly host. This is one of the first psalms that hint of the universality of God that became fully known to the eighth century Hebrew prophets.

Sons of God

I have said, Ye are gods; and all of you are children of the Most High. Ps. 82:6.

Prior to the flood, the descendants of Seth were good and were known as the sons of God—that is, good men. Though they were the good men of the times, they were tempted by the beautiful daughters of men—that is, the descendants of Cain.[144]

Humans were created in the image and likeness of God; therefore, a true human is a child of God. In the modern Near East, good men are addressed as sons of God and bad men are called sons of the devil or Satan. Jesus admonished his disciples to pray to God and address him as their Father.

PSALM EIGHTY-FOUR

God's Ways

Blessed is the man whose strength is in thee; in whose heart are the ways of them. Ps. 84:5.

The ending of the psalm should read, "in whose heart are thy ways," that is, "God's way." The way of God is the true religion, which is based on justice and truth. When people walk in the ways of God, they are blessed, protected, and prosper in all that they undertake. On the other hand, man's way of life usually leads to greed, hatred, war, and destruction.

The Valley of Weeping

Who passing through the valley of Baca make it a well; the rain also filleth the pools. Ps. 84:6.

Aumka debkhatha means "the valley of weeping." The Eastern Aramaic text reads: "They have passed through the valley of weeping, and have made it a dwelling place; the Lawgiver shall cover it with blessings."

The valley of weeping must have been a place through which the captives were taken away into exile, or a valley in which some massacre had taken place. Then again, when children were taken from their parents to be sold as slaves, both the parents and their children wept vehemently.

Selah

O Lord God of hosts, hear my prayer: give ear, O God of Jacob. Selah. Ps. 84:8.

---

[144]Gen. 6:2.

The term *selah* has been a riddle to students of the Bible. No doubt the meaning of this word was understood in biblical days, when both Aramaic and Hebrew languages were spoken by the Jews. However, it does not occur in the Eastern Aramaic text.

The term *selah* appears in the book of Psalms, other portions of the Bible, and in Jewish liturgical books. Various explanations have been given as to its meaning. Some authorities believe it was used as an indication to lift the voice in a doxology. In those ancient days, psalms were sung with musical accompaniments.

Selah might have been written with the letter *tsadeh* instead of *semkat.* The psalms were composed orally and then written, and the two letters would be pronounced alike. *Selah,* spelled with a *tsadeh*, would mean "to incline the ear, give heed, pray."

Dr. Lamsa was inclined to think that it meant "heed, give attention, or be ready." Some of the psalms were sung during battles. *Selah* might have meant, "Be ready to charge" or "Give ear to the command." In Turkish military drills, the term *selah* was used, meaning "Be ready." When this word was uttered, the soldiers placed their guns in position as though they were ready to charge. (In the Turkish language, the term *selah* was used for weapon or gun.)

That *selah* was used as a rubric, there is no doubt. Many times rubrics and titles were incorporated into the verses by the scribes, translators, and copyists. It may have been used as a marginal note later.

The Lord Is a Sun

For the Lord God is a sun and shield: the Lord will give grace and glory: no good thing will he withhold from them that walk uprightly. Ps. 84:11.

The Eastern Aramaic text reads: "For the Lord God is our supply and our helper . . ." The sun supplies all basic human needs. In the Near East, God is often likened to the sun. This is because the sun is the source of life-giving energy, heat, and light, and is symbolic of God. In other words, these attributes of the sun are similar to the attributes of God: life, nourishment, and impartiality. Just as the whole universe depends on God for its existence, so humans and the universe depend on God for harmony and well-being. When God's truth (light) is manifested, darkness and falsehood flee.

In the gospel of John, Jesus is reported as saying: "I am the light of the world; he who follows me shall not walk in darkness, but he shall find for himself the light of life."[145]

PSALM EIGHTY-FIVE

Kiss of Peace

Mercy and truth are met together; righteousness and peace have kissed each other. Truth shall spring out of the earth; and righteousness shall look down from heaven. Ps. 85:10-11.

These verses are written in poetic style. Kissing is an indication of deep love and affection. Near Easterners kiss one another while greeting. When enemies reconcile, they also kiss one another.

The prayers of the Jews who were exiled were answered. King Cyrus of Persia had granted them permission to return to their own country and to rebuild Jerusalem and the temple. Cyrus had been magnanimous in extending his mercy and grace to these exiles.

PSALM EIGHTY-SIX

There Is None like God

Among the gods there is none like unto thee, O Lord; neither are there any works like unto thy works. Ps. 86:8.

The first part of the verse in the Eastern Aramaic text reads: "There is none like thee, O Lord my God . . ." The Israelites feared other gods, but they believed that their God, who was called Yahweh, was the greater god. The God of Israel was called the God of gods.

It took the Hebrew prophets centuries of teaching and warning to destroy polytheism in the minds of the people. Despite their admonitions and revelations, the belief in pagan gods and idolatry persisted until after the second captivity. The weird pagan rituals and immoral Baal worship was a great temptation and a stumbling block to the children of Israel.

---

[145]Jn. 8:12, Eastern Aramaic Peshitta text, Lamsa translation.

PSALM EIGHTY-EIGHT

Resurrection

Wilt thou show wonders to the dead? shall the dead arise and praise thee? Selah. Shall thy loving-kindness be declared in the grave? or thy faithfulness in destruction? Ps. 88:10-11.

The question of resurrection and life hereafter was not yet crystallized when the early (pre-exile) psalms were written. This question came to be the subject of debate during the exile and the post exile. The belief in resurrection was taught by some of the early prophets and by Job.

"Thy dead men shall live, their dead bodies shall arise. Those who dwell in the dust shall awake and sing, for thy dew is a dew of light, and the land of the giants thou shalt overthrow."[146]

"Although devouring worms have covered my skin and my flesh, yet, if my eyes shall see God, then my heart also will see the light; but now my body is consumed."[147]

During the time of the Hebrew patriarchs there was little faith in the life hereafter. The early Hebrews considered death an end, believing that when someone died he or she was cut off from the Living God. People continued to live only through their posterity or nation.

The notion of the resurrection was proclaimed more openly by Daniel during the exile. People who had suffered injustices were to rise and enjoy a new life, and the wicked were to rise so that they could be condemned for their evil deeds. This doctrine was upheld by the Pharisees, but disputed by the Sadducees. Jesus, like Daniel, Isaiah, and Job, proclaimed the resurrection of the dead and eternal rewards.

PSALM EIGHTY-NINE

"The Proud," Not "Rahab"

Thou hast broken Rahab in pieces, as one that is slain; thou hast scattered thine enemies with thy strong arm. Ps. 89:10.

---

[146]Isa. 26:19, Eastern Aramaic Peshitta text, Lamsa translation.

[147]Job 19:26-27, Eastern Aramaic Peshitta text, Lamsa translation. See also Job 7:7, Eastern Aramaic text.

"Rahab" in the King James Version should not be confused with Rahab, the harlot, in Joshua 2:1. The Eastern Aramaic text of this verse reads: "Thou hast humbled the proud as those that are slain . . ."

There was a city called Rahab, but like many other cities, it was destroyed and never rebuilt.[148] In Isaiah 51:9, "Rahab" is confused with *rabba,* meaning "great."

Understanding of God

Blessed is the people that know the joyful sound: they shall walk, O Lord, in the light of thy countenance. Ps. 89:15.

The opening section of the verse in the Eastern Aramaic text reads, "Blessed is the people that understand thy glory," that is, the people who praise the Lord instead of praising idols made of silver and gold.

People who understand God's glory understand the divine laws and ordinances and walk in the sure way. The blessings come from loyalty to the true God, the Creator of the heavens and earth, who knows the thoughts of humanity and rewards them according to their deeds.

Speaking in Visions

Then thou spakest in vision to thy holy one, and saidst, I have laid help upon one that is mighty; I have exalted one chosen out of the people. Ps. 89:19.

Most of God's communications and revelations with the holy prophets and seers were in visions and dreams. The reference is to the Messiah, who was predicted by the prophets and holy men as the Savior of Israel and of the world. The Messiah was to be exalted above all the kings and princes of the world and was to be endowed with power and wisdom. The Messiah, Christ, is the heir of the Davidic kingdom, the spiritual realm of God.[149]

Dominion—Power

I will set his hand also in the sea, and his right hand in the rivers. Ps. 89:25.

---

[148]Ps. 87:4.
[149]Jer. 33:17.

The hand, in Semitic languages, is symbolic of power and dominion. It is also used as a token of blessing[150] and for chastisement.[151]

"I will set his hand also in the sea, and his right hand in the rivers" means that he shall have dominion over the islands in the sea and the lands of the rivers, namely Egypt and Assyria. This suggests that the kingdom will be a great land and sea power.

This is a messianic psalm. The reference is to the dominion that the Messiah will have over the world and his everlasting throne.[152] In biblical days, neither Israel nor Judah was a great naval power. Today the messianic kingdom embraces all lands, islands, and great rivers. The Messiah/Christ is the everlasting king and high priest.[153]

Man Not Created in Vain

Remember how short my time is: wherefore hast thou made all men in vain? Ps. 89:47.

The Eastern Aramaic text reads: ". . . for thou hast not created all men in vain." The error was caused by the mistranslation of negative *la* (not). The first part of the verse reads, "Remember me from the time I was created"; that is, God is mindful of man from the time he forms him.

According to Scripture, humans were made in the image and likeness of God. They were not created in vain or by chance but with a spiritual mission on this earth; therefore, God is constantly mindful of them.

According to the Eastern text, this is one of the psalms of David that was sung by the people who were in Babylon, asking God for comfort and blessings, and reminding God of their mission in life.

PSALM NINETY

Temporal Life

Thou carriest them away as with a flood; they are as a sleep: in the morning they are like grass which groweth up. Ps. 90:5.

---

[150]Ezra 7:9; Neh. 2:18.
[151]Dt. 2:15; Job 2:10.
[152]See verses 28 and 29.
[153]Jer. 33:17-18.

The Eastern Aramaic text reads: "The span of their life will be as a sleep; in the morning they are like grass which changes." The reference is to generations that come and quickly pass away.

In their growth, humans change like grass, which today is green and tomorrow is yellow and dry. In the Near East grass sometimes grows on the walls of houses, housetops, and other places in the towns. This grass grows quickly but withers when the sun is hot.[154] Such is temporal life; it withers like the grass on the housetops, which today is and tomorrow is gone.

Sins Before God

Thou hast set our iniquities before thee, our secret sins in the light of thy countenance. Ps. 90:8.

"Thou hast set our iniquities before thee" means, "You are constantly mindful of our evil deeds." This is because nothing that humans do is ever hidden from God. The Eastern Aramaic text reads "the sins of our youth" instead of "our secret sins."

God sees and feels every human action that is contrary to the good. Whenever the children of Israel turned from the ways of truth, God saw that the divine laws and ordinances were violated. On the other hand, when men and women did good, God was cognizant of that as well. Evil and wickedness prevail when goodness is lacking.

Human sins and iniquities remain in the presence of God until people repent and seek forgiveness. Then they are no longer in the presence of God. According to the psalmist, God sees and remembers even the sins of our youth.

PSALM NINETY-ONE

Shadow—Divine Protection

He that dwelleth in the secret place of the Most High shall abide under the shadow of the Almighty. Ps. 91:1.

In Semitic languages, "shadow" is often used figuratively, meaning "protection." The term "shadow" originally was derived from the shadow

---

[154]James 1:10-11.

of the trees under which weary travelers and the sick sought refuge and relief during the hot hours of the day. In those days, just as today in some Near Eastern countries, trees are venerated and visited as sacred shrines by the sick and the suffering. In biblical days trees and groves were worshiped. The tree, through its inner energies, produces a cool shadow that helps the weary travelers and the sick.

In the Near East, when a king is good to his people they say, "We are under a good shadow," meaning "protection." On the other hand, dark shadows are symbolic of fear and uncertainty. "The valley of the shadow of death," for instance, means "instant death." "A secret place" in Aramaic means "fortress," the place where the warriors defend the town—that is, the strongest and most secure place in a town or a city. Kings and princes have secret places to hide themselves from their enemies.

God's Feathers

He shall cover thee with his feathers, and under his wings shalt thou trust: his truth shall be thy shield and buckler. Ps. 91:4.

The psalmist portrays God as a loving mother bird that tenderly shelters her brood under her soft feathers and covers them with her wings. The psalmist, being a shepherd and living in the outdoors, had carried newly born sheep under his thick woolen mantle and had seen, during times of danger, little birds taking refuge under their mother's wings.

Wings are symbolic of mercy, grace, protection, and trust. God has no wings but protects with goodness and loving kindness. This is symbolized by the everlasting wings constantly spread over all creation, and especially over those who take refuge under them, for God is our refuge and our everlasting fortress (protection).

Conspiracy

Nor for the pestilence that walketh in darkness; nor for the destruction that wasteth at noonday. Ps. 91:6.

The Aramaic word *miltha* in this verse means "conspiracy." "Pestilence that walketh in darkness" is a mistranslation of the Aramaic idiom, *miltha dam halkha bheshokha,* meaning "the conspiracy that spreads in darkness." Conspiracies are generally devised in secret and spread during the dark hours of the night when most people are asleep.

Viper and Adder

Thou shalt tread upon the lion and adder: the young lion and the dragon shall thou trample under feet. Ps. 91:13.

"Viper and adder" are used symbolically, meaning "deadly enemies" or "evil forces." The lion and the dragon, metaphorically, are wicked men and oppressors who rebel against God and oppress the people of the Lord.

Serpents and other deadly reptiles are symbolic of Satanic forces—that is, evil forces—and of men who are the enemies of God and spiritual truth. Jesus told his disciples that they could handle serpents and drink any deadly poison, meaning that they could handle the enemies of his gospel of God's kingdom and overcome all kinds of attacks and defamation of their names.[155]

The reference is to the Messiah, who had the power to overcome all obstacles in his way and to prove that, in the end, truth triumphs over evil forces.

PSALM NINETY-THREE

The Rivers Are Full

The floods have lifted up, O Lord, the floods have lifted up their voice; the floods lift up their waves. Ps. 93:3.

The Eastern Aramaic text reads: "The rivers are full flowing, O Lord; the rivers have lifted up their voice; the rivers are flowing with purity." Floods, generally, are symbolic of calamities.

"The rivers" symbolize great powers and abundance. They could mean Assyria or Beth-Naharin, the land between the two rivers, the Tigris and Euphrates. Assyria had invaded all the lands west of the River Euphrates. Nearly all kingdoms, both large and small, were conquered or made tributaries. Thousands of people were taken captive. The Assyrian power, like a flooded river, was capturing everyone. Jeremiah, in his visions, saw the rise of Babylon like a swollen river sweeping everything ahead of it.

---

[155]Mk. 16:18.

"The rivers have lifted up their voice" means that the Assyrians had lifted up their voices and defied the other nations and their gods.[156] But later, when both Assyria and Babylon were gone, the rivers were flowing with purity. Persian kings were magnanimous in their decrees, granting the restoration of the Jews. This psalm is a prophecy concerning God's abundant help to restore the exiles to their homeland.

PSALM NINETY-FOUR

Material Thoughts

The Lord knoweth the thoughts of man, that they are vanity. Ps. 94:11.

The last part of the verse in the Eastern Aramaic text reads: ". . . they are like a breath." The Aramaic word *laha* means "breath" or "vapor." This metaphor is used to indicate that human thoughts and aspirations are of short duration. This is because an individual's life is so short when compared with spiritual values that endure forever.

Human material and temporal thoughts vanish like a breath and like a vapor, but a human being's spiritual ideas and aspirations endure forever and are handed down from one generation to another.

PSALM NINETY-FIVE

God of Gods

For the Lord is a great God, and a great King above all gods. Ps. 95:3.

The early Hebrews believed in the existence of other gods—the gods of the Gentiles—but maintained that the God of Israel was the God of gods, a greater God. The Hebrew religion was different from that of the Gentiles in that they believed in one God and not a pantheon, and because their deity was a mighty God, they felt they had no need for other gods. But after they were defeated in battle, they often turned to pagan deities for help.

On one occasion when they lost the battle against the Moabites, they blamed it on their God, believing that their Lord was a God of the

---

[156] 2 Ki. 19:10-13.

mountains and therefore could not direct a battle in the plains.

Again and again the Israelites went after other deities and forsook the God of their fathers, the living God. It took many centuries of defeats, two captivities, and much suffering, before a pure concept of God was crystallized. In other words, the Hebrews became monotheistic in their concept of God. The God of Israel was the Creator of the heavens and the earth and all that is.

PSALM NINETY-SIX

Gift Offerings

Give unto the Lord the glory due unto his name: bring an offering, and come into his courts. Ps. 96:8.

The Israelites never visited their holy places with empty hands. They always took an offering of the flocks or herds, or a basket of bread or fruits. Even in modern times, when Near Easterners visit holy places or men of God who act as healers, they take offerings or gifts with them.

The offerings were used to take care of the priests and Levites and to feed the needy ones who came from long distances to worship.[157] This ancient custom is still practiced by members of the church of the East.

Some of the offerings were known as thanksgiving offerings, peace offerings, and sin offerings, while others were in payment for vows.[158]

PSALM NINETY-SEVEN

God Is the Author of Laws

His lightnings enlightened the world: the earth saw, and trembled. The hills melted like wax at the presence of the Lord, at the presence of the Lord of the whole earth. Ps. 97:4-5.

The reference is to the appearance of God's glory upon Mount Sinai. Mount Sinai was in smoke because the Lord God descended upon it in fire.

---

[157]Mal. 3:10.

[158]Lev. 1:9. See Errico and Lamsa, *Aramaic Light on Exodus through Deuteronomy*, "Offering Sacrifices to Deity," pp. 92-93.

The whole mountain quaked. There were also thunder and lightning and a thick cloud.[159]

"Earth" refers to the ground or the land in the vicinity of Mount Sinai. Such terms of speech as "the earth melted" are used metaphorically in describing the presence of the Lord and the glory of his majesty as compared with the mountains, hills, and even the earth itself. In biblical days people believed, and many still believe, that thunder, rain, winds, and quakes were the acts of God.

Heavenly Harmony

The heavens declare his righteousness, and all the people see his glory. Ps. 97:6.

The reference is to universal harmony. All planets and other heavenly bodies travel harmoniously in their own orbits. No planet gets out of its orbit without causing disturbances in the universe. Sun, moon, and stars are so firmly established that we can hardly notice a change in their long courses.

Our concept of peace, justice, righteousness, and harmony is derived from the heavenly order. Jesus said, "Thy will be done in earth, as it is in heaven."[160] If human beings would mind their own business and travel on their own paths, many of the difficulties and evils of this world would be eliminated.

The Light of God

Light is sown for the righteous, and gladness for the upright in heart. Ps. 97:11.

The Aramaic word *denakh* means "has shone"; that is, "light has shone on the righteous." The righteous are always associated with the light, which is symbolic of truth, understanding, and good works; the wicked are associated with darkness, which is symbolic of ignorance and evil forces.

The error in the King James Version may have been caused by a defective manuscript that had suffered from constant use and humidity, or it might be a printer's error. "Shone" and "sown" could be easily confused.

It was believed the righteous are always blessed by God, that their

---

[159]Ex. 19:16-18.
[160]Mt. 6:10.

offspring prosper and they are spared during times of calamity. The light of God causes the darkness to flee.

PSALM ONE HUNDRED TWO

Eaten Ashes like Bread

For I have eaten ashes like bread, and mingled my drink with weeping. Ps. 102:9.

In many parts of biblical lands, Arabia and other regions, where the tribal peoples migrate from one place to another, ovens are unknown and bread is baked on coals of fire. The baking is done so hastily that, at times, the dough is mixed with ashes. When the nomad peoples are hungry, they eat the ashes that are on the bread. "For I have eaten ashes like bread" means, "I was poor and hungry." The poor and hungry do not stop to examine the food they eat. Sometimes they weep when they eat and drink, and their tears mingle with the water and bread. "My tears have been my bread."[161]

An Error in a Pronoun

He weakened my strength in the way; he shortened my days. Ps. 102:23.

The Eastern Aramaic text reads: "For they have weakened my strength on earth; they warned me of the shortage of my days." "They" refers to the enemies of Israel. Their enemies had carried Israel captive and sold the people in the market places.

PSALM ONE HUNDRED FOUR

The Greatness of God

Who maketh his angels spirit; his ministers a flaming fire. Ps. 104:4.

The psalmist relates the greatness of God and the divine wondrous creations. Angels are God's spiritual creations, that is, God's counsels. They carry the divine messages everywhere. They are powerful and swift like fire. In Aramaic, people often say: "He is like a flame of fire." This

---

[161]Ps. 42:3, Lamsa translation. See also Ps. 80:5.

means he is a genius and speedy in his actions and deeds.

The Lord Clothed the Earth

Thou coveredst it with the deep as with a garment: the waters stood above the mountains. At thy rebuke they fled; at the voice of thy thunder they hasted away. They go up by the mountains; they go down by the valleys unto the place which thou hast founded for them. Thou hast set a bound that they may not pass over; that they turn not again to cover the earth. Ps. 104:6-9.

About two-thirds of the surface of the earth is water. Water covers high mountains in the ocean, some of which are higher than some of the mountains on land. The reference is to the seas and lakes that were formed on the tops of the mountains. In verse 9, the psalmist praises God's wisdom for setting bounds that the water may not cover all the earth. One probably will never be able to explain the wonders, wisdom, and creative power of God. Valleys, plateaus, plains, and hills were all formed by God.

According to the book of Genesis, the lands that now lie under the oceans and seas once were dry and, therefore, could be seen. But the Lord commanded that all the waters should gather together.[162]

The Lord clothed the earth with glory and majesty. The great oceans and seas around us are full of beauty and life. Water is one of the four precious elements that makes life possible and the earth beautiful.

Wine, Oil and Bread

And wine that maketh glad the heart of man, and oil to make his face to shine, and bread which strengtheneth man's heart. Ps. 104:15.

"Wine" is another word for "joy." The moderate use of wine was permitted during religious feasts. Wine was, and still is, used moderately with food, especially in places where water was scarce or polluted. But wine and strong drink were forbidden by Muhammad.

When Abraham returned from defeating the five kings, Melchizedek, king of Salem, brought forth bread and wine to greet Abraham and to

---

[162]Gen. 1:9-10.

rejoice with him in his triumph. Wine was drunk as a symbol of joy.[163]

In the book of Judges we are told that wine cheers God and man, which means that it rejoices God and man when it is consecrated and drunk as a symbol of communion with God. We all know that God is the Eternal Spirit, and Spirit does not need or use wine to rejoice.." The term "wine" in the book of Judges is used to signify eternal joy. This is because bread and wine were offered by Near Easterners to their guests as a token of hearty welcome and rejoicing. This is why wine was used in offerings, symbolizing the joy of being in the presence of God.[164]

Jesus also sanctioned the use of wine by drinking it and giving it to his disciples at the Lord's Supper.[165] But in the Near East, wine was made from pure grape juice. Even before World War I, the alcoholic content was very small.

Scriptures condemn the excessive use of wine. It was prohibited to the Nazarites.[166] Many of the prophets, Jesus, and his apostles condemned drunkenness.[167] Drinking is a cause of much evil and unnecessary tragedy.

Near Easterners consume considerable butter and olive oil. Some men drink them like water. They believe that oil makes men's faces shine. Bread is known as the staff of life. In the Near East no table is complete without high stacks of bread upon it. No matter how much other food is upon the table, the lack of bread would cause the host considerable embarrassment.

PSALM ONE HUNDRED FIVE

A Small Tribe

When they were but a few men in number; yea, very few, and strangers in it. When they went from one nation to another, from one kingdom to another people. Ps. 105:12-13.

When the Hebrews crossed the River Euphrates they were a small tribe.

---

[163]Gen. 14:17-18; 1 Sam. 1:24. See also Ecc. 10:19, Eastern Aramaic Peshitta text, Lamsa translation.

[164]Ex. 29:40; Lev. 23:13.

[165]Mt. 26:29.

[166]Num. 6:3.

[167]Isa. 5:11; Eph. 5:18; 1 Tim. 3:3; Titus 1:7; 1 Pet. 4:3.

For many years they continued to wander from one place to another, seeking grass and water for their large flocks and herds. In biblical days there were many small kingdoms in the land of Canaan. Even small sedentary tribes were known as kingdoms. In a short space of time, Joshua conquered thirty-one kingdoms, but the whole area of these kingdoms would not be more than three or four thousand square miles. At times, even a city with a few villages around it was called a kingdom. For example, the kingdoms of Jericho and Ai consisted of a few hundred acres of grazing land.

Everywhere the Hebrews went, God was with them and they also found favor with the kings of these small kingdoms. These Gentile tribal leaders welcomed them, traded with them, and did them no harm. No doubt the grace of God went in advance of the Hebrew patriarchs, who were called by God to play a great and important role in human history.

To Discipline

To bind his princes at his pleasure; and teach his senators wisdom. Ps. 105:22.

The Aramaic word *nerdey* means, "to instruct, chastise, or discipline." "Bind" is a wrong translation. The Eastern Aramaic text reads: "To discipline [instruct] the governors at his pleasure and to teach the elders wisdom."

In those days kings, princes, governors, and elders acted as judges in settling disputes among the people. They were guided by the law of God and the Holy Scripture. Every prince and elder was taught the laws and ordinances.

The prophet Samuel and other Hebrew leaders acted as judges, teachers, and arbitrators. All the kings of Israel and Judah were judges and were accessible to their subjects. Even poor men and women appeared before them for judgment. This psalm is an admonition to the people and a reminder of the glorious past when God's favor was with Israel.

Prosperous and Healthy

He brought them forth also with silver and gold: and there was not one feeble person among their tribes. Ps. 105:37.

This passage appears somewhat contrary to what we read in the first chapter of the book of Exodus, where the Israelites were poverty-stricken, oppressed, and living in misery. However, a closer reading of the book of Exodus might tell another story. For example, in Exodus 13:18 we read that Israel went up armed out of the land of Egypt. The suffering and oppression might have been exaggerated. It seems that the people were well-to-do, healthy, and happy. The Israelites believed that God was on their side and that their faith in him protected them from disease.[168]

The Hebrews, like other nomad people in the Near East, looked with disdain on manual labor. Pastoral people consider any kind of labor and regimentation as oppression. This is because nomad tribes lived in tents and had no knowledge of laying bricks, making roads, or digging canals. They also abhorred houses and palaces.

Seemingly, the Egyptian oppressors were not as bad as the oppressors of our day. They even loaned the Israelites their jewelry of gold and silver, costly garments, and other articles.[169] The Israelites left Egypt as strong, prosperous, and healthy people, so the Egyptians may not have been as bad as they are pictured in the early portion of the book of Exodus.

Rock Bored

He opened the rock, and the waters gushed out; they ran in the dry places like a river. Ps. 105:41.

The reference is to Exodus 17:6 and Numbers 21:16. The Aramaic text reads *tar ana,* "flint." The word "open" means "uncovered" or "bored through" the hard rock.

Many of the water sources were hidden under rocks to conserve the water. Then again, water was often found in dry, flinty places where the people did not expect to find any water. Even during World War I, wells were hidden, poisoned, and filled to prevent the enemy from advancing. Wise Arab shepherds knew where the water was. Prophets and men of God were divinely guided to find it.[170]

---

[168]See Errico and Lamsa, *Aramaic Light on Exodus through Deuteronomy,* "Persecution Exaggerated," pp. 2-3. Also see "The Israelites were Armed," p. 34.

[169]Ex. 3:22. See the same commentary "Borrowing Clothes," p. 13.

[170]See Errico and Lamsa, *Aramaic Light on Exodus through Deuteronomy,* "Beer–A Well," pp. 148-149, Num. 21:16-18.

PSALM ONE HUNDRED SIX

Abundance

And he gave them their request; but sent leanness into their soul. Ps. 106:15.

The last section of this verse in the Eastern Aramaic text reads: " . . . and he supplied them with abundance." Like many other passages of Scripture, this mistake is due to mistranslation. The Aramaic word *sabaa* means "fullness."

The reference is to the period when the Israelites were wandering in the desert for forty years. God granted them their request and provided abundant food. Nevertheless, at times they were ungrateful and complained against Moses and Aaron.

Revolt Against Moses

The earth opened and swallowed up Dathan, and covered the company of Abiram. Ps. 106:17.

The psalmist refers to the revolt in the wilderness under the leadership of Dathan and Abiram.[171] These men challenged Moses and Aaron and questioned their leadership. Many leaders and laymen who were unable to face the desert hardships and were discontent tried to persuade the people to return to Egypt. They blamed their plight on Moses and Aaron.

Moses placed the matter in God's hands and asked his enemies to come forth before the Lord with their censers in their hands to see which groups the Lord would choose. As they started to offer incense, an earthquake took place, and the ground opened under the rebels so that they and their families were swallowed. According to the biblical text, this incident proved that Moses and Aaron were innocent and that God was with them.[172]

Moses was divinely guided about the earthquake, just as Lot was guided in his days when Sodom and Gomorrah (Amorah) were destroyed by the earthquake and fire.[173] All these regions in Arabia contained oil and pitch, and eruptions like this are not uncommon. But when people are guided by

---

[171]Num. 16:31-32; Dt. 11:6.

[172]Num. 16:1-35.

[173]Gen. 19:24-25.

God, they are warned to escape disaster. The rebels who were swallowed by the earth had revolted against God's commandment. That is why they perished. It was a great wonder and a triumph for Moses and Aaron, because it happened when these insurgents came to offer incense before the Lord. The rebel leaders were Reubenites. They were not permitted to offer incense. When men and women break God's laws and rebel, strange things may happen whereby they suffer the consequences.

Egypt

Wondrous works in the land of Ham, and terrible things by the Red sea. Ps. 106:22.

"In the land of Ham" means Egypt. The Egyptians were the descendants of Ham from his son Mizraim. Ham himself never dwelt in Egypt, but his descendants migrated southward. The descendants of Japheth went northward, and the descendants of Shem, the firstborn, remained in their ancestral land.

The term "ham" in Aramaic means "heat." When we say "Hamites," we mean "the people of the hot regions."

Sacrifice for the Dead

They joined themselves also unto Baal-peor, and ate the sacrifices of the dead. Ps. 106:28.

The reference is to Baal-peor, or the Baal of Peor, when some of the Israelites took part in this pagan immoral ritual at Shittim. Twenty-four thousand died with venereal disease. The Israelites participated in the sacrifices that the Moabites were offering to their pagan gods and the sacrifices for the dead.

The sacrifices were an ancient institution. The pagans sacrificed animals in memory of the departed ones. They also offered their children as burnt offerings to their idols. Many of these ancient customs were borrowed and practiced by the Israelites when they forsook their God and went astray after pagan deities.[174]

---

[174]See Errico and Lamsa, *Aramaic Light on Exodus through Deuteronomy*, "Baal-Peor," p.159, Num. 25:2-3.

Agriculture

They did not destroy the nations, concerning whom the Lord commanded them. Ps. 106:34.

The Hebrews, prior to the occupation of the land of Canaan by Joshua, were commanded by Moses to destroy all the inhabitants of the land who worshiped images and sacrificed to idols. But when the Hebrews conquered a territory, they knew nothing about agriculture or the city life. The generation that had left Egypt was dead, and the new generation that was born and reared in the wilderness was ignorant of sowing, planting, and raising crops. They knew nothing about the proper seasons for planting.

For a long time, then, the Israelites depended on the natives of the land for plowing, sowing, and pruning the vineyards. This is why they did not totally destroy the worshipers of Baal, the god of agriculture. These inhabitants of the land, despite their pagan practices, were highly experienced in raising crops, building, and other arts unknown to the semi-nomads. They were indispensable to the Israelite conquerors. This is also true of the Turks when they conquered lands in the Near East. Being a nomad people, they spared the inhabitants of the land, treated them well, and entrusted them with high government tasks, such as trading, raising food, manufacturing, and banking. Even today the desert Arabs know nothing about raising crops. Some of them have never seen a wheat or barley field.

Had the Hebrews destroyed the inhabitants of the land, they would have confronted many difficulties in building cities, planting trees, and vineyards, pruning, grafting, and many other things of which the desert people are ignorant. In those days textbooks were unknown and knowledge was handed down from one person to another.

Human Sacrifices

Yea, they sacrificed their sons and their daughters unto devils. Ps. 106:37.

The Canaanites, like other pagans, sacrificed some of their children whom they had vowed to sacrifice to their idols. These idols were also referred to as demons by the Hebrews. The children were slain and burned on the altars. This ancient custom of sacrificing to demons (*shedeh,* "devils") was prevalent in Canaan. Four centuries earlier, Abraham had been admonished to offer a ram instead of his son Isaac. The Hebrews never sacrificed their children to idols when they were in Egypt. Seemingly, human sacrifices began after the conquest of Canaan. The Israelites went astray after the gods of the Gentiles. Pagan worship, practices, and sacrifices, introduced by some of the kings of Israel and Judah, persisted until the second captivity, 586 BCE.

The Mosaic code states that every Israelite shall redeem all the firstborn males. This law was revealed and written so that the Israelites might not sacrifice their children to idols. In addition to this, the Ten Commandments prohibited the worship of other gods and images.[175] Nevertheless, the Israelites often left their pure worship for pagan practices.

PSALM ONE HUNDRED SEVEN

Dry Rivers

He turneth rivers into a wilderness, and the watersprings into dry ground. Ps. 107:33.

In Jordan and other lands adjacent to the Arabian desert, most of the rivers, brooks, and other sources of water dry up in the early summer months. The dry rivers are called "wadies." During the long droughts, water becomes so scarce that cattle and sheep perish from the lack of it.

In the Near East, long droughts are usually attributed to the sins of the people. During the reign of King Ahab there was a drought that lasted for three years. Many flocks of sheep and herds of cattle perished.[176]

PSALM ONE HUNDRED EIGHT

Washpot

Moab is my washpot; over Edom will I cast out my shoe; over Philistia will I triumph. Ps. 108:9.

"Moab is my washpot" means, "Moab is my slave." A washpot is an unclean vessel and is greatly despised. This is because people wash their

---

[175]Ex. 20:1-6.

[176]1 Ki. 18:5.

hands and feet in it.

The Aramaic text reads that "Edom will loosen my shoe." In the Near East when a guest enters a house, generally a servant will untie the shoelaces of the guest. When John was baptizing Jesus, he said he was not even worthy to untie the shoelaces of the Master.

Moab, Edom, and Philistia were to be humbled and made servants to Judah. These nations had fought against the Israelites and always sided with Israel's enemies.

PSALM ONE HUNDRED NINE

Praying for Enemies

For my love they are my adversaries; but I give myself unto prayer. Ps. 109:4.

The Eastern Aramaic text reads: "For my love they reproach me; but I have prayed for them." The psalmist declares that Israel has been rewarded evil for good; nevertheless, Israel prayed for its enemies and tried to make peace.

According to the gospel of Matthew, Jesus said: "Love your enemies, bless anyone who curses you, do good to anyone who hates you, and pray for those who carry you away by force and persecute you."[177] Prayer is strengthened by good deeds and right action and often overcomes the opposition and evil intent.

Satan on Right Hand

Set thou a wicked man over him: and let Satan stand at his right hand. Ps. 109:6.

Near Easterners believe that every person has a guardian angel on the right hand and Satan on the left. The angel guides humans in the way of God, but Satan causes them to go astray. "Let Satan stand at his right hand" means, "Let him receive wrong counsel," or "Let Satan become his counselor."

---

[177]Mt. 5:44, Eastern Aramaic Peshitta text, Lamsa translation.

PSALM ONE HUNDRED TEN

Messiah, King and Priest

The Lord said unto my Lord, Sit thou at my right hand, until I make thine enemies thy footstool. Ps. 110:1.

The reference is to the anointed king, a greater king than David. It is a royal psalm. The psalmist saw that a spiritual ruler was to replace the political kingdom of David, and he was to conquer and rule all the enemies of the Jews, not with force but with the arm of God, with truth and understanding. God was to make the Messiah both lord and Messiah/Christ.[178]

According to the gospel of John, Jewish leadership rejected Jesus as Messiah/Christ on the grounds that he was not from the house of David.[179] But Jesus challenged their literal interpretation of this psalm, contending that these words were spoken about himself, the Messiah, and not about David.[180]

"Right hand" is an Aramaic idiom meaning "power" or "trust"; that is, all things in heaven and on earth were to be entrusted to Messiah/Christ. The enemies are those who had departed from God's way of life and truth. In due time, error was to be defeated and the truth was to triumph once and for all time.

Messiah/Christ was to rule over the new theocracy. He was destined to be a king and priest forever in the order of Melchizedek, the king of Shalem (Salem). No one knows who ordained Melchizedek; nevertheless, he was a priest and king when Abraham defeated the five kings. "And Melchizedek king of Salem brought forth bread and wine: and he was the priest of the most high God."[181]

Beauty of Holiness

Thy people shall be wiling in the day of thy power, in the beauties of holiness from the womb of the morning: thou hast the dew of thy youth. Ps. 110:3.

---

[178]Acts 2:34-36.

[179]Jn. 7:40-42.

[180]Mt. 22:41-46; Lk. 20:41-44; Mk. 12:35-37.

[181]Gen. 14:18 and Heb. 7:1-2, K.J.V.

The Eastern Aramaic text reads: "Thy people shall be glorious in the day of thy power: arrayed in the beauty of holiness from the womb, I have begotten thee as a child from the ages."

The Lord God promises to be with the Messiah and his people. "I have begotten thee as a child from the ages" is a prophecy concerning the dispensation of the anointed one/Messiah.

PSALM ONE HUNDRED FOURTEEN

Jordan Driven Back

The sea saw it, and fled: Jordan was driven back. The mountains skipped like rams, and the little hills like lambs. What ailed thee, O thou sea, that thou fleddest? thou Jordan, that thou wast driven back? Ps. 114:3-5.

"The sea saw it, and fled" is a poetic expression and means that the sea was turned back by a strong wind, so the children of Israel could cross it.[182] Some authorities attribute this event to the holding back of the Jordan by landslides damming the narrow river. According to Scripture, the Lord God cleared every obstacle before the Israelites—causing the waters of the sea to go backward and drying up the River Jordan—so they might cross into Canaan.

The Jordan is a small river but was the first body of water the Israelites saw when they came from the Sinai Desert. Water was very scarce in the desert, and some of the natives did not know what a river was. The Israelites who had been born in the desert had never seen moving water such as the river Jordan.

"The mountains skipped like rams, and the little hills like lambs" means that the earth rejoiced at the presence of the Lord.[183] All nature shared in the great joy, simply because the Israelites had left Egypt trusting in God and, thus, overcame all the difficulties they had to face.

Rocky Place

Which turned the rock into a standing water, the flint into a fountain of waters. Ps. 114:8.

---

[182] Ex. 14:21.

[183] See verse 7.

The reference is to Exodus 17:6, when Moses struck the rock—that is, found the water system that had been hidden by roaming tribes, or struck a new well in a rocky place.

Moses was guided by God where to test the ground, and when Moses struck the rock on the top of the well, the princes and the nobles of the people who were with him uncovered the well with their staves.[184] Flint is abundant in in the Sinai Desert, where water is scarce and droughts common. ". . . who brought thee forth water out of the rock of flint."[185]

God helped Moses discover what was hidden from the eyes of men. When Moses turned to God and prayed, God directed him to the places where there was water, grass, and food. God, as a loving Father, is always ready to lead and to answer the prayers of those who seek divine aid.[186]

PSALM ONE HUNDRED SIXTEEN

A Righteous Death

Precious in the sight of the Lord is the death of his saints. Ps. 116:15.

Precious is the death of righteous people in the sight of the Lord because they gave their lives for a good cause and therefore will never be forgotten. Many martyrs were put to death because of their belief in the living God.

PSALM ONE HUNDRED EIGHTEEN

Builders and Stones

The stone which the builders refused is become the head stone of the corner. Ps. 118:22.

Builders in the Near East refuse to use large, heavy, unhewn stones in walls. This is because they are difficult to lift and it takes a long time to hew them. After a conference with the owner of the house, they may agree to use them for foundation stones.

---

[184]Num. 21:16-18.

[185]Dt. 8:15.

[186]See Errico and Lamsa, *Aramaic Light on Exodus through Deuteronomy*, "Beer–A Well" pp. 148-149, Num 21:16.

Stones and all other materials for building are provided by the owner of the house. The builders are hired to set the stones together; therefore, the builders and the owner of the project must agree on the type of stones to be used in the walls. Generally, the owner of the building wishes to see large stones hewn and placed in the walls where they will be seen. The builders argue that the large stones should be placed on the corner. The builders know better than the owner of the house. The large and unhewn foundation stones are more important than the smooth stones that rest upon them. They bear the weight of the whole building.

Truth is the foundation of a religion because everything rests upon it. But there are certain important truths that cannot be understood, and therefore they are rejected.

According to New Testament writers, Jesus of Nazareth was the stone that the builders rejected, but he became the cornerstone of a new building.[187] Jesus' teaching was alien to the ears of the Jewish priests and scribes. It was hard for them to love their enemies and to pray for those who hated them.

Processions

God is the Lord, which hath showed us light: bind the sacrifice with cords, even unto the horns of the altar. Ps. 118:27.

The Eastern Aramaic text reads: "O Lord, our God, enlighten us; bind our festival processions as an unbroken chain, even to the horns of the altar." "Bind our festival processions" means to make them orderly and permanent; that is, "Keep our ritual in perfect order throughout all generations."

The Israelites, during their festivals and thanksgiving for victory, marched in an orderly manner to the altar where the thanks sacrifice was offered. The people implored the Almighty to give them light and understanding so that they might worship him, pray before him, and make offerings to him continually, orderly, and faithfully without fear.[188]

---

[187]Mt. 21:42; Isa 28:16.
[188]Isa. 33:20.

PSALM ONE HUNDRED NINETEEN

The Faithful

My soul breaketh for the longing that it hath unto thy judgments at all times. Ps. 119:20.

The Eastern Aramaic text reads: "My soul is pleased and desires thy judgments at all times." The Aramaic word *saba* means "to be pleased, to be desirous, or to long for something." The psalmist implies that his soul longed to keep God's judgments at all times.

Many Hebrews in exile were forced to break the ordinances of their God and to bow to images. But most of them remained loyal, and some of them, like Daniel, were willing to die for the way of their God rather than break God's commandments.

An Enlarged Heart

I will run the way of thy commandments, when thou shalt enlarge my heart. Ps. 119:32.

The Eastern Aramaic text reads: "I have walked in the way of thy commandments, because thou hast made me joyful." "Enlarge my heart" is an Aramaic idiom, and it means to be made happy or joyful.

A Solemn Oath

My hands also will I lift up unto thy commandments, which I have loved; and I will meditate in thy statutes. Ps. 119:48.

"My hands also will I lift up unto thy commandments" means, "I will take an oath with thy commandments." When praying, Near Easterners lift their hands above their heads. Lifting up the hand may be a gesture or threat of striking or punishing. But in this case the term "hand" is used figuratively. When people make a solemn oath, pledge, or vow, they lift up one or both hands. The lifting of the hand signifies that what is to be uttered is the truth.

"And Abram said to the king of Sodom, I have lifted up mine hand unto the Lord, the most high God,"[189] which means "I have sworn by God." "My mouth hath kissed my hand."[190] Also when people wish to exonerate themselves of guilt, they wash their hands.

Bottle in the Smoke

For I am become like a bottle in the smoke; yet do I not forget thy statutes. Ps. 119:83.

The first part of the verse in the Eastern Aramaic text reads literally: "I have become like a frozen sheepskin." This means, "I have suffered all disgrace," or "I was harassed." In the Near East sheepskins are used as containers for water, milk, and wine. During cold seasons, in the early morning when the temperature is low, empty sheepskins may become frozen. The skin becomes wrinkled and hard like a stone. Bottles made of glass were unknown in biblical days. Even in the modern Near East, sheepskins are still used as containers among the nomads and the migratory tribes in Kurdistan, Iran, and the Arabian desert.

Near Easterners, when describing difficulties, humiliations, and persecutions they have gone through or awful tales they have heard, say, "My skin wrinkled on my bones." This idiom is still popular today in vernacular speech. The psalmist is asking God for his speedy judgment on those who persecute him. In other words, Israel is praying for vengeance against her enemies.

Wise Elders

I understand more than the ancients, because I keep thy precepts. Ps. 119:100.

Near Easterners look up to their elders for wisdom, counsel, and guidance. In some parts of the Near East where primitive customs and manners still prevail, the words of an elder are respected and obeyed as the words of a book of law. In these ancient parts of the world, age and gray hair speak with authority, and the counsel of a young man is scorned.

Job says, "With the ancient [elders] is wisdom; and in length of days

---

[189]Gen. 14:22, K.J.V.

[190]Job 31:27, K.J.V. See p. 82 of this volume, "Good Luck" for the meaning of the idiom "My mouth hath kissed my hand."

understanding."[191] "Days should speak, and multitude of years should teach wisdom."[192]

The psalmist understood more than the elders, because he was guided by God's commandments. In truth there is no age, but age is important because young men lack experience and are unfamiliar with God's laws and ordinances.

A Lamp unto My Feet

Thy word is a lamp unto my feet, and a light unto my path. Ps. 119:105.

Light is symbolic of enlightenment and education, and darkness is symbolic of ignorance and lawlessness. The streets in the ancient cities of biblical lands were narrow and crooked, and the pavement was rough. Even in the daytime, people had to watch their steps while walking. Moreover, there were holes and rubbish in the streets, which often caused people to fall and injure themselves. In the ancient days, just as today in some parts of the Near East, city ordinances were unknown and the streets were neither swept nor repaired—except when a ruler, a prince, or a member of the royal family planned to visit the city. Then the streets were cleaned and repaired in honor of the royal visitor.

In the evening and during the dark hours of the night, when people were walking in the city, they generally carried a lamp with them. The ancient lamp was a small, earthen vessel in the shape of a small saucer. The wick was on one end and the oil or butter on the other. Noblemen were led by a servant who carried a lamp in his hand. The bearer of the lamp bent one arm down so that the light of the lamp might fall at the feet of his master, and as he walked ahead, he bent down once in a while, turning the light of the lamp to the path ahead of him to see if there were any holes or rubbish in the road.

God's laws and words lighten our path and keep our feet from falling into temptations. Life is full of difficulties like a dark and crooked path. God's laws and ordinances direct our steps to the straight path of life and protect us and lead us into safety, for only through God's light do we see the light.

---

[191]Job 12:12, K.J.V.
[192]Job 32:7, K.J.V.

Trusting in God

My soul is continually in my hand: yet do I not forget thy law. Ps. 119:109.

The Eastern Aramaic text reads: "My soul is continually in thy hands." The Aramaic word *naphsha*, "soul," also means "life" and, at times, is used to mean "the spirit." The Aramaic word *edek,* "thy hands," has been confused with *edi,* "my hand." The reference is to life. The psalmist has entrusted his life into the hand of God, and, therefore, is able to keep God's commandments.

Life without God's help is not secure, nor can one walk in the way of God without entrusting one's life into God's hands. This is because life is full of difficulties, and God's truth has many enemies and much opposition. Many of those who have tried to walk in God's way have been persecuted and put to death.

Jesus quoted this phrase when he said, "Father, into thy hands I commend my spirit."[193] When we entrust our spirit into the hands of God, we are sure of ultimate victory over opposition and the forces of evil.

My Eyes Looked for Salvation

Mine eyes fail for thy salvation, and for the word of thy righteousness. Ps. 119:123.

The Aramaic word *saki* means "hoped, longed for, looked forward to, expected." "Fail" is a mistranslation. This verse should read: "My eyes look forward to [or hope for] thy salvation." In the Near East when people are in danger, they look around to see if any help is coming. And when no help comes, then they look up to heaven and implore God to save them.

"Eyes" in this instance are used figuratively, meaning "mind." The eyes are the agents of the mind. What the psalmist means is that Israel had been looking forward to God's salvation and deliverance from the hands of the oppressors. In times of oppression and distress, the people lifted up their eyes and looked to Zion for salvation and for the reign of God.

---

[193] Lk. 23:46.

Time to Repent

It is time for thee, Lord, to work: for they have made void thy law. Ps. 119:126.

This verse should read: "It is time to serve the Lord; for they [the wicked] have nullified thy law." When wickedness was prevalent, the prophets and the pious called on the people to turn to God and to keep the divine laws.

The psalmist calls not on God to work, but on the people to repent and serve the Lord. The Lord, like a loving Father, was always ready to receive the penitent—it was never too late. On the other hand, the suffering and hardships were caused by the people who had forsaken God's law and gone after pagan gods.

Understanding from God

The entrance of thy words giveth light; it giveth understanding unto the simple. Ps. 119:130.

The Eastern Aramaic text reads: "Make plain thy word and enlighten and give understanding to the simple." The terms "children" or "babies" are used in referring to the unlearned, simple people. Jesus said the truth was hidden from the learned, but revealed to the simple, the little children. Without understanding from God and the power of the Holy Spirit, we cannot unlock the Scriptures and grasp their inner meaning.

Wept Bitterly, Vehemently

Rivers of waters run down mine eyes, because they keep not thy law. Ps. 119:136.

"Rivers of waters ran down my eyes" is an idiom that means, "I wept vehemently," or "I washed my bed with my tears." Such sayings are common in Near Eastern languages and are well understood by the people even today. They know that no one can literally wash a bed with tears.

The psalmist was sorry and wept when he saw that the people were not heeding God's admonitions and keeping his commandments. He mourned over the lack of religion and the failure to keep the law of God. This is because religion and God's law were the dearest things in the hearts of the faithful Jews. They meant more than their children, their wives, and their earthly possessions.

Prevented the Dawning

I prevented the dawning of the morning, and cried: I hoped in thy word. Ps. 119:147.

"I prevented" means "I went before" or "rose up before dawn." This word was well understood a century ago, but now it has become obsolete and hard to understand. It means "preceded," "went before," or "in advance." In a number of other passages it is translated, "I rose up early and sent prophets." It should read, "I sent prophets in advance." Near Easterners often pray at dawn, and some pray at midnight when "the heavens declare the glory of God."[194]

Prayer Seven Times

Seven times a day do I praise thee, because of thy righteous judgments. Ps. 119:164.

Seven was a sacred number among the Israelites and was often used symbolically. God ended work on the sixth day and rested (ceased) on the seventh day.[195] Pharaoh, in his dream, saw seven cows and seven ears of corn.[196] Seven priests with seven trumpets marched seven days around Jericho.[197] The number seven was a well-known number and was used frequently by biblical scribes and authors.

In the Near East people pray many times a day. Some of the pious men and women pray at midnight, in the morning, at noon, and in the evening. The Muslims pray five times a day. But in praying, it is not the hour or the number of times that counts but sincerity and pious devotion. Great is the power of the prayer of the righteous.

---

[194]See verse 148 and verse 1 also.
[195]Gen. 2:2.
[196]Gen. 41:2-7.
[197]Josh. 6:4.

PSALM ONE HUNDRED TWENTY

Long Sojourn

Woe is me, that I sojourn in Mesech, that I dwell in the tents of Kedar! Ps. 120:5.

"Mesech" is not present in the Eastern Aramaic text. The first part of the verse should read: "Woe is me, that my sojourn is prolonged." The Jews were taken captive to Assyria and Babylon. Many of them longed for the return to Zion.

PSALM ONE HUNDRED TWENTY-ONE

Looking up to Zion

I will lift up mine eyes unto the hills, from whence cometh my help. Ps. 121:1.

The reference is to Jerusalem and Mount Zion, the city that had been chosen for God's holy habitation. Jerusalem is built on Mount Zion, the highest mountain, which is situated on the south-westernmost part of the city, the hill of the Jebusites.

The holy temple was built on Mount Moriah. The terms "hills" and "mountains" are often used indiscriminately in the Bible. "Why leap ye, ye high hills?"[198] "Yet have I set my king upon my holy hill of Zion."[199] The oppressed people of Israel looked to Zion, the high hills, for salvation. High hills are symbolic of God's glory, power, and majesty, which are higher than all the realms of men. In those days people worshiped in high places in order to feel closer to God.

Israel Established

He will not suffer thy foot to be moved: he that keepeth thee will not slumber. Ps. 121:3.

The Aramaic word *zaweta,* "moved," also means "tremble." "His foot moves" is a Near Eastern idiom which means, "He is not firm." In other

---

[198]Ps. 68:16, K.J.V.
[199]Ps. 2:6.

words, he is trembling because of fear and uncertainty. But "his foot is firm" means that he is well established and confident.

Israel was to be reestablished in the land. The captives were to return once more to the holy land, but this time they were to be settled permanently. They would be so firm that nothing could ever disturb them or cause them to move from one place to another.

This prophecy was fulfilled during the reign of the Persian kings when the second Jewish commonwealth was established in the fourth century BCE.

Smitten by the Moon

The sun shall not smite thee by day, nor the moon by night. Ps. 121:6.

Many calamities and catastrophes were attributed to the heavenly bodies. The junction of the stars and their relation to the moon predicted certain omens; therefore, people feared that they might be smitten by the moon. Furthermore, people were smitten by the sun during the hot hours of the day and sometimes became blind. Both the sun and the moon were worshiped as deities and feared by the people. It was the study of the stars and other heavenly bodies that gave rise to astrology.

PSALM ONE HUNDRED TWENTY-THREE

Waiting for God's Help

Behold, as the eyes of servants look unto the hand of their masters, and as the eyes of a maiden unto the hand of her mistress; so our eyes wait upon the Lord our God, until that he have mercy upon us. Ps. 123:2.

To "look to the hand" of masters and mistresses is an Aramaic idiom that means to depend upon them—to wait for their masters or mistresses to give them their hire and food and to extend favors to them. Moreover, the Aramaic term *eida*, "hand," also means "help" or "aid."

Servants waited patiently for the master or mistress to give them orders, food, clothing, and their wages. They respected and revered their masters and mistresses. The psalmist portrays Israel as depending upon the hand of God for direction, guidance, mercy, and blessing.

PSALM ONE HUNDRED TWENTY-SIX

Sow in Tears

They that sow in tears shall reap in joy. Ps. 126:5.

In many Near Eastern lands where grain is scarce, farmers hide some of the grain for seed. Seed stores and salesmen were unknown, so every farmer took care of his own seed.

Generally, wheat supplies were exhausted during the long winter months. The spring months were the hardest months of the year for the family to get through. Nearly all the scanty provisions the family had stored were gone, and bread and other food supplies became very scarce. Bread was carefully rationed. As the scanty supply of wheat was exhausted, the children would cry for bread, but there was little or no bread to give them.

In the spring when the farmer sowed the wheat, he would weep; although his children were crying for bread, he must use what grain was left for seed. So he would scatter the precious seed in the ground with tears running down his cheeks.

On the other hand, during the months of harvest, the sowers and reapers and their families were happy. The bread supplies were once more replenished and everybody rejoiced. ". . . they joy before thee as those who rejoice in the harvest . . ."[200]

In America a farmer may worry during harvest, not knowing where to store his new and abundant supplies of wheat, or what to do with the grain that is left from the year before. In the Near East, however, the farmers usually received only a small portion of the crops. Most of the produce was taken by the owner of the land. Moreover, high taxes and tithes reduced the farmer's portion. In some cases their wheat supplies were plundered.

The Israelites were subjected to many hardships and privations by their ruthless foreign oppressors. But they always looked to the bright day, the day of God's deliverance and the day of abundance.

---

[200]Isa. 9:3, Eastern Aramaic Peshitta text, Lamsa translation.

PSALM ONE HUNDRED TWENTY-NINE

Plowed upon My Back

The plowers plowed upon my back: they made long their furrows. Ps. 129:3.

The Eastern Aramaic text reads: "They have scourged me upon my back; they have made long their oppression." The psalmist expresses his difficulties using metaphors and figurative speech. He compares himself to a man who has been beaten with straps and punished severely.

PSALM ONE HUNDRED THIRTY-TWO

God's Promise to David

The Lord hath sworn in truth unto David; he will not turn from it; Of the fruit of thy body will I set upon thy throne. Ps. 132:11.

The Lord had promised David, saying, "There shall not fail thee a man [an heir] in my sight to sit on the throne of Israel." However, this promise is conditional. The descendants of David who were to sit upon his throne were admonished to take heed of their ways so they would not depart from the way of the Lord. They were told to walk before him faithfully as David had walked.[201]

The "seed of David" also means the teaching of David—that is, the things for which David stood. Despite his many weaknesses, King David's faith in God never wavered, nor did he serve other gods. David was the symbol of true loyalty to God.

Zedekiah was the last descendant of David who sat upon his throne. From the year 586 BCE, when Judah was conquered by the Chaldean army, to the present day, no descendant of David has ever reigned in Jerusalem. This is because David's descendants forsook their God and went after pagan gods. They also made alliances with pagan kings, so they disqualified themselves as the true heirs of David.

Spiritually, these promises were fulfilled through Jesus of Nazareth, the spiritual heir for the throne of David. The Davidic kingdom was symbolic

---

[201] 1 Ki. 8:25.

of a universal state and the kingdom of God with its reign of justice.

PSALM ONE HUNDRED THIRTY-THREE

Collar of His Robe

It is like the precious ointment upon the head, that ran down upon the beard, even Aaron's beard: that went down to the skirts of his garments. Ps. 133:2.

The Aramaic word *bar sora* means "the collar." The Eastern Aramaic text reads: ". . . the beard . . . that went down to the collar of his robe." In biblical lands, the collar of some of the robes comes down to the man's chest.

The Aramaic word for "skirt" is *shipola.* No man could grow a beard to reach to the skirt of his garment. Most beards are trimmed short. But the priests grew long beards that came down to the collar of their robes as a token of dignity. Even today, the beards of the elderly priests reach to the collar of their robes.

PSALM ONE HUNDRED THIRTY-FIVE

Jacob Chosen

For the Lord hath chosen Jacob unto himself, and Israel for his peculiar treasure. Ps. 135:4.

Jacob was chosen, not because the Lord hated Esau, but because the latter was not interested in the promises that God had made to his grandfather, Abraham. Esau was more interested in hunting than in religious devotion and sacred family traditions.

On the other hand, Jacob, from the outset, was interested in the spiritual religion, laws, and ethics of his grandfather. He wanted to hand them down from generation to generation, so that the Abrahamic blessings might be fulfilled and his teaching become a light to the Gentile world.

God did not reject Esau. He disqualified himself. This is why his birthright was given to Jacob. Being the firstborn, he had the chance to carry on the spiritual mission of his people, but he rejected it because the material world meant more to him.

Jacob was loved more by his mother and Esau more by his father. But

God does not choose by a person's appearance. God chose the one who was qualified for the divine purposes. Nevertheless, Esau was also blessed. His descendants included twelve kings and princes. God revealed the Word to Jacob but God's statutes and judgments to Israel.[202]

PSALM ONE HUNDRED THIRTY-SEVEN

An Eye for an Eye

O daughter of Babylon, who art to be destroyed; happy shall he be, that rewardeth thee as thou hast served us. Happy shall he be, that taketh and dasheth thy little ones against the stones. Ps. 137:8-9.

The people of the captivity hated Babylon. The Jews remembered how they were uprooted from their homes and taken to a strange land. Every generation related to the younger generation the cruelties of the Babylonians (Chaldeans). The captives could not forgive Babylon for its evils and for having given such a deadly blow to their state.

Israel thought that anyone who would dash a Babylonian child against a stone would be blessed for such an act. After all, the Babylonians had done these atrocities to their young ones. The people, at that time, had no knowledge of the power of forgiveness. Jesus reversed the concept of an eye for an eye and told the people that they should love their enemies and not hate them. Little children did not do any evil; why should they suffer for the deeds of their forefathers.

Moses, the great lawgiver, taught that children should not be put to death for the sins of their fathers, nor should the fathers be put to death for the sins of their children.

PSALM ONE HUNDRED THIRTY-EIGHT

Kings

I will praise thee with my whole heart: before the gods will I sing praise unto thee. Ps. 138:1.

The middle portion of this verse in the Eastern Aramaic text reads:

[202]Ps. 147:19.

"before the kings will I sing praise to thee." The term "gods" was generally used when speaking of the idols or human deities that were worshiped instead of God.[203] Moreover, good people who represented God were sometimes called children of god. "I have said, You are gods; all of you are children of the most High."[204]

The prophets and poets of Israel, when praising their God, spoke of him as God of gods, King of kings, and Lord of lords. At times, the Israelites were misled by false prophets and priests who, for the sake of worldly gain and sensualities, had embraced pagan religions and worshiped their gods. The pagans had many deities. Also, most of the kings and emperors were worshiped as gods.

PSALM ONE HUNDRED THIRTY-NINE

Human Conduct

Thou knowest my downsitting and mine uprising; thou understandest my thought afar off. Ps. 139:2.

"My downsitting and mine uprising" means, "my conduct of life" or "my behavior." In the Near East when a noble or wise man was praised, people said, "He knows how to sit down and how to rise up"; that is, he is cultured and knows etiquette. Noblemen, pious men, and the cultured never sat in the chief places. They sat in the low places or stood until they were seated by the host.

Near Easterners were known and esteemed for their correct behavior. "But I know thy abode, and thy going out, and thy coming in . . ."[205] The psalmist here implies that the Lord knows the conduct of people and the thoughts of their hearts.[206]

Descending into Hell

If I ascend up into heaven, thou art there: if I make my bed in hell, behold, thou art there. Ps. 139:8.

---

[203]Dt. 32:16.

[204]Ps. 82:6, Eastern Aramaic Peshitta text, Lamsa translation.

[205]2 Ki. 9:27.

[206]See verses 7-10.

"Hell" is not correct. The Aramaic and Hebrew word is *Sheol* (the resting place for departed souls). The word for hell is *gehenna*, derived from the valley of Hinnom. Gehenna was a place outside the walls of Jerusalem where rubbish was burned, a place where the pagans had sacrificed their children to idols. The Eastern Aramaic text reads: ". . . If I descend into Sheol, behold, thou art there also."

The Hebrews thought that *Sheol* was the place of the dead, an isolated place beyond the jurisdiction of the living God. "In Sheol who shall give thee thanks?"[207] Today we understand that there is no place in the universe that is not under the jurisdiction of God, no place that is hidden from the divine presence.

God Is Everywhere

If I take the wings of the morning, and dwell in the uttermost parts of the sea; Even there shall thy hand lead me, and thy right hand shall hold me. Ps. 139:9-10.

Prior to the eighth century BCE, some of the Hebrew prophets, such as Amos, Hosea, and Isaiah, proclaimed the universality and omnipresence of God. The eternal and living God was no longer perceived to be a local deity like pagan gods but the God of all nations and people, the Lord of the mighty empires and the small kingdoms. In the past, Abraham, Isaac, and Jacob knew that their God was the only Creator of the heavens and the earth and all that exists.

Years later this pure concept of the universality of God was lost. The Hebrews had spent 400 years in Egypt, and the Egyptians were idolaters. They had many gods with diverse duties and jurisdictions. The Egyptians were opposed to the idea of a single deity.

The Hebrew prophets knew that no man could escape or hide himself from the presence of God. Nearly all great Hebrew prophets believed in the universality of their God. Prior to the eighth century BCE, the Hebrews believed that their God was the Creator of the heavens and of the earth, but they also thought of the pagan deities as lesser gods. In other words, their God was the God of gods. Jonah declared that the Hebrew God, YHWH, "made the sea and the dry land."[208]

With this clear Hebrew concept of the universality of God so plainly

---

[207]Ps. 6:5, Eastern Aramaic Peshitta text, Lamsa translation.
[208]Jonah 1:9.

expressed in the above verses, we can see that no Hebrew prophet could have hidden himself or fled from God. And when they did, they did it in a vision or in a dream like those of Ezekiel and Daniel. All communication between God and the prophets took place in visions and dreams.

Light of God

If I say, Surely the darkness shall cover me; even the night shall be light about me. Yea, the darkness hideth not from thee; but the night shineth as the day: the darkness and the light are both alike to thee. Ps. 139:11-12.

This passage should read: "If I say, Surely the darkness shall be as light upon me; even the night shall be light before my face." Darkness and light are relative terms. Darkness is caused by the turning of the earth. Symbolically, darkness represents ignorance, evil, and paganism, and light symbolizes God's truth and the divine way of life. When one knows the truth, even the night shall be light before his face. Just as light dispels darkness, so truth dispels error. And just as the darkness is the absence of light, evil is the absence of truth.

PSALM ONE HUNDRED FORTY-ONE

Prayer as Incense

Lord, I cry unto thee: make haste unto me; give ear unto my voice, when I cry unto thee. Let my prayer be set forth before thee as incense; and the lifting up of my hands as the evening sacrifice. Ps. 141:1-2.

This psalm was sung by the exiles who were in Babylon. They implored God to stand by them and to strengthen them, that they might not incline to evil things in a strange land.

The Aramaic word for incense is *bisma*, and the Aramaic word for health and satisfaction is *basam*. When incense is cast on the fire, the smoke with its aroma rises up to heaven. Their prayer and supplication was to rise up above all the materialism, confusion, and paganism in Babylon.

The evening sacrifice referred to here was a meat offering that consisted of lambs, which were offered daily, in the morning and in the evening.[209]

---

[209]Ex. 29:38-41; Num. 28:4.

Righteous Teachers

Let the righteous smite me; it shall be a kindness: and let him reprove me; it shall be an excellent oil, which shall not break my head: for yet my prayer also shall be in their calamities. Ps. 141:5.

The Eastern Aramaic text reads: "Let the righteous teach me and reprove me; let the oil of the wicked not anoint my head since my prayer has been against their evils."

Near Easterners never refused chastisement and reproof from the mouths of pious men; they looked upon it as dew on dry land. But they refused admonition and discipline from the wicked. The righteous, elderly men, and teachers of religion, discipline people who have gone astray, and they correct and punish the youth. The parents are pleased and grateful when their children are chastised and punished by the elders.

Oil was used for healing. In the Near East, where Western medicine was unknown, oil was poured on wounds. The heads of guests were anointed with oil to refresh them. Because water was scarce, bathing in some of the arid lands was unknown. People anointed their heads and parts of their bodies with butter or olive oil to prevent the skin from cracking.[210]

Pious men would refuse the admonition and the hospitality of the wicked, because they condemn the evil deeds of such men.

A Strong Hand

When their judges are overthrown in stony places, they shall hear my words; for they are sweet. Ps. 141:6.

This should read: "When their judges are stopped [or hindered] by a strong hand . . ." The reference is to the wicked judges and oppressors who perverted justice and thus defrauded the poor. Only a strong hand, the hand of God, could restrain these wicked judges from oppressing the people. God was the only hope of the pious men who longed for justice and righteousness. Nothing else could stop the oppression, extortion, and prevailing evil. Under such circumstances, the words of the law of God were sweet.

---

[210]Lk. 7:46.

Vengeance upon the Dead

Our bones are scattered at the grave's mouth, as when one cutteth and cleaveth wood upon the earth. Ps. 141:7.

The Eastern Aramaic text reads: "Like the ploughshare that scatters the earth, let their bones be scattered at the mouth of the grave."

When cities were occupied by enemy forces, dead bodies were often dug out of their graves and burned or otherwise desecrated. Moreover, the graves of kings and princes were sometimes dug up by treasure seekers, and they would leave the bones of the dead scattered around the graves. The sepulchers of the princes and kings usually contained costly objects of gold, silver, and precious stones. For centuries, therefore, sepulchers and graves of the kings have been violated by treasure hunters. Josiah took the bones of the pagan priests out of their sepulchers and burned them.[211]

The Jews who were oppressed were cursing their enemies and wanting God's vengeance upon them and even upon their dead bodies.

PSALM ONE HUNDRED FORTY-THREE

Dwelling in Darkness

For the enemy hath persecuted my soul; he hath smitten my life down to the ground; he hath made me to dwell in darkness, as those that have been long dead. Ps. 143:3.

This is not the song of a poet as it may seem, but a song of the people who were in Babylon, beseeching God's mercy and protection in the land of their enemies. All references are to the state—that is, to Israel. The term "servant" means the exiles (Israelites) who were captive in Babylon. The psalm might have been composed by King David and sung by the exiles.

Political Israel was crushed and the people were in despair in a pagan land. The enemy had destroyed both the state and the temple and done away with the law, which was the light and the very life of the Jewish people. Now the Israelites were living in darkness, in lands where paganism was the official religion. The hopes of restoration were dim, and the people felt that there was nothing worthwhile to live for.

---

[211] 2 Ki. 23:16.

The exiles were remembering their glorious past, the days of old, when they were living in their own land and worshiping in God's temple.

PSALM ONE HUNDRED FORTY-FOUR

God Is Not Partial

Blessed be the Lord my strength, which teacheth my hands to war, and my fingers to fight. Ps. 144:1.

All acts of triumph in battle were attributed to God. For example, an expert bowman believed that God had given him dexterity in his fingers to make him a straight shooter.

Jesus changed this concept and belief. God is not the author of war, defeats, or triumphs. God, being the Father of all humanity, is impartial.

Strange Children

Send thine hand from above; rid me, and deliver me out of great waters, from the hand of strange children. Ps. 144:7.

The Aramaic word *awaleh,* "wicked, ungodly men," has been confused with *aweleh*, "little children, babies." The Aramaic word for wickedness is *awla*; the Hebrew is *awel.* These words in Semitic languages are written alike but pronounced differently. The word for child or baby has two dots under it, and the word for wicked or ungodly men has one dot under it.

When the Old Testament was translated into Greek about 300 BCE, vowels and dots were unknown. They were introduced in the fifth century after Christ by the learned men in the church of the East (wrongly called Nestorian) and later were adopted by the Jews. Note that the Aramaic and the Hebrew alphabets are the same. Thus the words were confusing and difficult for the translators, especially to foreigners. At times, flies placed more dots on a manuscript than had been placed there by the scribe! Western versions were based on Hebrew or Masoretic texts of the ninth century, and these texts contained dots or vowel signs. The oldest Aramaic texts of the Peshitta, written in Estrangela characters, have no vowels.

No one would even think to pray for deliverance from the hands of children. The people ask God for complete delivery from their enemies.[212]

PSALM ONE HUNDRED FORTY-SIX

Son of Man

Put not your trust in princes, nor in the son of man, in whom there is no help. Ps. 146:3.

"Son of man" means an ordinary human being; that is, a man should put his trust in God instead of trusting in a human being.

The Aramaic words *bar-nasha,* "son of man," or *barnasha,* "a human being" or "humanity in general," are similar. *Barnasha* is often used collectively, meaning "humankind."

The title *breh-dnasha,* "the Son of man," was frequently used by Jesus when he referred to himself.[213] Jesus used this term more often than the title "Son of God." He did this as a token of his humility and as proof that he was both an ordinary and meek man and at the same time demonstrated the works of God. *Breh-dnasha,* "the Son of man," was used by Jesus about forty times. The term was also used by the prophet Ezekiel.[214]

According to the book of Genesis, earthly man was made from dust, and into dust he returns. But spiritual man is the image and likeness of the living God. Physical man, being weak and subject to temptations, cannot be relied upon for help. Therefore, God is humanity's only hope, its trust and its salvation.[215] Human help is temporal, but God's help endures from one generation to another.

Spiritual Blindness

The Lord openeth the eyes of the blind: the Lord raiseth them that are bowed down: the Lord loveth the righteous. Ps. 146:8.

Hebrew prophets healed the sick, cleansed the lepers, raised the dead, and performed other wonders, but there is no mention in the Bible that they

---

[212]See verse 11 in the Lamsa translation.

[213]Mk. 2:10; 14:62.

[214]Ezk. 2:1.

[215]Ps. 131:3; 146:5.

ever opened the eyes of the blind.

When Jesus restored the sight of a man who was born blind, a few of the Jewish religious leaders rejected the miracle and tried hard to prove that the blind man had not been born blind and therefore was not healed by Jesus. This is because they had never heard that anyone could open the eyes of a blind person. It was hard for them to believe that a prophet from Galilee could perform greater miracles than those wrought by their great prophets, Elijah and Elisha. But the man was born blind and he was healed by Jesus.

The blind man argued to prove that Jesus must be a man of God to have opened his eyes: "From ages it has never been heard that a man opened the eyes of one who was born blind. If this man were not from God, he could not have done this."[216]

"Blind" is also often used to mean dull-minded. This expression was used by both Isaiah and Jesus. "Eyes they have, but they cannot see." "Their eyes have become blind and their hearts darkened, so that they cannot see with their eyes and understand with their hearts; let them return and I will heal them."[217]

"I was eyes to the blind," declared Job, by which he meant that he was a guide to men who were carried away with the material world.[218] Spiritual blindness is worse than physical blindness. A physically blind man may have keen spiritual sight and be pleasing in God's sight, but a spiritually blind man cannot even know God. He is blind to truth and justice, and his evil influence may lead others astray.

---

[216]Jn. 9:32-33, Eastern Aramaic Peshitta text, Lamsa translation.

[217]Jn. 12:40, Eastern Aramaic Peshitta text, Lamsa translation.

[218]See Job 29:15.

INTRODUCTION TO THE PROVERBS

The Aramaic word *mathleh* means "parables or proverbs." *Mathleh* is something formulated by the mind—a mental picture. Parables, axioms, and riddles are devised by the wise and educated. During their discourses, debates, and preaching, Near Easterners use parables and proverbs to convey their meaning and to impress that meaning vividly on the minds of their hearers. Some of the great teachers and preachers never spoke or preached without first telling a parable or composing a proverb.

The book of the Proverbs, no doubt, was composed largely by King Solomon, the wisest king in Israel.[1] This is why the book bears his name. They are called the Proverbs of Solomon, the son of David, the king of Israel. There was only one king in Israel by the name of Solomon.

Solomon prayed for wisdom and understanding instead of for wealth and power, and according to the biblical epic, the Lord answered his prayer and gave him both wisdom and riches. Nevertheless, some of these sayings might be the works that Solomon had collected from other wise men.

Most of the sayings in the book of Proverbs are expressed in axioms in order to leave a lasting impression on people's minds. The parables and proverbs served to guide the young and the old in their ways of life and to warn them against evils.

Jesus illustrated most of his teachings by parables, metaphors, and figures of speech; in fact, he rarely spoke without parables. This is why the four Gospels are more widely read and understood than all other portions of the Bible put together.

CHAPTER ONE

The Law of Compensation

Therefore shall they eat of the fruit of their own way, and be filled with their own devices. Prov. 1:31.

"Therefore shall they eat of the fruit of their own way" is an idiom in

---

[1]Modern scholars hold to the idea that most of the Proverbs are from other sages at different time periods. They posit that the actual Solomonic authorship of any part of the book is doubtful.

Semitic languages that means they will be punished by the results of their own evil devices. It is the law of compensation. One reaps what one has scattered. That is, one who sows wheat, reaps wheat; those who sow tares, reap tares. Nothing can change the essence of a seed or the essence of an act. The Hebrew prophets and poets were familiar with the law of compensation, for they had seen it work in their own tribal life. In the Near East it is often said, "I will make him eat a beating," meaning, "I will punish him." The term "eat" is also used for embezzlement.

The gospel of Matthew reports Jesus saying: "Woe to you, scribes and Pharisees, hypocrites! for you embezzle [eat or devour] the property of widows, with the pretense that you make long prayers; because of this you shall receive a greater judgment."[2]

CHAPTER TWO

Reverence to God

Then shalt thou understand the fear of the Lord, and find the knowledge of God. Prov. 2:5.

The Aramaic word *dikhelta* means "reverence, fear, worship" and in most cases should read "reverence," that is, the reverence of the Lord God. *Dikhelta* also means "worship," and worship is reverence to God. *Dighlatha di ammey* refers to the worship of the images of the Gentiles.

Kings and princes in the Near East demanded great reverence from their subjects and officials. The people bowed to the ground and then stood up in awe in their presence. This is because pagan kings were worshiped as gods and therefore were greatly feared.

God is a loving Father, who loves and cares for everyone. Scripture admonishes the reader to revere and put God first in one's heart and to walk in the divine ways of justice and peace. One who reverences another individual also loves that person. But when one fears an individual, hatred will result in one's heart. Reverence produces love, but fear creates hatred. To be afraid of God would do no one any good. All over the world in different nations thousands of people are afraid of dictators, and the more they are afraid of them, the more they hate them.

---

[2]Mt. 23:13, Eastern Aramaic Peshitta text, Lamsa translation.

We revere God because God is the Father of all humanity—the beloved One and our Creator. The reverence of God is the foundation of all wisdom.

CHAPTER THREE

Wisdom

Happy is the man that findeth wisdom, and the man that getteth understanding. Prov. 3:13.

Wisdom and understanding are two separate matters. Wisdom is the source of knowledge; understanding is knowing how to carefully and properly use wisdom. Therefore, wisdom without understanding is dangerous.

For instance, atomic energy is a blessing to humankind, but without understanding, humans may use it to their own destruction. This is also true of money and power. One has to gain knowledge and understanding in order to use them constructively. For example, when religion is understood, it is a great blessing to humanity; when it is not understood, it can be a curse. Peace, harmony, and brotherly love are fruits of the understanding of religion and worship. On the other hand, strife and religious wars are the fruits of misunderstanding. Wisdom must be tempered with the love of God which passes all limited human reasoning and knowledge.

The Wicked Bless Themselves

The curse of the Lord is in the house of the wicked: but he blesseth the habitation of the just. Prov. 3:33.

The wicked prosper, but not by the blessing of the Lord. They bless themselves and flourish for a time, but sooner or later they lose their way in life. It was believed that the Lord, being patient, grants them time to turn from their crooked ways, and when they refuse to mend their deceitful ways, they destroy themselves.

Job says: "The tabernacle of robbers shall be removed, and the confidence of those who provoke God; for there is no God in their heart."[3] Justice sooner or later catches up with those who crookedly gain wealth.

[3]Job 12:6, Eastern Aramaic Peshitta text, Lamsa translation.

"I will bring it forth, saith the Lord of hosts, and it shall enter into the house of the thief, and into the house of him that sweareth falsely by my name, and it shall remain in the midst of his house, and shall consume it with the timber thereof and the stones thereof."[4] "The ungodly are not so: but are like the chaff which the wind driveth away."[5]

CHAPTER FOUR

Wine

For they eat the bread of wickedness, and drink the wine of violence. Prov. 4:17.

"Wine" is used metaphorically, meaning "extortion, rage" and many other evil things that dominate the lives of the wicked and cause them to oppress the poor and the needy.

Wine was used for drink offerings and for human rejoicing. Wine causes people's hearts to rejoice, but it also destroys them when they drink to excess. "Wine is a mocker, strong drink is raging: and whosoever is deceived thereby is not wise."[6] People can be drunk with wine, with inspiration, with hatred, pride, anger, and other evil ways.

A Clear Day

But the path of the just is as the shining light, that shineth more and more unto the perfect day. Prov. 4:18.

The word "perfect' in this passage of scripture refers to a clear or cloudless day. The righteous, being unblemished, let their light shine in their communities. The good works and genuine kindness shine like light where darkness prevails.

Look Straight in the Eyes

Let thine eyes look right on, and let thine eyelids look straight before thee. Prov. 4:25.

---

[4]Zech. 5:4, K.J.V.
[5]Ps. 1:4, K.J.V.
[6]Prov. 20:1, K.J.V.

"Let thine eyes look right on" is a Near Eastern saying that means to be honest, sincere, and look people straight in their eyes. Eyes are the windows of the soul. Pious and sincere persons are not ashamed to look straight into the faces of other people. On the other hand, liars and crooked persons usually cannot even look straight into the faces of their friends. They look down because they are hypocrites and know their acts are evil.

Evil Paths

Ponder the path of thy feet, and let all thy ways be established. Prov. 4:26.

The Eastern Aramaic text reads: "Keep your feet away from evil paths; then all your ways shall be firm." Evil paths refers to broad and dangerous ways that are full of temptation; they are ways that lead one to destruction. Jesus said: "Enter ye in at the strait gate: for wide is the gate, and broad is the way, that leadeth to destruction, and many there be which go in thereat: because strait is the gate, and narrow is the way, which leadeth unto life, and few there be that find it."[7]

Those who keep away from evil paths will avoid all the stumbling blocks in the way. Interestingly, the word "way" is also a Near Eastern term that means "religion," that is, a way of life and human conduct.

CHAPTER FIVE

Immorality Discouraged

Drink waters out of thine own cistern, and running waters out of thine own well. Let thy fountains be dispersed abroad, and rivers of waters in the streets. Prov. 5:15-16.

The Eastern Aramaic text reads: "Drink water out of your own well, and running water from your own spring. Let your water overflow into your streets, let it be disbursed abroad." This is a Near Eastern saying used commonly in vernacular speech and means, "Love your own wife and keep away from other women." Water, in this instance, is symbolic of love

---

[7]Mt. 7:13-14, K.J.V.

between a husband and wife and the children that are born to them.[8]

"Rivers of waters in the streets" means many children playing in the streets. Love, like precious water, must be zealously guarded. The author of the Proverbs warns the Israelites not to waste their semen with strange women because the children they beget would not be their own. Adultery was strongly condemned by the Mosaic law, and the Israelites were warned against cohabiting with strange women. They were the offspring of Israel, called and sanctified for a holy mission. They were not to mix with other races. Because of their calling they were to keep their posterity pure.

Water in the holy land and the Arabian desert is so scarce and precious that some are reluctant to let strangers, and at times even neighbors, draw water from their wells. This is also why the proverb likened children to rivers of water.

CHAPTER SIX

Becoming Surety

Thou art snared with the words of thy mouth, thou art taken with the words of thy mouth. Do this now, my son, and deliver thyself, when thou art come into the hand of thy friend; go, humble thyself, and make sure thy friend. Prov. 6:2-3.

The Eastern Aramaic text reads: "Then you are snared with the words of your mouth, you are caught with the words of your lips. Do this now, my son, and deliver yourself because, for the sake of your friend, you have fallen into the hands of your enemies; go, therefore, and stir up your friend for whom you have become surety to meet his obligation."

King Solomon admonishes his son in case he has become responsible for his friend's debt and thus fallen into the hands of his enemies. The son is told to stir up his friend to pay the debt for which he had become a surety. In the Near East, a good man's word is accepted as surety. At times, a man may become surety for a poor friend who is unable to give collateral.

The good man may incur the enmity of the lender because of his friend's failure to pay his debt. Most lenders would hold the pledge at a high rate of interest until the debt was paid by the borrower or by the one who has been security for him. On the other hand, some borrowers take advantage

---

[8] See verses 17-18.

of good men who become surety for them, and they refuse to pay the debt.

Slothfulness

So shall thy poverty come as one that traveleth, and thy want as an armed man. Prov. 6:11.

The Eastern Aramaic text reads: "And then poverty shall come upon you, and distress shall overtake you; become a successful man." The reference is to a sluggard who spends most of his days in idleness, playing, and sleeping. Sooner or later, these men are overtaken by poverty and want. The translators were unable to translate certain Semitic words and terms of speech in this verse. The Aramaic word *tadrekhakh,* "shall come upon you, shall catch up with you" has been confused with "the traveling man" or "an armed man."

Some people were poverty-stricken simply because they were heavily taxed and exploited. But a great many were poor because they were unwilling to work. Some, who considered themselves noble, would choose death rather than work in the field or in the street.

Winking

A naughty person, a wicked man, walketh with a froward mouth. He winketh with his eyes, he speaketh with his feet, he teacheth with his fingers. Prov. 6:12-13.

An individual who was intending to do evil would wink with his eyes, signal with his feet, and make signs with his fingers. When in the presence of government officials and judges, Near Easterners keep still but impart their thoughts by means of signs made by their fingers, feet or eyes. "He who winks with his eyes deceitfully causes sorrow; but he who reproves openly makes peace."[9]

Also women in the Near East never talk to men, but they make gestures. They know how to convey their motives when making dates with men by using certain bodily movements and signals.

---

[9]Prov. 10:10, Eastern Aramaic Peshitta text, Lamsa translation.

Law Is a Light

For the commandment is a lamp; and the law is light; and reproofs of instruction are the way of life. Prov. 6:23.

Lamps and candles in the Near East were used not only to lighten the dark houses but also to lighten the paths in the crooked, narrow streets during the night. People carried lamps or candles while walking at night.

God's commandments are likened to a lamp, because life is full of difficulties and stumbling blocks. It is necessary to have the light of God in order to be sure of one's steps.

CHAPTER SEVEN

A Reminder

Bind them upon thy fingers, write them upon the table of thine heart. Prov. 7:3.

"Bind them upon thy fingers" is a Near Eastern idiom that means, "Do not forget them." People tie a string on the finger as a reminder of an admonition or of something to be done.

The Israelites, like other Near Eastern people, carried amulets containing passages from the Scriptures to protect them from evil spirits and as signs to remind them of promises and vows.[10] Amulets are still used by modern Near Eastern people. The reminder is placed in a small silver amulet and fastened to a chain or silken cord and worn around the neck or placed in a necklace and worn by women.

Harlot's Enticing

For at the window of my house I looked through my casement . . . And behold, there met him a woman with the attire of an harlot, and subtil of heart. Prov. 7:6, 10.

It should read *adikath,* meaning "she looked out" and not *adiketh,* "I looked out." The difference between these two words is a single dot over

---

[10]Dt. 6:8.

or under the letter "t."

The reference is to a prostitute who sits at her window trying to lure young men. As Near Eastern women did not dare converse with men, harlots beckoned with their eyes and nodded their heads to men who passed by their houses.

Harlots seldom walked the streets. In some places they sat at the doors of their houses. They were also found in camps and small villages, and some of them sat on the highways far off from the villages.[11]

CHAPTER EIGHT

Prudence the Product of Wisdom

For wisdom is better than rubies; and all the things that may be desired are not to be compared to it. I wisdom dwell with prudence, and find out knowledge of witty inventions. Prov. 8:11-12.

It should read: "I, wisdom, have created prudence . . ." The Aramaic word *bereth,* "I have created," has been confused with *beth,* "house, dwelling place." Prudence and knowledge are the products of wisdom.

Wisdom is the source of power, honor, glory, and riches. Then again, justice and righteousness are determined by wisdom and understanding. Wisdom is more precious than rubies and other costly stones. Only with wisdom can one distinguish between evil and good, false and real. King Solomon, in his prayer, asked for wisdom because wisdom is more precious than gold and silver.

Wisdom, the Source of Good

My fruit is better than gold, yea, than fine gold; and my revenue than choice silver. Prov. 8:19.

From time immemorial the world's economic systems, wealth, and commerce have been based on wisdom and understanding. Wisdom has made silver and gold the mediums of exchange. Moreover, all our inventions are fruits of wisdom.

---

[11]See Gen. 38:14.

CHAPTER NINE

Stolen Water and Secret Bread

Stolen waters are sweet, and bread eaten in secret is pleasant. Prov. 9:17.

When water turns brackish and wells and brooks dry up, especially during the early summer, water becomes precious and, at times, was stolen. People who dwelled in arid lands might suffer thirst, and the sheep and cattle might perish because of the lack of water. In many cities in the Near East water was sold in the marketplaces.

In the Europe and America, where people are blessed with abundant water, no one would think of stealing water. But in biblical lands and Arabia, during droughts when wells and springs dry up and water is hard to obtain, thirsty people often steal water. The water is usually stored in a skin that is hung on a pole in the tent. At times it is hidden under bed--clothing, for it is so scarce that it is given only to little children. The adults may go to sleep thirsty.

Stolen water is sweet simply because the person who steals it is suffering from thirst, and it is obtained without paying anything for it. However, the reference here is to stolen love—those who neglect their wives and satisfy their desires by secretly loving the wives of others. Anything stolen or deceitfully obtained may taste sweet but sooner or later turns bitter.

When Near Eastern men were on a journey, they tried to conserve their provisions. According to Eastern custom, whenever a man sat down to eat he must invite all those who happened to be near him. Therefore, some men, in order to avoid inviting others to share their scanty supply of bread, eat secretly. That is, they do not sit down; they eat while they are walking. The loaves of bread are kept hidden in their garments. Other food supplies are kept in their large sashes. The person who eats secretly enjoys the bread because he knows some of the men who are with him are hungry.

Bread, being scarce on a journey, tastes good, but when bread is abundant, it is no longer a delicacy.

CHAPTER TEN

Riches

The blessing of the Lord, it maketh rich, and he addeth no sorrow with it. Prov. 10:22.

Riches are the result of spiritual understanding of life and keeping God's commandments. It is believed that God blesses those who walk in God's ways and do the divine will. God entrusts wisdom to one and riches to another to be distributed to others. Thus, riches are gifts of God, that man may rejoice in his labor, have his portion in this life, and offer thanks to his Creator. "The Lord gave, and the Lord hath taken away," says Job.[12] According to Near Eastern philosophy, God sets one up high and puts down another.

The Hebrew patriarchs who walked in God's way were blessed with wealth. Their sheep and cattle multiplied exceedingly, and they were led by God to green pastures and prolific wells.

Extreme wealth is just as dangerous as extreme poverty. When riches multiply, some people forget God. They may attribute their wealth to their own power and wisdom and thus are destroyed by them.[13] The secret of wealth is not the in the quantity but in the joy, the blessing, and the contentment that it brings to those who possess it.

CHAPTER ELEVEN

Gold Cannot Redeem

Riches profit not in the day of wrath: but righteousness delivereth from death. Prov. 11:4.

"The day of wrath" is "the Day of the Lord," that is, the day of reckoning when all will be rewarded according to their deeds. On that day, silver and gold will not count, nor will it ransom those who possess it. "They shall cast their silver into the streets, and their gold shall be despised; their silver

---

[12]See Job 1:21.

[13]Dt. 8:13-14; Mt. 13:22; Mk. 10:21-22.

and their gold shall not be able to deliver them in the day of the wrath of the Lord . . ."[14] On that day, works and righteousness will count for the deliverance of the soul.

Good Counsel

Where no counsel is, the people fall: but in the multitude of counselors there is safety. Prov. 11:14.

The Eastern Aramaic text reads: "A people who have no leader shall fall; but in the multitude of counsels there is deliverance." The Aramaic word *medabrana* means "a leader, ruler, high priest." The Aramaic word for counsel is *molhana,* derived from *melakh,* "to give counsel."

Israel was often portrayed as a flock without a shepherd.[15] Whenever the people lacked a good ruler and faithful counselors, they suffered defeats, exile, poverty. The rise and fall of a kingdom or a people lies in the hands of those to whom the people have entrusted themselves, their welfare, and future.

The Pious Man

The merciful man doeth good to his own soul: but he that is cruel troubleth his own flesh. Prov. 11:17.

The first part of the verse in the Eastern Aramaic text reads: "The pious man does good to his soul." The Aramaic word *khasia* means "unblemished, pious, one whose sins are forgiven." The Aramaic word for "merciful" is *merakhmana.*

A pious man does good to his own soul by his good behavior, charity, and character. But an evil man destroys his own body by his depraved conduct. A pious man whose sins are forgiven is greater than a merciful man. Even the wicked have mercy toward one another. But the pious is unblemished in all his ways.

---

[14]Ezk. 7:19.
[15]1 Ki. 22:17.

The Blessing of Substance

There is that scattereth, and yet increaseth; and there is that withholdeth more than is meet, but it tendeth to poverty. Prov. 11:24.

The Eastern Aramaic text reads: "There is he who scatters his own seed abroad, and yet brings in plenty; and there is he who gathers that which is not his, and yet has less." The reference is to a man who scatters his substance in doing good. He helps his neighbors, feeds the hungry, clothes the needy, and yet he has plenty. King Solomon implies the blessing of substance when used rightfully.

Then, there is another who has acquired wealth through evil method—that is, by charging exorbitant interest, accepting bribes, and worshiping material possessions—and yet in the end has less. This is because his wealth had been gathered wickedly and lacked God's blessings. Scripture says that if God does not build the house, the laborers work in vain.

Merciful Grain Dealers

He that withholdeth corn, the people shall curse him: but blessing shall be upon the head of him that selleth it. Prov. 11:26.

The Eastern Aramaic text reads: "He who holds back grain in the day of distress shall fall into the hands of his enemies; but a blessing shall be upon the head of him who sells it." During famines and droughts, many wicked rich refused to sell their grain. They stored it and kept it to sell at a higher price. They knew that when people are hungry, they will pay any price for food. In the Near East most of the grain and other food supplies were in the hands of the wealthy and greedy landowners. They refused to sell until the people were at the point of starvation.[16]

The Egyptians lost their houses, their cattle, and their fields during the famine, but the lives of the people were spared.[17]

Near Easterners believe that what is gathered deceitfully and unjustly will be scattered away by God's justice like dry stubble before the wind.

---

[16]Gen. 41:56.
[17]Neh. 5:1-5.

A Good Tree

The fruit of the righteous is a tree of life; and he that winneth souls is wise. Prov. 11:30.

"Tree of life" is used figuratively, meaning "family," that is, one's posterity. Vine is symbolic of a race, and a cedar tree of a ruler. Good men who trust in God and obey his commandments are likened to the trees planted by the waters, which spread out their roots by the stream and give good fruit in their seasons.[18] "The trees of the Lord are full of sap; the cedars of Lebanon, which he hath planted."[19]

A good tree brings forth good fruits, and a bad tree bad fruits. Jesus sometimes spoke of people figuratively as trees.[20] The importance of a tree is its fruit, and not the tree itself. When a tree fails to bring forth good fruit, it is cut down.[21] People are judged by their works. The wicked are cut off from the face of the earth.[22]

CHAPTER TWELVE

Wicked Are Overthrown

The wicked are overthrown, and are not: but the house of the righteous shall stand. Prov. 12:7.

The wicked may prosper for a while, but sooner or later they destroy themselves and are no more. This passage confirms what Job wrote: "The tabernacle of robbers shall be removed, and the confidence of those who provoke God; for there is no God in their heart."[23] But the rendering of that verse in the King James Version is a contradiction of Proverbs 12:7.

---

[18]Ps. 1:3; Jer. 17:8.
[19]Ps. 104:16, K.J.V.
[20]Mt. 7:17.
[21]Mt. 7:19.
[22]See Prov. 12:7; Job 36:6, Eastern Aramaic Peshitta text, Lamsa translation.
[23]Job 12:6, Eastern Aramaic Peshitta text, Lamsa translation.

CHAPTER THIRTEEN

Posterity

The light of the righteous rejoiceth: but the lamp of the wicked shall be put out. Prov. 13:9.

"Light" in this instance means "posterity." The "lamp" is symbolic of an heir; that is to say, the posterity of the righteous shall rejoice, but the posterity of the wicked shall be extinct.

Near Easterners often say, "God has given him a lamp" and "May God preserve your lamp." In 1 Kings 15:4, we read: "Nevertheless for David's sake did the Lord his God give him a lamp in Jerusalem, to set up his son after him, and to establish Jerusalem."

When families mourn over the death of their heirs or beloved persons, their tents are dark. They sit in darkness as a token of mourning.

Worship of Riches

Much food is in the tillage of the poor: but there is that is destroyed for want of judgment. Prov. 13:23.

In the King James Version, this verse is unclear. Evidently, the translators confused the Semitic Aramaic word *aomrah,* "life span, manner of life," with *eborah,* "wheat, food". The Eastern Aramaic text reads: "Those who do not understand the manner of life are destroyed by riches; yea, many men are destroyed completely."

The proverb refers to men whose worship of wealth has deprived them of enjoying their lives. Many people lose their lives pursuing riches and material things. Life is more important than things. Spiritual and eternal life should not be jeopardized for the sake of material goods that are temporal.[24]

---

[24]See Ezk. 10:19, Eastern Aramaic Peshitta text, Lamsa translation.

CHAPTER FOURTEEN

Household of the Wicked

The house of the wicked shall be overthrown: but the tabernacle of the upright shall flourish. Prov. 14:11.

"House" in this instance means "household." Near Eastern overlords and oppressors have large households and many servants. Moreover, some of them have their own private tax collectors and armies. These wicked lords had enriched themselves at the expense of the poor. They believed they would continue to exert power forever. The houses and the tabernacle of the wicked are overthrown at the end, but the upright shall flourish.[25]

Interestingly, this passage (verse 11) is longer in the Eastern Aramaic text. It reads: "A heart which has understanding knows its own bitterness; and a stranger does not share in its joy. The house of the wicked shall be destroyed; but the tabernacle of the upright shall flourish."

Rich in Wisdom

The crown of the wise is their riches: but the foolishness of fools is folly. Prov. 14:24.

Aothra, "riches," is often used figuratively, meaning "rich in wisdom, intelligence, and understanding." *Miathra* means "excellent." Educated men in the Near East are addressed as *Miathra,* "Excellency," which denotes their vast scope of knowledge.

On the other hand, not all wise men are blessed with material goods. Near Eastern men who were in search of knowledge and understanding generally neglected their business affairs and overlooked gaining the material world. Some of these wise religious men were so engrossed in their studies that they became poverty-stricken. Nevertheless, they were highly respected for their wisdom. Thousands of men and women were blessed by their wisdom and understanding.

---

[25]Job 8:15.

People Are Important

In the multitude of people is the king's honor: but in the want of people is the destruction of the prince. Prov. 14:28.

The Eastern Aramaic text reads: "In the abundance of population is the king's honor; but in the destruction of the people is the ruin of the king."

This refers to the increase in population and the welfare and prosperity of the people. During famines and plagues many people perish; consequently, the king becomes impoverished and weak. The prophet Isaiah says: "Thou hast multiplied the people, and thou hast increased its joy."[26]

Anger Kills

A sound heart is the life of the flesh: but envy the rottenness of the bones. Prov. 14:30.

The Aramaic word *de mepaig* is the active participle of *paag, piga,* "to cool, abate, mitigate." The Eastern Aramaic text reads: "He who cools down his anger is a healer of his own heart; but wrath is the rottenness of the bones."

The reference is to those who control their anger and thus heal their hearts. Anger and resentment are destructive forces that result in pain and suffering. Job says: "For anger kills the foolish man, and enmity slays the silly one."[27]

The Wicked Perish

The wicked is driven away in his wickedness: but the righteous hath hope in his death. Prov. 14:32.

The last part of this verse reads differently in the Eastern Aramaic text: ". . . he who is confident that he is without sin is a righteous man." The word "death" is not found in the Eastern text.

The reference is to those who have done good deeds throughout their

---

[26]Isa. 9:3, Eastern Aramaic Peshitta text, Lamsa translation.
[27]Job 5:2, Eastern Aramaic Peshitta text, Lamsa translation.

lives and are confident in their hearts that at the end they will be rewarded for their good works and therefore declared pious. But the wicked are overthrown in their wickedness. They remember the evil they have done and expect nothing but ultimate judgment, condemnation, and destruction.

CHAPTER FIFTEEN

Spiritual Truths

A wholesome tongue is a tree of life: but perverseness therein is a breach in the spirit. Prov. 15:4.

The latter part of the verse is mistranslated in the King James Version. The Eastern Aramaic text reads: ". . . and he who eats of its fruit shall be filled with it." The Aramaic word *akhel* means "eat." *Akhel* also has several other meanings, such as "devour, decay, embezzle."

The fruits of a wholesome tongue are spiritual truths and a wise counsel, which lead people to the way of God. The souls of those who heed the admonitions of wise and pious men are satisfied with spiritual food.

Love Essential

Better is a dinner of herbs where love is than a stalled ox and hatred therewith. Prov. 15:17.

The Eastern Aramaic text reads: "Better is a dinner of vegetables where love is than fatted steer and hatred with it."

In the Near East, poor families who cannot afford meat and other luxuries eat vegetables. Most of the vegetables grow wild and abundantly. On the other hand, the wealthy slaughter sheep and oxen and do not eat any vegetables. They broil the meat over the fire and eat dainty food. They so deplore vegetables that when angry with a neighbor, the worst insult is to say: "Eat turnips."

The author states that it is better to be poor and have love than to have abundant meat and other fine foods and have no love in the family. Love is greater than anything in life. It cannot be purchased with money or good food. Love has to be mutual. Many rich lack love, while a poor family with love has everything.

CHAPTER SIXTEEN

Loyalty to Friends

Every one that is proud in heart is an abomination to the Lord: though hand join in hand, he shall not be unpunished. Prov. 16:5.

The Aramaic word *moshit* is derived from *yeshat,* "to stretch out." The Eastern Aramaic text reads: "Every one who is proud in his heart is an abomination to the Lord; and he who stretches out his hand against his neighbor shall not be pardoned because of this evil."

"Stretch out his hand against his neighbor" in this instance means to do evil or harm to his neighbor. People can be on guard against enemies, but few suspect that their friends or neighbors would harm them. An enemy can be forgiven, but a friend cannot be forgiven or declared innocent when doing evil to a friend.

Early Rain

In the light of the king's countenance is life; and his favor is as a cloud of the latter rain. Prov. 16:15.

The latter part of the verse should read: "And his favor is like a cloud of the early rain." The Aramaic word *bakherata* means "the first." The early rain is most welcome in Near Eastern countries and is received with joy by both farmers and pastoral people. This rain is held by a thick cloud and lasts for many days. It softens the parched ground for the sower and causes grass to grow. On the other hand, the later (latter) rains often destroy the ripening crops.

Near Easterners watch for the rain patiently, especially when the land has suffered a long drought.[28] Droughts are very common and sometimes last two or three years.

The unexpected favor of a king is like the appearance of a cloud heralding the downpour upon the parched ground. People rejoice to receive favors and commendations from their rulers. They also rejoice when they see the cloud that heralds the early rain.

---

[28] 1 Ki. 18:14-45.

Wisdom Is Precious

How much better is it to get wisdom than gold! and to get understanding rather to be chosen than silver. Prov. 16:16.

Wisdom is more precious than costly jewels. Without wisdom and understanding, people would not be able to discern the value of things. They would not know the difference between pearls and glass beads. They invent new things to meet their growing needs.

The values of material articles are determined by wisdom and understanding. It is wisdom that declares gold more valuable than silver and brass. Wisdom is the essence of prosperity and happiness.

Jesus said, "And yet wisdom is justified by its works."[29] The works of the wise are manifested and praised, and the works of fools detested and scorned.

Disgrace Comes First

Pride goeth before destruction, and an haughty spirit before a fall. Prov. 16:18.

The Eastern Aramaic text reads: "Disgrace goes before destruction, and pride before misfortune." That is to say, a wicked man is disgraced before his fall, and his pride is gone before his misfortune.

In the ancient days, when justice caught up with wicked people, they were humiliated in the presence of the people before they were reduced to poverty and put to death.

Poor in Pride

Better it is to be of an humble spirit with the lowly, than to divide the spoil with the proud. Prov. 16:19.

The Eastern Aramaic text reads: "It is better to be humble and lowly in pride than he who divides spoil with the mighty." "An humble spirit" in this instance means a meek or humble person. In the Near East people who were unassuming and unconscious of their noble racial ancestry were

---

[29]Mt. 11:19, Eastern Aramaic Peshitta text, Lamsa translation.

known as *ruha makikhta,* "humble people." Jesus said, "Blessed are the humble," that is, "those who have no racial pride."[30]

The Aramaic word *ruha,* "pride," also means "spirit, temper, wind, and rheumatism." At times *ruha* may be used to mean "a person."

Self-Control

He that is slow to anger is better than the mighty; and he that ruleth his spirit than he that taketh a city. Prov. 16:32.

The Eastern Aramaic text reads: ". . . he who conquers himself than he who takes a city." The Aramaic word *naphshah,* "soul," also means "self," *naphsheh,* "himself."

In the Near East people who controlled their anger and restrained themselves from doing evil hastily were considered wise. Many good people were noted for their patience and self-control.

"Be not hastily angry, for anger rests in the bosom of the fools."[31] Jesus spoke concerning anger when he said: ". . . whosoever is angry with his brother without a cause shall be in danger of the judgment."[32] The prophet Isaiah says, "Shun the man who is hasty for of what account is he?"[33]

CHAPTER SEVENTEEN

Feasting

Better is a dry morsel, and quietness therewith, than a house full of sacrifices with strife. Prov. 17:1.

The Aramaic term "sacrifices" in this case means "feasting." In the Near East when people were blessed and their substance multiplied, they offered sacrifices to display their wealth. Sheep and oxen were slaughtered and the meat was distributed among the people, who feasted and enjoyed themselves. The house of the rich man was filled with guests, the women

---

[30]Mt. 5:3, Eastern Aramaic Peshitta text, Lamsa translation.

[31]Ecc. 7:9, Eastern Aramaic Peshitta text, Lamsa translation.

[32]Mt. 5:22, Eastern Aramaic Peshitta text, Lamsa translation.

[33]Isa. 2:22, Eastern Aramaic Peshitta text, Lamsa translation.

busy cooking and baking bread, and servants serving food. Wealthy Semites were lavish in their banquets. On the other hand, the poor seldom offered sacrifices and other offerings, nor did they entertain.

Generally there was more quarreling and strife in the houses of the rich, where money was abundant and food plentiful, than in the houses of the poor. Many of the rich in the Near East married more than one wife, but most of the poor had to settle for one. Therefore, in the houses of the rich one would not be surprised to see strife and rivalry between women and children who were jealous of one another. Many women whose husbands had more than one wife preferred to live in poverty and to work hard rather than to live in a household where there was constant quarreling and strife.

Peace of mind is more important than riches, for without peace there is no contentment and life becomes meaningless. Peace and harmony can create wealth, but riches cannot buy peace.

Meditation

Let a bear robbed of her whelps meet a man, rather than a fool in his folly. Prov. 17:12.

The Eastern Aramaic text reads: "Meditation and reverence are suitable for a wise man; but a fool meditates in his folly." There is nothing in the Eastern text about a bear. The translators may not have been able to understand the Semitic words *napel renya odekheltha legabra.*

A fool cannot meditate or give counsel. There is nothing in his secret treasure to bring forth but folly.[34] His friendship and advice may cause a great deal of damage or even endanger the lives of those with whom he associates, for a fool will give advice in his folly. But the mind of the wise pours out wisdom and good counsel.

CHAPTER EIGHTEEN

Words Are as Deep Waters

The words of a man's mouth are as deep waters, and the well-spring of wisdom as a flowing brook. It is not good to accept the person of the wicked, to overthrow

[34]Prov. 18:2.

the righteous in judgment. Prov. 18:4-5.

Just as deep waters may cause humans to drown, so the deceitful words of a person may cause people difficulties and sorrows. The reference is to damaging words and false testimony in courts. Pious people do not respect a wicked person nor those who pervert justice for the sake of a bribe or because of fear. They are like deep and turbulent waters around a person who cannot swim. A word is probably the most powerful thing in the world. It goes on and on, and can be used for good and for evil. But words of wisdom and truth are like the gentle water of a spring which refreshes thirsty and weary travelers and laborers.

The Power of a Bribe

A man's gift maketh room for him, and bringeth him before great men. Prov. 18:16.

In biblical lands, the term "gift" is another name for a bribe. Many recipients of bribes prefer to call them gifts. The word gift occurs many times in the Bible and should be distinguished from the true meaning of a gift or present offered voluntarily without thought of any gain.

In those days, judges, governors, and other government officials were seldom paid for their services; they depended on gifts or bribes for their livelihood. When people wanted to visit a certain high judge or official, they sent a gift in advance of their arrival; some people took the gifts with them, but those who went empty-handed were not received. This is why the wicked judge refused to see the widow until she wore him out by calling on him again and again.[35]

Ezekiel upbraids Jerusalem for corruption, bloodshed, and bribes. "In thee have they taken gifts to shed blood."[36] ". . . and their right hand is full of bribes."[37] A very few people refused to accept bribes.[38]

Bribes blinded the eyes of the judges and government officials and perverted justice. True presents are always presented with the right hand as a token of loyalty and sincerity.

---

[35]See Lk.18:1-5.
[36]Ezk. 22:12, K.J.V.
[37]Ps. 26:10, K.J.V.
[38]See Isa. 33:15.

A Brother Is Protection

A brother offended is harder to be won than a strong city: and their contentions are like the bars of a castle. Prov. 18:19.

The Eastern Aramaic text reads: "A brother helped by a brother is like a city helped by its fortifications; and his helpers are like the bars of a castle." A brother who is depending on help from his brother is like a city that is dependent on its fortifications. Near Easterners often say, "My brother has been a fence to me," which means that he is a defense and protection.

Brothers renders help to one another. They lend money to and fight for each other. This is a sacred obligation that no brother can easily shirk. Brotherly love and kindness are highly recommended by Scripture.[39]

CHAPTER NINETEEN

Hasty Feet

Also, that the soul be without knowledge, it is not good; and he that hasteth with his feet sinneth. Prov. 19:2.

The Eastern Aramaic text reads: "He who has no knowledge of his own soul, it is not good for him; and he who is hasty with his feet sins."

People must first examine themselves before passing judgment on others. At times some individuals overestimate themselves and think they are better and more righteous than they really are. How can a person who does not know himself understand others?

A man with "hasty feet" is ready to commit crimes or do other evil things. This is a common idiomatic expression among Semites of the Near East. Many people regret what they have done hastily. It is always wise to examine the matter before taking any action."Be not rash with thy mouth, and let not thine heart be hasty to utter any thing before God . . ."[40]

---

[39]Heb. 13:1; 2 Pet. 1:7.

[40]Ecc. 5:2, K.J.V.

A Rich Liar

The desire of a man is his kindness: and a poor man is better than a liar. Prov. 19:22.

The latter portion of this passage of scripture in the Eastern Aramaic text reads: ". . . and a poor man is better than a rich man who lies." That is to say, a poor man who makes his living honestly is better than a rich man who acquires his riches by cheating, lying, and other deceitful means.

In the Near East every businessman is suspected of lying and cheating. Measuring short and having diverse weights and balances is a great problem. This is because the merchants and prospective buyers bargain and take oaths. And many of them lie about prices in order to make large profits. The poor buyer is always at the mercy of the rich seller.

CHAPTER TWENTY

Wine a Mocker

Wine is a mocker, strong drink is raging: and whosoever is deceived thereby is not wise. Prov. 20:1.

Most Near Easterners, especially pastoral and nomadic peoples, seldom drink wine or strong drink. As a general rule, those who do drink do not drink heavily. But at banquets, feasts, and weddings they drink until they are dead drunk. When they drink excessively, after the festivities they stagger through the streets cursing and uttering shameful remarks. Then they are mocked by the people, who gather around them to amuse themselves.

A man who is drunk does not know what he is doing. While intoxicated some even expose themselves and do other disgraceful things. When Noah was drunk, he slept in his tent naked and uncovered. However, his sons Shem and Japheth covered him.[41] Lot, when he was inebriated, slept with his daughters, not knowing what he was doing, and both of his daughters conceived and bore sons by him, Moab and Ammon.

Isaiah condemns drunkenness. He says, "Woe unto them that are mighty

---

[41]Gen. 9:21-23.

to drink wine, and men of strength to mingle [mix] strong drink."[42] "But these also have erred with wine, and with strong drink are gone astray; the priests and the prophets have erred with strong drink, they are overcome with wine, they stagger with strong drink, they err in judgment with drunkenness, they eat immoderately."[43]

Surety for Deceitful Gain

Bread of deceit is sweet to a man; but afterward his mouth shall be filled with gravel. Prov. 20:17.

The Eastern Aramaic text reads: "He who becomes surety for a man by means of deceitful gain will afterwards have his mouth filled with gravel."

At times greedy men became surety for bandits, murderers, and men of bad reputation and credit. Even though they knew that the person for whom they had become a surety was a risk, they did it because of the large sum of money they received and for political reasons. When the crooked men failed to carry out their promises and pledges, the man who had become surety for them had to make good the losses. At times, even honest and pious men were victimized.

"To have a mouth filled with gravel" is a Semitic idiom which means that the person cannot give an answer or exonerate himself for his evil deed. In the Near East small stones and gravel are often found in bread and food, and, at times, they cause people to choke. This is because wheat that comes from the threshing floor contains gravel, soil, and other impurities.

Cursing Father or Mother

Whoso curseth his father or his mother, his lamp shall be put out in obscure darkness. Prov. 20:20.

Cursing father and mother was a capital crime and punishable by death. "He who curses his father or his mother shall surely be put to death."[44]

The Aramaic word *sheraga,* "lamp," is used metaphorically, meaning

---

[42]Isa. 5:22, K.J.V.

[43]Isa. 28:7, Eastern Aramaic Peshitta text, Lamsa translation. See also Gen. 19:32-25; Prov. 23:20-22.

[44]Ex. 21:17 and Lev. 20:9, Eastern Aramaic Peshitta text, Lamsa translation.

"posterity or heir." In Aramaic a son or an heir is often called "a lamp." "Nevertheless for David's sake did the Lord his God give him a lamp in Jerusalem, to set up his son after him."[45]

According to Scripture, the Lord is displeased with haughty eyes, a proud heart, and the posterity of wicked people. When the Lord rejected wicked kings, their posterity was cut off from the land of the living. Those who cursed their father or their mother were counted among the wicked, and their posterity was to be cut off.

Vows Fulfilled

It is a snare to the man who devoureth that which is holy, and after vows to make inquiry. Prov. 20:25.

The Aramaic word *nader* means "to vow or make a vow." The Eastern Aramaic text reads: "It is a snare for a man who vows to give something to a holy place, and regrets after he has vowed."

The Scriptures admonished the Israelites to fulfill their vows as soon as possible. Near Easterners were afraid to delay or cancel their vows. Generally, vows were made by people who were sick or in difficulties, or traveling, or praying for the birth of a male child. The animals or money vowed were given to the priests or distributed among the poor. The vow was a reminder of God's favor and blessings in time of need. God does not need the things that are vowed, but poor people who know about the vows look forward to having the meat of the animals and bread.

"When you vow a vow to God, do not delay in fulfilling it; for he has no pleasure in fools; but as for you, pay that which you have vowed. It is much better that you should not vow than that you should vow and not fulfill it."[46] "And you shall make your prayer to him, and he shall hear you, and you shall fulfill your vows."[47]

Sickness Result of Evil

The blueness of a wound cleanseth away evil: so do stripes the inward parts of the belly. Prov. 20:30.

---

[45]1 Ki. 15:4, Eastern Aramaic Peshitta text, Lamsa translation.
[46]Ecc. 5:4-5, Eastern Aramaic Peshitta text, Lamsa translation.
[47]Job 22:27, Eastern Aramaic Peshitta text, Lamsa translation.

The Eastern Aramaic text reads: "Misery and torment befall the evil men; and wounds smite the inner parts of their bodies." It was commonly believed that evil sooner or later manifested itself in the bodies of evildoers, and misery and torment took possession of their physical forms. In other words, wicked men received their evil rewards just as good men received their good rewards in this world.

Evil obscures the mind, which is the lamp of the body. Jesus said, "When thine eye is single, thy whole body also is full of light."[48] "Single" means clear. When the mind is clear, the whole body is lighted and well. But when the mind is obscured by evil thoughts and acts, the body is in darkness and helpless to heal itself.

CHAPTER TWENTY-ONE

A Quarrelsome Woman

It is better to dwell in a corner of the housetop, than with a brawling woman in a wide house. Prov. 21:9.

Near Easterners, when lacking a place in the house, live anywhere they can find a space to put their heads. Indeed, it is not unusual to see men and women eating in the streets, or holding councils and sleeping on the housetops.[49] Dwelling places have always been scarce in biblical lands. One can see small houses crowded with three or four families. The family traditions are so sacred that as long as the father and mother are living, both their married and unmarried sons live with them.

"It is better to dwell in a corner of the housetop, than with a brawling woman in a wide [spacious] house" means that it is better to remain single and to sleep anywhere than to be married to a quarrelsome woman and live in a spacious house with luxuries.

Lack of Gift Stirs Wrath

A gift in secret pacifieth anger: and a reward in the bosom, strong wrath. Prov. 21:14.

---

[48]Lk. 11:34, K.J.V.
[49]Mt. 10:27.

The last portion of the verse is mistranslated in the King James Version. It should read: ". . . but he who is sparing with his gifts stirs wrath."

"Gift" in many cases means "bribe." Prior to World War I, bribery was prevalent in the Near East. Many litigations and disputes were settled in advance by means of bribes. When people transgressed the law and incurred the anger of the officials, they often pacified the officials by means of lavish gifts. Small gifts, or bribes, were rejected and those who offered them were rebuked and punished.

In biblical days, "tribute" was often called "a gift." Kings in biblical lands presented gifts to the kings of Assyria, Babylon, and Egypt in order to win their favor and to get protection against their enemies. But when they failed to present gifts, they were invaded and taxed more heavily.

Bribery is condemned by the Mosaic law and the prophets. Bribes obscure the eyes of judges and other government officials and pervert justice.

Wealth

There is treasure to be desired and oil in the dwelling of the wise; but a foolish man spendeth it up. Prov. 21:20.

The Eastern Aramaic text reads: "A coveted treasure and ointment are in a dwelling place; but the wisdom and understanding of men shall dispense it." That is to say, they will spend it wisely. The reference is to the houses of pious men who revere the Lord and who are blessed with abundance.[50]

"Treasure" in this instance means a good accumulation of silver, gold, and precious stones. Until recent days, Near Eastern men stored gold and silver in the houses or buried them in fields or caves. Banks were unknown; therefore, a house or a field was the safest place to store money.

From time immemorial, oil and butter have been an important part of the economy in biblical lands, especially in the ancient days when money was scarce and buried in the ground or lying idle in the treasuries of the rich. Olive oil and butter were used as mediums of exchange. Jesus told a parable about an unjust steward who reduced the debts of his lord, which he had loaned to the people in oil.[51]

---

[50]Ps. 112:3; Prov. 15:6.
[51]Lk. 16:5-8.

Those who have a treasure of silver, gold, and oil are wise and rich. They spend it with wisdom and understanding. The unwise spend their money and oil in riotous living and suddenly become poor.[52]

CHAPTER TWENTY-THREE

Knife on Your Throat

And put a knife to thy throat, if thou be a man given to appetite. Prov. 23:2.

"Knife" in this instance is used allegorically to mean "poison." When people eat something bad or poisonous, they say, "It cuts me like a knife." The poison injures the throat of the victims who eat it in food or drink it in wine. The verse needs to be understood in its entire setting. "When you sit to eat with a ruler; consider diligently what is set before you. That you may not put poison in your mouth. And if you are a man given to excessive appetite, Be not desirous of his food . . . "[53]

In many Near Eastern lands, a person who wishes to do away with an enemy gives a lavish banquet in his honor and poisons his food or drink. Kings, princes, and rich men generally employ food-tasters, who try the food first. Some men examine the food secretly before they put it into their mouths. Years ago this practice was so common that many men who were invited to such banquets were reluctant to accept.

Doing away with one's enemies by means of poison is an old Eastern custom. Alexander the Great was poisoned at a banquet in Babylon. Muhammad was poisoned by a woman whose relatives were slain in the battle against him. Hundreds of prominent men and government officials have met with such horrible deaths.

In his prayer, Jesus asked God to let the cup pass away from him.[54] Because of poisoning men at banquets, the term "cup" has become symbolical of treachery, and guests at banquets are often fearful and hesitate to drink.

---

[52]Prov. 21:17-18.

[53]Prov. 23:1-3, Eastern Aramaic Peshitta text, Lamsa translation..

[54]Mt. 26:39.

Beware of Hypocrites

Eat thou not the bread of him that hath an evil eye, neither desire thou his dainty meats. Prov. 23:6.

The Aramaic word *khawara* means "hypocrite," and this verse should read: "Do not eat with a hypocrite, neither desire his food." This is because hypocrites are dangerous to associate with.

Some wicked people used their tables to snare the innocent. They entertained lavishly for ulterior purposes. Some of them did away with their enemies and rivals by poisoning their food. "Let their table become a snare before them," says the psalmist.[55] This is because many plots and conspiracies are planned at the table, and at times the conspirator himself is caught and punished.

Swallow Pitch

For as he thinketh in his heart, so is he: Eat and drink, saith he to thee; but his heart is not with thee. Prov. 23:7.

The Eastern Aramaic text reads: "For he is like him that swallows pitch; in like manner you will eat and drink with him, but his heart is not with you."

"Swallows pitch" is an idiom which means that he is a superb liar; he can make you believe that he is your sincere friend, whereas he is your enemy. Pitch is hard to swallow, but a liar can convince people that he can do it. In the Near East, magicians claim that they can do what the people cannot do. A liar is the same, and his big lies seemingly are convincing.

Hypocrites Reject Truth

The morsel which thou hast eaten shall thou vomit up, and lose the sweet words. Speak not in the ears of a fool: for he will despise the wisdom of thy words. Prov. 23:8-9.

"Vomit up" is an Eastern idiom meaning that you shall pay for it or it

---

[55]Ps. 69:22.

shall be exacted from you by force or deceitful means. That is, when you eat the bread of a hypocrite and associate with him, you put yourself in danger. Sooner or later you will pay double for it.

The good counsel which the guest has given will also be lost. This is because fools and hypocrites despise the truth and words of wisdom. Jesus said, "Do not give holy things to the dogs; and do not throw your pearls [words of wisdom] before swine [fools], for they might tread them with their feet, and then turn and rend you."[56]

A Harlot Is a Trap

For a whore is a deep ditch; and a strange woman is a narrow pit. Prov. 23:27.

The Aramaic word *gomasa* means "a deep pit used as a trap." A prostitute traps men by her smooth words and cunning until they are caught in her net. The "strange woman" here means any woman not his wife. She is likened to a narrow and dry well with mud in its bottom. In those days, dry wells were used to imprison men. Once a man is in it, it is hard to pull him out. Jeremiah spent numerous days in a muddy well, and it took many strong men to pull him out.

Red Eyes

Who hath woe? who hath sorrow? who hath contentions? who hath bubbling? who hath wounds without cause? who hath redness of eyes? Prov. 23:29.

Redness of eyes is symbolic of drunkenness and also of material prosperity. When Jacob blessed his son Judah, he said, "He washed his garments in wine, and his clothes in the blood [juices] of grapes: His eyes shall be red with wine, and his teeth white with milk."[57] This saying is still used in vernacular speech—"His eyes are red; he is drunken."

The woe here is against those who drink wine to excess and mix wine with strong drink. These men have sorrows that alcoholic beverages have brought upon them. "For at the last it bites like a serpent and stings like an

---

[56]Mt. 7:6, Eastern Aramaic Peshitta text, Lamsa translation.
[57]Gen. 49:11-12.

adder."[58]

Red Wine

Look not thou upon the wine when it is red, when it giveth his color in the cup, when it moveth itself aright. Prov. 23:31.

The last part of the verse in the Eastern Aramaic text reads: ". . . but meditate on righteousness." In the Near East red grapes were scarce; therefore, red wine was enticing and coveted more than white wine, which was abundant. During banquets and wedding feasts, red wine sold at a premium. Also, the color red was popular in biblical lands. Most of the women were arrayed in red garments with stripes. And during feasts, banquets, and weddings, most women wore red. "O daughters of Israel, weep over Saul, who clothed you in scarlet and dyed garments."[59]

The author of Proverbs admonishes us not to covet after the color of red wine but to think of righteous things and good works that are edifying.

A Drunkard Is Lost

Yea, thou shalt be as he that lieth down in the midst of the sea, or as he that lieth upon the top of a mast. Prov. 23:34.

The last portion of the verse in the Eastern Aramaic text reads: ". . . or as a sailor in a tempest." "Lieth down in the midst of the sea" is a Near Eastern idiom that means he is lost or does not know what he is doing. The reference here is to drunkenness. Drunkards lose their senses.[60] In a raging storm, sailors lose direction and do not know what to do.[61] In those days ships were small and the sea hazards many. Compasses were unknown. The sailors relied on the sun and stars for finding their way.

---

[58]See verse 32, Lamsa translation and also Prov. 20:1.
[59]2 Sam. 1:24, Eastern Aramaic Peshitta text, Lamsa translation.
[60]See verses 29-32.
[61]Verse 35.

CHAPTER TWENTY-FOUR

Wisdom Crushes the Fool

Wisdom is too high for a fool: he openeth not his mouth in the gate. Prov. 24:7.

The Aramaic word *ramiah,* "to crush," is confused in the King James Version with the Aramaic adverb *ramah,* "high." This verse should read: "Wisdom crushes a fool." Wisdom cannot grace the mind of a fool, because he does not value it.

"He openeth not his mouth in the gate" means that he never gave counsel when he sat with the elders at the gate. In the Near East, important meetings and councils are held at the gate of the city where the people gather to discuss the affairs of the town, settle disputes, and receive the judgments of the rulers.[62] Squares and parks were unknown, and the streets were too narrow for gatherings. The gate was the only adequate place for meetings of this nature.

The wise and prudent men tried to show their knowledge at the gate. This was because the words spoken at the gate were published in the town and countryside and were quoted by the wise men. On such occasions fools were rebuked when they started to speak or attempted to give counsel.

Admonition to Kings

My son, fear thou the Lord and the king: and meddle not with them that are given to change. Prov. 24:21.

The Eastern Aramaic text reads: "My son, fear [revere] the Lord and give good counsel; and meddle not with the fools." The Aramaic word *amlikh* means "to give counsel, to reign." The king is advising his son to reverence the Lord when he reigns over the people. The term "king" in Aramaic means "a counselor." At the outset, kings were chiefs of the tribes. They gave counsel and led the tribal people during their wanderings.

Without wisdom and reverence for the Lord, no ruler would execute justice. When kings and princes revere God they refrain from doing evil and oppressing the poor.

---

[62]Ruth 4:1-4; 1 Ki. 22:10

Moreover, Solomon admonishes his son not to associate with fools. Nevertheless, his son Rehoboam, who reigned in his place, rejected the good advice of the elders who had acted as counselors to his father, and he accepted the counsel of young men who had grown up with him.[63]

Golden Rule

Say not, I will do so to him as he hath done to me: I will render to the man according to his work. Prov. 24:29.

This verse is the foundation of the Golden Rule. King Solomon, in his long reign as a king and judge over Israel, found out that to render evil for evil did more harm than good. His statement here was a departure from the Mosaic law ". . . but life shall be for life, eye for eye, tooth for tooth, hand for hand, foot for foot."[64]

The author of the Proverbs admonishes the people to leave vengeance to God, who is the only true judge. "Do not say, I will recompense evil; but wait for the Lord that he may save you."[65] Many of the Hebrew prophets found out that evil for evil was the cause of Israel's long struggle with the Gentile world. They also disagreed with Mosaic ordinances and man-made laws.

Jesus went further in reversing the Mosaic ordinances. He admonished his followers ". . . that you should not resist evil; but whoever strikes you on your right cheek, turn to him the other also."[66] ". . . Love your enemies, bless anyone who curses you, do good to anyone who hates you . . ."[67] A good man does not wish to do to others what he does not wish to be done to him.

Sluggard

So shall thy poverty come as one that travelleth; and thy want as an armed man. Prov. 24:34.

---

[63] 1 Ki. 12:13-14.

[64] Dt. 19:21, Eastern Aramaic Peshitta text, Lamsa translation

[65] Prov. 20:22, Eastern Aramaic Peshitta text, Lamsa translation.

[66] Mt. 5:39, Eastern Aramaic Peshitta text, Lamsa translation.

[67] Mt. 5:44, Eastern Aramaic Peshitta text, Lamsa translation.

The Eastern Aramaic text reads: "So shall poverty come upon you, and want shall overtake you suddenly like a runner." The sluggard at last becomes the victim of poverty and want which, in due time, catch up with him. In biblical days, letters and other royal messages were dispatched by fast runners.

CHAPTER TWENTY-FIVE

Near Eastern Etiquette

Put not forth thyself in the presence of the king, and stand not in the place of great men: For better it is that it be said unto thee, Come up hither; than that thou shouldest be put lower in the presence of the prince whom thine eyes have seen. Prov. 25:6-7.

In the Near East uncultured men sometimes tried to stand in high places when in the presence of kings and princes. These places belonged to the wealthy and noblemen. Indeed, it made a great deal of difference where a guest stood or sat. Customarily the ministers of state, princes, and noblemen did not sit down in the presence of a king unless they were invited to do so.

This was also true of assemblies, wedding feasts, and banquets. Some men came very early and occupied the high places where food was more abundant. The host was generally busy welcoming the guests, chatting with them, and seeing that the food was plentiful. But when all the guests were seated and some of the prominent guests had arrived, he might ask those who had occupied the prominent seats to get up and move to lower places. This would be an embarrassing moment for those who must rise in the presence of seated guests and walk to a lower seat.

The wise noblemen sit low so that they may be asked to rise up and sit higher. This would be considered a great honor. The guest would be accompanied by the host, and all other guests watch.

Jesus knew Near Eastern etiquette. He admonished his disciples not to occupy high seats in the synagogues or at wedding feasts, but to sit in low seats so that the host might ask them to rise up and go to sit in more prominent places.[68]

---

[68]Lk. 14:8-10.

The Unruly Person

As he that taketh away a garment in cold weather, and as vinegar upon nitre, so is he that singeth songs to a heavy heart. Prov. 25:20.

The Eastern Aramaic text reads: "As he who takes away a garment from his neighbor in cold weather, as one who drops sand on the string of a musical instrument, as he who afflicts a broken heart, as a moth on a garment, and as a boring-worm on a tree: such is the effect of sorrow on a man's heart."

In the Near East, good mantles or robes were given by the poor as pledges of surety when borrowing money from a stranger. Some of the wicked moneylenders would take the robe of the borrower as a pledge even on a cold day. Thus the lender had no mercy upon the poor borrower, who needed the garment on a cold day as much as he needed the money he borrowed. The poor and the strangers sleep with their garments. They lie on the floor and cover themselves with their robes or mantles. The Mosaic law forbids keeping a neighbor's mantle or raiment during the night. ". . . you must give them back to him by sunset."[69]

"Dropping of sand on the string of a musical instrument" is an Aramaic idiom that means "wasting time." This is because sand cannot stand on the string of a musical instrument. It is just like saying, "placing an orange on a telephone wire."

The broken heart needs no affliction. Sorrow is likened to a moth on a garment and a boring-worm on a tree. They cause suffering within the person. In the Near East one says, "They eat the inside."

Doing Good to Your Enemy

If thine enemy be hungry, give him bread to eat; and if he be thirsty, give him water to drink: For thou shall heap coals of fire upon his head, and the Lord shall reward thee. Prov. 25:21-22.

"Heap coals of fire upon his head" is a Near Eastern idiom that means to embarrass him or cause him to suffer. Nothing would embarrass an enemy more than having to accept bread and water from someone he has hated or

---

[69]Ex. 22:26-27, Eastern Aramaic Peshitta text, Lamsa translation.

wronged. The enemy guest burns inside; that is, he regrets the wrongs he has done to the host. And on such occasions the guest may confess his evil deeds, forget the enmity, and become a sincere friend of the host.[70]

Moreover, during droughts, famines and natural calamities, enmities were forgotten and food and water were shared. This is especially true of tribal people who are constantly dependent on one another.

CHAPTER TWENTY-SIX

Thorns in Hand of a Drunkard

As a thorn goeth up into the hand of a drunkard, so is a parable in the mouth of fools. Prov. 26:9.

The first part of the verse in the Eastern Aramaic text reads: "Thorns spring up in the hand of a drunkard . . ." Biblical lands are noted for thorns and briers. Barren fields and grazing lands are full of thorns. Shepherds, reapers, and people who walk barefooted suffer from them.

Then again, during the wintertime all those who handle dry grass suffer from thorns. Leather gloves were unknown in that part of the world. Thorns were a problem in the summer and winter.

The author of Proverbs uses this analogy simply because a drunkard's difficulties multiply day by day. His substance is wasted in drinking. At first he does not feel the pinch of poverty, just as he does not feel the thorn when it goes into his hand if he is drunk, but sooner or later he finds himself facing money problems. This is also true of the fool; he does not know how to relate a parable so that those listening to him may understand its meaning.

The Fool Repeats His Folly

As a dog returneth to his vomit, so a fool returneth to his folly. Prov. 26:11.

Dogs in the Near East are seldom fed, especially in lands where dogs are considered as unclean and are not wanted. The exception to this custom is shepherds, who live outdoors and need them. Generally dogs roam around

---

[70]Ps. 23:5; Rom. 12:20.

the city hungry, howling and searching for food in vain.

At times, dogs find dead animals which are thrown away, and they eat until they are satiated. Some of them regurgitate the food and later, when they are hungry, eat it again. The fool, likewise, repeats his mistakes and folly. He refuses to learn from them and abhors discipline and correction.

The Slothful

The slothful hideth his hand in his bosom; it grieveth him to bring it again to his mouth. Prov. 26:15.

"Hides his hand in his bosom" is an Eastern idiom that means, "He is lazy." In the Near East idle men generally keep their hands in their chest area or pockets. One often hears people saying, "His hands are in his pocket," meaning that he is unwilling to work.

"It grieves him to bring it again to his mouth" means that he is so lazy that he would rather stay hungry than lift his hand to his mouth. This portion of the verse is used sarcastically in denouncing the slothful.

CHAPTER TWENTY-SEVEN

Oil and Ointment

Ointment and perfume rejoice the heart: so doth the sweetness of a man's friend by hearty counsel. Prov. 27:9.

The Eastern Aramaic text reads: "As oil and perfume rejoice the heart, so does the sweetness of a man's friend by hearty counsel."

In the Near East ointment is made of oil, perfume, wax, and balm, and is placed on sores to keep the skin soft and to heal it. Because of the scarcity of water to drink, bathing was very rare and in some places unknown. Sores on hands and feet and other parts of the body were very common, and they often became infected and wide open. A little oil or ointment softens the dirt and removes it from the skin.

This is also true of the good counsel given by a faithful friend. It relieves the person of his worries and troubles. The good counsel sinks into the mind and heals it, just like oil sinks into dry skin and cures the wound.

Flattery

He that blesseth his friend with a loud voice, rising early in the morning, it shall be counted a curse to him. Prov. 27:14.

The Eastern Aramaic text reads: "He who blesses his friend with a flattering loud voice is not different from him who curses." The Aramaic word *beshopra-notha* is derived from *shapar,* "flattery." It is confused in the King James Version with *shapraiotha,* derived from *shapar,* "early dawn." Flattery is condemned in the Near East and looked upon as a brand of hypocrisy.

The flatterers usually speak loudly when showering praises upon their unworthy friends. Flattery is deceitful and harmful both to the flatterer and to the one who is flattered.

A Quarrelsome Woman

A continual dropping in a very rainy day and a contentious woman are alike. Prov. 27:15.

In many parts of the biblical lands, houses were covered with timber and branches of trees, and the branches were covered with straw and earth. During the rainy season, water might drip from the ceiling into the house. Vessels were placed on the floor to catch the water. Beds were also moved from one place in the house to another to escape the dripping. The roof was so weak that no one knew where the next drops would fall.

Moreover, during the rainy season families might suffer considerably from the leaks; clothes and valuable articles were spoiled and bed clothing soaked. There is a Near Eastern parable that is very common: "He fled from the rain and sat under the dropping." This means that he fled from a minor annoyance only to suffer from a greater one.

Quarrelsome women were feared like a dripping ceiling. They were an annoyance to their husbands as well as to their neighbors. They always found fault and were dissatisfied with life.

No Two Hearts Are Alike

As in water face answereth to face, so the heart of man to man. Prov. 27:19.

The Aramaic word *damin* means "to be alike or resemble." The last part of the word resembles the Aramaic word for water. The Eastern Aramaic text reads: "As faces do not resemble faces, so hearts do not resemble hearts."

It is said that no two persons look alike. The author of the Proverbs states that no two hearts are alike. Probably no two people think alike. God has created everything in its own pattern.

Good Shepherd

Be thou diligent to know the state of thy flocks, and look well to thy herds. Prov. 27:23.

The Eastern Aramaic text reads: "When you are feeding the sheep, know their faces and set your mind on the flock." This is true of all good and experienced shepherds in the Near East. They know both the names and the faces of their own sheep and of most of the flock that is entrusted to them. Women who milk the sheep know their own sheep by their faces and call them by their names. When a sheep is lost, they search the whole flock for it, and when they fail to find it, they rush to the shepherd.

The sheep, likewise, know the shepherd and their owners, and they follow them. But they refuse to follow a stranger.

Jesus must have read this passage in the original Old Testament written in ancient Aramaic. He says: "And when he has brought out his sheep, he goes before them; and his own sheep follow him, because they know his voice. The sheep do not follow a stranger, but they run away from him, because they do not know the voice of a stranger."[71] "I am the good shepherd, and I know my own, and my own know me."[72]

CHAPTER TWENTY-EIGHT

Confessing of Sins

He that covereth his sins shall not prosper: but whoso confesseth and forsaketh them shall have mercy. Prov. 28:13.

---

[71]Jn. 10:4-5, Eastern Aramaic Peshitta text, Lamsa translation.

[72]Jn. 10:14, Eastern Aramaic Peshitta text, Lamsa translation.

The term "confessing" means "to acknowledge," that is, to reveal what one has done and, if possible, make restitution. Confessions were made in court, in public, before God, and in the house or in a place of worship. "I have acknowledged my sin unto thee, and mine iniquity have I not hid from thee."[73] Confession of sins relieves one of the burden of bearing them every day. True confession must come from a sincere heart and be followed by sincere repentance.

A person confessing sins pledged not to commit them again. Habitual sinners could hardly obtain mercy. And forgiveness of sins cannot be purchased with money. The Mosaic law demanded confession before receiving forgiveness and mercy from God. "If they shall confess their iniquity and the iniquity of their fathers, with their wickedness with which they transgressed against me, and also that they have walked contrary to me."[74] James says, "Confess your faults one to another."[75]

CHAPTER TWENTY-NINE

Servants a Problem

If a ruler hearken to lies, all his servants are wicked. Prov. 29:12.

In the Near East, servants usually were jealous of one another and were constantly complaining against the other servants. Most wise rich men dismiss the gossip and things that they hear about the servants. They know their servants envy one another. But if they listen to the lying charges about their servants, then all the servants would be considered wicked. This is because one servant accuses another. Jesus even told a parable about a so-called unfaithful servant against whom others had lied.[76]

Wicked as a Majority

Where there is no vision, the people perish: but he that keepeth the law, happy is he. Prov. 29:18.

---

[73]Ps. 32:5, Eastern Aramaic Peshitta text, Lamsa translation.
[74]Lev. 26:40, Eastern Aramaic Peshitta text, Lamsa translation.
[75]James 5:16, Eastern Aramaic Peshitta text, Lamsa translation.
[76]Lk. 16:1-8.

The Eastern Aramaic text reads: "When the wicked men multiply, the people are ruined; but he who keeps the law, blessed is he." The error in the King James Version is probably due to copyists who confused the Hebrew word *khazan,* "vision," with *khayaz,*"to cut asunder." The Aramaic word is *me-terra,* "to break in pieces, to cause to ruin."

Corrupt politics, immorality, drunkenness, and evil deeds have been the cause of the fall of many great empires and kingdoms. When the wicked multiply and become a majority, they take over and then start to destroy what good men have built.

CHAPTER THIRTY

Marginal Note

The words of Agur the son of Jakeh, even the prophecy: the man spake unto Ithiel, even unto Ithiel and Ucal. Prov. 30:1.

The Eastern Aramaic text reads: "These are the words of Agur the son of Jakeh, who prophesied and received power. He said to Ithiel . . ."

This first verse of chapter thirty is a marginal note that was copied into the text. The note was written in order to identify the book and its writer. Such marginal notes are found throughout the entire Bible and are numerous. For example: "The vison of Isaiah, the son of Amoz, which he saw concerning Judah and Jerusalem in the days of Uzziah, Jotham, Ahaz, and Hezekiah, kings of Judah:"[77] These notes that were written later by a scribe became an integral part of the text.

Tampering with Scripture

Add thou not unto his words, lest he reprove thee, and thou be found a liar. Prov. 30:6.

This ordinance was given so that the people might revere the inspired Word and refrain from adding to it or changing it. The Ten Commandments were to be handed down from one generation to another, intact, without revisions, additions, or changes. The words that the Lord uttered on Mount

[77]Isa. 1:1, Eastern Aramaic Peshitta text, Lamsa translation.

Sinai were perfect and eternal. The ordinances and statutes were also to be safeguarded against forgeries, additions, omissions, and unnecessary revisions so that the truth the law contains might be preserved intact.

Muslims, Jews, and Near Eastern Christians (wrongly called Nestorians) never dare to change a letter in their Scriptures, nor have they ever revised any portion of them or ever added or omitted a word. This is because revisions and deliberate forgeries have been the causes for many disputes, false theological doctrines, and divisions among the Western Christians.

In the Near East when a sacred book or a Bible is copied, every word of the copy is compared with the text from which it is copied. Even the letters are counted, so that no error might creep into the Scriptures.

"You shall not add to the commandment which I command you, neither shall you take from it, but you must keep the commandments of the Lord your God which I command you."[78] "Everything that I command you, that you must be careful to do; you shall not add nor take from it."[79]

"I testify to every man who hears the words of the prophecy of this book, If any man shall add to these things, God shall add to him the plagues that are written in this book; and if any man shall take away from the words of the book of this prophecy, God shall take away his portion from the tree of life and from the holy city and from the things which are written in this book."[80]

Knives

There is a generation, whose teeth are as swords, and their jaw teeth as knives, to devour the poor from off the earth, and the needy from among men. Prov. 30:14.

Table knives and forks were unknown in the Near East until recent years. The people used their front teeth to cut off pieces of meat. The reference here is to the oppressors who exploit the poor and the needy. These men were known as having sharp teeth like swords. In American slang they are called "sharks."

When the Israelites forsook the way of the Lord and transgressed his commandments, their rulers and judges became wicked. They oppressed the poor and corrupted justice. These wicked men had no knowledge of

---

[78]Dt. 4:2, Eastern Aramaic Peshitta text, Lamsa translation.

[79]Dt. 12:32, Eastern Aramaic Peshitta text, Lamsa translation.

[80]Rev. 22:18-19, Eastern Aramaic Peshitta text, Lamsa translation.

God, neither did they fear the Most High.[81]

It is said of princes or government officials who defraud or exploit their people that they have devoured [eaten] the poor and the weak. Job says: "And I broke the jaws of the wicked, and snatched the prey out of his teeth."[82]

Jesus used the same Aramaic metaphor: "Woe to you, scribes and Pharisees, hypocrites! for you embezzle [Aramaic 'eat'] the property of widows . . ."[83]

Young Men

The way of an eagle in the air; the way of a serpent upon a rock; the way of a ship in the midst of the sea, and the way of a man with a maid. Prov. 30:19.

The last part of the verse in the Eastern Aramaic text reads: ". . . and the way of a man in his youth." *Balemothey,* "in his youth," is confused with *alemtha,* "a maiden." Until recent days, unmarried men in the Near East never kept company with women, and in some parts of the East this ancient custom still prevails. Marriages were arranged by the parents of the bridegroom and those of the bride.

Young men found it difficult to make decisions or to know what to do or what not to do. It took a long time before a young man came to himself. When people spoke of young men, they said, "They are in the air"; that is, "they do not know what they are doing," or "they do not know the head from the tail." This is why until young men reach the age of thirty, they cannot speak in the council. Jesus was thirty years old when he began to preach and teach. That is the reason we know so little of his early life.

Wrath Produces Strife

Surely the churning of milk bringeth forth butter, and the wringing of the nose bringeth forth blood: so the forcing of wrath bringeth forth strife. Prov. 30:33.

The second clause is a mistranslation. The Aramaic word *khetta* means

---

[81]Ps. 10:4.

[82]Job 29:17, Eastern Aramaic Peshitta text, Lamsa translation.

[83]Mt. 23:13, Eastern Aramaic Peshitta text, Lamsa translation.

"a grain of wheat," and it should read: ". . . and if you press your hand on a raw grain of wheat, it will bring forth juices; thus out of the strife goes forth judgment."

Butter is made by churning. Buttermilk is placed in a goatskin that is hung on a tripod. Two women stand, one on each side of the tripod, and shake the skin until the butter is separated from the buttermilk. This process takes about an hour.

The author of the book of Proverbs likens the storing of wrath to the churning of buttermilk. Wrath and anger generate power, which, in due time, brings forth strife.

One should not allow room in his or her heart for wrath, for it is like a double-edged sword; it cuts both ways.

CHAPTER THIRTY-ONE

Wine to Mourners

Give strong drink unto him that is ready to perish, and wine unto those that be of heavy hearts. Prov. 31:6.

The Aramaic word *abileh* means "mourners," that is, those whose hearts are heavy and sorrowful. The root of the verb is *abal,* "to mourn." The Eastern Aramaic text reads: "Let strong drink be given to those who mourn, and wine to those who are of heavy heart."

Near Easterners mourn over their dead for a long period.[84] Some of the mourners, because of their grief, inflict injuries upon their bodies. They also wear old garments and are silent and sad. In some places the mourners are comforted after the burial; they are given food and drink.

Wine is given to the mourners so that they may forget their grief.[85] Near Easterners, except at weddings and feasts, drink very little wine. In some areas, wine is never drunk, and strong drink is unknown. Pastoral and nomad peoples drink milk and buttermilk.

---

[84]Gen. 50:3; Num. 20:29; 2 Sam. 3:31.

[85]Ps. 104:15; Ecc 10:19.

A Virtuous Woman

She perceiveth that her merchandise is good: her candle goeth not out by night, Prov. 31:18.

A few decades ago people in biblical lands went to bed at sunset and rose at dawn and worked from dawn to sunset. Some people went to bed at seven or eight in the evening. Therefore, lamps were lighted for only a short duration. Only the extravagantly rich kept their lamps burning all night.

"Her lamp does not go out all night" is a Near Eastern saying that means she works all during the night clear to the early morning hours. Industrious women worked at night, spinning, weaving cloth and rugs, sewing, and doing other housework.

When the virtuous woman found that her merchandise was good and in great demand, she worked during the night to supply the need. This kind of woman was pious, wise, and industrious; she prospered and was emulated.

Known in the Gate

Her husband is known in the gates, when he sitteth among the elders of the land. Prov. 31:23.

In those days trials were held at the town gate. City gates were used for gatherings of the elders and noblemen and for other meetings. The houses were too small and the streets too narrow for such assemblies. Then again, because the woman baked bread and cooked food, the house was often filled with smoke. When the king of Israel and the king of Judah wanted to discuss war against Syria, they met at the gate.[86]

Until recently, many trials were held in the gate or other open places where noblemen were able to assemble. The judges were appointed from among these noble elders. When Boaz wanted to settle the question of Naomi's field, he went and sat at the gate. "And he took ten men of the elders of the city, and said, Sit ye down here. And they sat down."[87] When Hamor and Shechem, his son, wanted to discuss with the people of their

---

[86]1 Ki. 22:10.
[87]Ruth 4:2, K.J.V.

city the question of circumcision, they went to the gate.[88]

Noblemen and prosperous men were usually found idle at the gate. The husband of the virtuous woman was well dressed and well fed. He wore new garments and new sashes that his wife had made for him. Consequently, he was well known and admired in the town.

A Skillful Woman

She maketh fine linen, and selleth it; and delivereth girdles unto the merchant. Prov. 31:24.

In the Near East, until recent days, sashes, gloves, and stockings were made by women during their spare time and sold to merchants. Most other articles of clothing were woven on looms by male weavers.

Women retained the price of the articles they made as their own possession. The family purse is kept by men. Some women gave the money thus gained to their husbands, or spent it on their children, or made it into necklaces, earrings, and bracelets for their daughters. Wise, pious, and skillful women of this type were admired and emulated in biblical lands.[89]

[88]Gen. 34:20.

[89]1 Ki. 10:1.

INTRODUCTION TO ECCLESIASTES

Ecclesiastes is a Greek word that means "the one who assembled." However, the Aramaic title for the book of Ecclesiastes is *Kohlat* (the Hebrew title, *Koheleth*), which means "the voice, the words," that is, "the preaching." It is the words of the Preacher, the son of David, King Solomon in Jerusalem. The first verse confirms the authorship of the book.[1]

King Solomon, through his long experience as a ruler, his constant study, and being a wealthy sovereign, had tasted all phases of life. But he came, at last, to the conclusion that life is vanity, all things under the sun are temporary, and humans come into this world naked and leave naked. The book of Ecclesiastes, like the book of Proverbs, contains wise sayings, axioms, admonitions, and instructions. The book is also known as a wisdom text that reflects on the nature of the world, the Creator, and the place of human beings in the divine creation.

CHAPTER ONE

The Preacher

The words of the Preacher, the son of David, king in Jerusalem. Ecc. 1:1.

As stated in the introduction, the book of Ecclesiastes in Aramaic is called *Kohlat*—that is, "the voice" or "the preaching." This is because the theme of the book is like a sermon, containing advice and admonitions, and transmitting the experiences of one generation to another.

King Solomon, the son of David, who was reigning in his father's stead in Jerusalem, was noted for his wisdom and understanding.[2] When God appeared to him in Gibeon in a dream and said to him, "Ask what I shall give thee?" Solomon asked for wisdom and understanding.[3] Moreover, when the queen of Sheba heard of the fame of Solomon and his wisdom, she came to see him to prove his wisdom with her dark sayings,

---

[1]As with the book of Proverbs, modern Old Testament scholars postulate that Ecclesiastes was written by many sages and not just King Solomon.

[2]Ecc. 2:9.

[3]1 Ki. 3:4-14.

axioms, and riddles.[4]

Solomon had a full share of this life. He knew much and saw plenty. He had abundant riches and a thousand wives. He had all that his heart desired, but when his material desires at last were gone, he found himself empty, despondent, and dissatisfied.[5]

Human Toil

What profit hath a man of all his labor which he taketh under the sun? Ecc. 1:3.

The Aramaic word *amel* means "he toils." This last part of the verse should read: ". . . at which he toils under the sun." "Taketh" is a mistranslation. "Sun" means "light." In the Near East when electricity was unknown, all work was done during the day. The dark hours of the night were for rest. Only a few women worked during the evening.

All human gains are left where they are wrought. One generation goes and another comes, but all mortal labor and gains are left upon the earth.

Wisdom Eternal

The thing that hath been, it is that which shall be; and that which is done is that which shall be done: and there is no new thing under the sun. Ecc. 1:9.

King Solomon hints that everything we now have has already existed, and everything that has been done will be done again. What he means is there will be constant changes—the rise and fall of different civilizations and cultures—when one thing is forgotten, another thing is born.

Wisdom is neither new nor old. It is what it is. Necessity is the mother of inventions and new ideas. Also, spiritual ideas are neither new nor old, but they are applied in new ways in time. For example, transportation in Arabia until recently was (and still is in some areas) by means of camel; in Europe, by means of steam engines. The Arabs had less to transport, but the idea behind both systems of transportation is the same. The Assyrians invented the wheel, but America made great use of it by manufacturing cars. This one idea served in both a large and small

---

[4]1 Ki. 10:1.

[5]See verse 8.

way in man's different dispensations.

Humankind Cannot Change Nature

That which is crooked cannot be made straight: and that which is wanting cannot be numbered. Ecc. 1:15.

The Eastern Aramaic text reads: "The chaotic [or crooked] cannot be made orderly; and he who is lacking knowledge cannot be supplied with it." The Aramaic word *mithmlaio,* "to be supplied," has been confused in the King James Version with *mithmnaio,* "to be numbered." The only difference between the two words is the letter "l" in the former and the letter "n" in the latter. These two letters are often confused. The "n" is slightly shorter than "l" in Aramaic. The error may have occurred during transcription, when the alphabet was changed, or is a copyist's mistake.

What the author of Ecclesiastes says is this: What is lacking—that is, what we do not have now—cannot be supplied. Humans can create from what God has already created but cannot create the substance for new things nor change the essence of that which God has created.[6]

Too Much Wisdom

For in much wisdom is much grief; and he that increaseth knowledge increaseth sorrow. Ecc. 1:18.

Much knowledge can create new problems that complicate life. It is so much easier for an individual to transport merchandise on the back of a camel than to build railroads. The railroads would usher in new problems. It would cause some to be extremely poor and others extremely wealthy. There would be accidents and deaths caused by new techniques with which humans are not familiar.

Human beings pay a costly price for everything new that wisdom introduces. Humankind has sacrificed thousands of lives on the altar of speed and on the altar of navigation and aviation. While some enjoy life through speed and other comforts of modern transportation, others mourn for those who have perished because of these modern inventions.

---

[6]Ecc. 7:13.

CHAPTER TWO

Eternal Values

I said in mine heart, Go to now, I will prove thee with mirth; therefore enjoy pleasure: and, behold, this also is vanity. Ecc. 2:1.

During the time of Solomon people had no idea about life hereafter. They believed that those who died were either cut off from life and the living God or they lived on in their posterity.

Solomon, during his peaceful and prosperous reign, gave himself to luxuries and indulged in everything that his heart desired. Pleasures and joys of this earthly life were the only realities to him.[7] Nevertheless, with all the wealth he had—that is, fame, wives, wine, and luxuries—he found his life empty and boring.[8]

Everything King Solomon had is now gone and forgotten, even the magnificent temple he built. The only thing that was left behind is his riotous life and his profound writings. The only permanent thing one can bequeath to posterity is the good one may leave behind. In that good a person lives forever because good, like God, is eternal and indestructible.

Understanding

I sought in mine heart to give myself unto wine, yet acquainting mine heart with wisdom; and to lay hold on folly, till I might see what was that good for the sons of men, which they should do under the heaven all the days of their life. Ecc. 2:3.

The Aramaic word *sacolthana* means "understanding" but also means "folly or stupidity." With a dot *over* the third letter, the word is pronounced *sacolthana,* "understanding"; with a dot *under* the same letter, the word is aspirated and thus is pronounced *sakhulthana,* "folly, stupidity."

Solomon is speaking of wisdom and understanding, for wisdom without understanding is dangerous. We can be wise but must know how to

---

[7]Ecc. 2:10.

[8]See verses 3-12.

use our wisdom; that is, understanding guides us and warns us when we produce something remarkable and powerful but dangerous. Wisdom can create an atomic bomb, but understanding declares it a dangerous device.

Solomon could not have sought wisdom and yet held onto folly. Through understanding, Solomon found that all human wisdom was folly and that there was nothing material under the sun to strive for or in which to find lasting happiness.[9]

Many Servants

I made me great works; I builded me houses; I planted me vineyards. Ecc. 2:4.

The Aramaic word *abdeh,* "servants," is confused in the King James with *abadeh,* "works." Both words are written alike but pronounced differently. King Solomon had many servants, eunuchs, court attendants, butlers, and herdsmen. He built his magnificent royal palace and the costly and beautiful temple in Jerusalem.

In the Near East all rich men, princes, and kings are noted for the number of their servants and the ministers, singers, musicians, and the palaces they maintain.

Butlers and Waitresses

I gathered me also silver and gold, and the peculiar treasure of kings and of the provinces: I got me men singers and women singers, and the delights of the sons of men, as musical instruments, and that of all sorts. Ecc. 2:8.

The Aramaic word *shakyatha* means "waitresses" or "female butlers." The Eastern Aramaic text reads: ". . . and I appointed for myself butlers and waitresses." The Bible mentions butlers, but this is the first mention of waitresses. Nehemiah was a butler who waited on Artakhshisht, king of Persia.[10]

Waitresses were employed by King Solomon to wait on the queens and princesses in his palace. The king had everything in the world that

---

[9]See verse 17.
[10]Neh. 2:1.

money could buy and power could acquire. But at the end of his life, he found that everything was vanity and very fleeting.[11]

CHAPTER THREE

Time

To every thing there is a season, and a time to every purpose under the heaven. Ecc. 3:1.

The Aramaic word for "time" is *zabna* (pronounced *zawna*). In the realm of the Spirit, there is no time and space. Time is relative to the movements of the earth, moon, stars, and other planets. The author of Genesis tells us that all of these heavenly bodies were created to bring light into the world and for marking the days, months, and years.

Humans buy time by working and creating events. Time is more precious than gold. All things are reckoned by time. Time can make an article precious, and time can also depreciate its value. Time graces the heads of kings with crowns, and time sends them away, disgraced and empty-handed.

It is appropriate for humans not to waste time in foolishness, for time is precious and like a one-way street. It comes only once and never returns.

God's Works Unchangeable

I know that, whatsoever God doeth, it shall be for ever: nothing can be put to it, nor any thing taken from it: and God doeth it, that men should fear before him. Ecc. 3:14.

God's laws and works are from everlasting to everlasting, and are unchangeable. No one can alter one of God's laws or change the essence of things; nor can anyone add to or take from what God has created.

God has done this so that humankind may revere the divine presence and glorify the holy name. The term "fear" should be "revere." God is revealed through divine, marvelous works. Heaven and earth declare God's glory, and humanity wonders over the work of God's hands.

---

[11]See verse 2.

The Persecuted

That which hath been is now; and that which is to be hath already been; and God requireth that which is past. Ecc. 3:15.

The last part of the verse in the Eastern Aramaic text reads: ". . . and God will avenge him who has been persecuted." The Aramaic word *redipa,* derived from *radap,* "to persecute, pursue, urge on," in this instance means "the persecuted"; that is, "God will seek him who is persecuted and who is an outcast." The persecuted are driven away by their enemies, but the Lord succors and gathers those who are persecuted and driven away unjustly. It was believed that God always avenges those who trust in him.

Immortality

For that which befalleth the sons of men befalleth beasts; even one thing befalleth them: as the one dieth, so dieth the other; yea, they have all one breath; so that a man hath no preeminence above a beast: for all is vanity. Ecc. 3:19.

During the time of King Solomon, the Hebrew concept of immortality was not yet crystallized. The Hebrews, like the pagans, thought that death was the end. There was a slight glimpse of life hereafter, but it had not yet become a doctrine.

The major preeminence that humans have over the animals is free will. Humans have the Spirit of God in them, and therefore are God's children. The spirit in people is eternal and indestructible because the spiritual essence of a human being is created in the image and likeness of God and is perfect and immortal.[12]

CHAPTER FOUR

A Miserable King

For out of prison he cometh to reign; whereas also he that is born in his kingdom becometh poor. Ecc. 4:14.

---

[12]See Ecc. 12:7.

The Eastern Aramaic text reads: "Out of prison he has come to reign, because also in his own kingdom he had been born miserable." The reference here is to a foolish king who has not been brought up well.

Foolish kings in the Near East at times were imprisoned and branded insane by their own rival brothers. When a king died his sons routinely fought over the throne, and the strongest one among them slew or imprisoned the others. Many of the imprisoned princes became insane. Then when the dynasty lacked an heir, one of these mentally challenged men would be brought out and set on the throne. The king had been born and reared in a palace with hundreds of rival and unfriendly half-brothers.

CHAPTER FIVE

Fulfilling of Vows

Better is it that thou shouldest not vow, than that thou shouldest vow and not pay. Suffer not thy mouth to cause thy flesh to sin; neither say thou before the angel, that it was an error: wherefore should God be angry at thy voice, and destroy the work of thine hands? Ecc. 5:5-6.

The Eastern Aramaic text reads "before God" instead of "before the angel." It was considered a sin in the Near East to make a vow and not fulfill it because a vow is a solemn promise made on the name of God, pledging and consecrating something to God. It is a sacred oath that cannot be violated, a promise to God that has to be met. God does not require that anyone make vows in the first place. It is much better not to make a vow than to vow and then delay to fulfill it, or to say, "I did not mean it," or "It was a mistake."

When people are at peace and secure, some of them forget, defer, or even conceal their vows. They may say a vow was made erroneously. Sometimes vows were beyond the ability of the person who made them to fulfill. Such violations were considered an offense before God. This is because Near Easterners met their obligations and paid their taxes and debts. In the modern world, as in the past, they make vows and then offer gifts of meat, bread, money, and other things to fulfill those vows.

CHAPTER SEVEN

Patience and Time

Better is the end of a thing than the beginning thereof: and the patient in spirit is better than the proud in spirit. Ecc. 7:8.

Time is the only thing that can determine the course of events. Some events appear to be inevitable; others are due to cause and effect.

Many events that people call tragedies have a meaning in life, and in the end one may find that they turned out to one's advantage. For example, the selling of Joseph to the Arabians, who in turn sold him in Egypt, at the outset seemed a tragedy for himself and his father, Jacob. But later it proved to be a blessing and salvation to Jacob, his sons, and their families. According to the storyteller, it seems that the tragedy was a part of the divine plan. Had Joseph not been sold, the twelve tribes of Israel would have perished of famine like other tribes that perished during the severe drought. Joseph himself acknowledged it as a part of the divine plan: "Now do not be grieved, nor displeased with yourselves, that you sold me here: for it was to provide for you that God sent me before you."[13] James says: "Blessed is the man that endureth temptation: for when he is tried, he shall receive the crown of life . . ."[14]

Patience and time are keys to much of what happens in life. Patience can solve many problems, avert wars and tragedies, and lead people into the true path of life. But to be patient, one has to be humble and wait for the fulfillment of matters and not be disturbed by their beginnings.

Wisdom Better than Weapons

Wisdom is good with an inheritance: and by it there is profit to them that see the sun. Ecc. 7:11.

The Eastern Aramaic text reads: "Wisdom is better than weapons; yea, it is better for those who see the light of the truth." This saying is still used in some parts of the Near East. One hears: "Wisdom is better than a gun." This is because wisdom offers protection to those who possess it,

---

[13]Gen. 45:5, Eastern Aramaic Peshitta text, Lamsa translation.

[14]James 1:12, K.J.V.

just as a weapon offers protection to the one who carries it. Wisdom is invaluable to those who know the truth and rely on God for protection, health, and prosperity.

In Aramaic "sun" metaphorically means "truth," "the true light of God." The sun is seen by all God's creatures. Even the wicked see the sun, but truth is hidden from them.

CHAPTER EIGHT

The Wise Men

Who is as the wise man? and who knoweth the interpretation of a thing? a man's wisdom maketh his face to shine, and the boldness of his face shall be changed. Ecc. 8:1.

The Eastern Aramaic text reads: "Who is like the wise man? And who knows the interpretation of a thing? A man's wisdom makes his face to shine, but he who is impudent shall be hated."

A wise individual is like a deep sea that cannot be measured with a line. The thoughts and imagination of his or her mind are like remote mountains that can be seen only from a distance.

Truly wise people are humble and lovable. Wisdom makes their faces to shine—that is, to radiate. In the Near East people rejoice to hear wise people speak, and they respect their counsel. But impudent and foolish people are hated when they speak or give counsel, and they cannot look straight into the face of the people.

Immortality Is Essential

Then I commended mirth, because a man hath no better thing under the sun, than to eat, and to drink, and to be merry: for that shall abide with him of his labor the days of his life, which God giveth him under the sun. Ecc. 8:15.

When this book was written ideas of immortality were in their infancy, and very few people thought seriously of another life in the hereafter. In those days life was uncertain and beset with so many difficulties and sorrows that people were reluctant even to consider the possibility of another life—on earth, or anywhere else.

Therefore, kings, princes, and the rich tried to make the best of everything. Their slogan was: "Today we eat, drink, and be merry, and tomorrow we shall die." Nevertheless, they failed to find satisfaction even in riotous living. Therefore, the philosophers and wise men concluded that eating, drinking, and the joys of this life were the only portions that people have on earth. But even that was vanity, because sooner or later people lose all their desires for material things. And just as a human being comes naked into this world, so naked he or she departs this life. Thus, all joys of life are temporal and life is meaningless without the hope of resurrection and life hereafter.

Wondrous Works of God

Then I beheld all the work of God, that a man cannot find out the work that is done under the sun: because though a man labor to seek it out, yet he shall not find it; yea further; though a wise man think to know it, yet shall he not be able to find it. Ecc. 8:17.

God's works are so great, marvelous, and unsearchable that humanity will never be able fully to understand their nature and objectives. This is because a human being is one of God's many wonders. Indeed, God's wisdom is so great and the works so wondrous that there is no way to search out divine wisdom and to expound spiritual understanding.

There are too many things which are wrought under the light of the sun that humans cannot fully discover or understand. Every day reveals new wonders of God. Nevertheless, human beings, during their short stay in this world, have found, understood, and made use of some of them. Hundreds of things that were a mystery in the days of Solomon are now well understood, and many others are partially known. Every day reveals new things, and every night brings forth new knowledge. Humankind lives in a progressive revelation. As one curtain is lowered, another curtain goes up.[15]

---

[15]Job 5:9; Isa. 40:28.

CHAPTER NINE

White Garments

Let thy garments be always white; and let thy head lack no ointment. Ecc. 9:8.

White garments symbolize honesty and piety. The wearer is known as a spotless person. In biblical days, kings, princes, and priests wore white linen garments. Jesus said that those who wear cotton live in palaces.[16]

Rich men, and even poor pious men, anoint their heads daily. Some use olive oil and others use butter. Oil is symbolic of the light of God. Oil also signifies wealth. There are many people who cannot afford to anoint their heads at all. On the other hand, where water is scarce and bathing is unknown, people anoint their heads and bodies frequently to protect them from the rays of the sun.

CHAPTER TEN

Flies and Ointment

Dead flies cause the ointment of the apothecary to send forth a stinking savor: so doth a little folly him that is in reputation for wisdom and honor. Ecc. 10:1.

In biblical lands, jars containing oil, honey, and ointments were often left uncovered or with the cover not secure. Due to unsanitary conditions and lack of water, flies were so abundant that they got into such things.

When ointment, honey, and butter were contaminated with flies, they were rejected by prospective buyers. This is also true of individuals who have wisdom and are honorable. One mistake or folly will be easily noticed by their followers and admirers. Wisdom and knowledge are like precious ointment; they must be kept secure and pure so that they may be imparted to future generations.

---

[16]Mt. 11:8.

Heart—Mind

A wise man's heart is at his right hand; but a fool's heart at his left. Ecc. 10:2.

"Heart" in this instance means "mind." That is to say: "A wise man thinks wisely." To say that a man "walks on the right hand" means that he goes straight. The right hand is symbolic of faithfulness, straightforwardness, and power. The left hand is symbolic of error, wrong thinking, and mistrust. Jesus said: ". . . and he shall separate them one from another, as a shepherd divideth his sheep from the goats; and he shall set the sheep on his right hand, but the goats on the left."[17]

The hearts of all people, whether they are wise or foolish, are of course in the same place. Right hand and left hand symbolize the right way and the wrong way—that is, right thinking and wrong thinking, the good and the bad, those who are chosen and those who are rejected. But it is the mind that is responsible for good and for evil. The mind is the master and the guardian of the body.

Pit and Hedge

He that diggeth a pit shall fall into it; and whoso breaketh a hedge, a serpent shall bite him. Ecc. 10:8.

"Pit" is often used figuratively for "evil" or "mischief." What this verse says is that whoever tries to do evil to his neighbor will himself become the victim of evil.

Pits were common in biblical days and are still seen in many isolated places where Western civilization has not yet penetrated. The pits were to be used as storage for wheat, turnips, and cheese. Some of them were about twelve feet deep and ten feet in diameter and were often left empty and open. They were dug sometimes in secret places by hunters to trap wild game. They were also dug by conspirators who wanted to do away with their enemies. These types of pits were generally covered and concealed so that even the man who dug them might fall into them.[18]

A grain pit might be dug in a village only a few feet from the house of

---

[17]Mt. 25:32-33, K.J.V.
[18]Ezk. 19:8.

its owner. During the winter and spring months when the pit was empty, both men and animals could fall into it, especially during the dark hours of the night.[19] Jesus called the Pharisees "blind guides."[20] When one blind person tries to lead another blind person, both may fall into a pit.[21]

"Hedge" in this instance means boundaries or landmarks. In some lands a hedge was the only landmark between two fields. Near Easterners were afraid to trespass the boundaries between houses and remove the landmarks between the fields. Snakes generally were found in hedges and in heaps of stones that were used as landmarks.

Buying and Selling

The labor of the foolish wearieth every one of them, because he knoweth not how to go to the city. Ecc. 10:15.

The Eastern Aramaic text reads: "The labor of fools wears them out because they do not know how to buy and sell in the city." "Knoweth not how to go to the city" is a Near Eastern idiom that means they were not wise enough to buy or sell when they were in the city. Until recent days, there were no commission houses or middlemen. Farmers, artisans, and pastoral people brought their produce to the city where they sold it or exchanged it themselves.

Bartering and bargaining were extremely difficult, especially for farmers and people who came to the cities from far off villages and country places. These simple peasants were often cheated. Even today when buying or selling, many Near Easterners seek the services of shrewd and experienced businessmen. The articles to be sold or exchanged have certain values, and the price is determined through bargaining. The foolish and the simple are easily duped by shrewd and wise merchants.

Eating in the Morning

Woe to thee, O land, when thy king is a child, and thy princes eat in the morning! Blessed art thou, O land, when thy king is the son of nobles, and thy princes eat in due season, for strength, and not for drunkenness! Ecc. 10:16-17.

---

[19]Ex. 21:33-34.
[20]Mt. 23:16-17.
[21]Mt. 15:14; Lk. 6:39.

Near Easterners seldom ate much breakfast. They arose early to go to work and were satisfied with just enough to break their fast. "Breakfast" in colloquial Aramaic is called *taamta,* "to taste." A morsel or a mouthful of bread and a little cheese or buttermilk was a sufficient breakfast. Meat, cereals, and eggs were seldom eaten. The heavy meal was eaten at noon.

In the modern Near East many men break their fast with a cup of Turkish coffee, a piece of bread, and a little cheese. But those who drink alcoholic beverages start the day with a heavy meal. This is because when Near Easterners drink, they also eat, and the more they eat, the more they drink. Breakfast is eaten not so much because they need the food but because of the wine or strong drink.

When the Apostles were accused of being drunk,[22] Peter said: "For these are not drunken, as ye suppose, seeing it is but the third hour of the day."[23]

Money Brings One Low

A feast is made for laughter, and wine maketh merry: but money answereth all things. Ecc. 10:19.

The Eastern Aramaic text reads: "Bread and wine are made for joy, and oil makes life merry; but money brings one low and causes him to go astray in all things." Evidently this passage was forged to encourage people to give more money to religious and other institutions. The passage is so simple, the error could not have been caused by translators.

Jesus called money the wicked mammon of this world. In his day most wealth was acquired by deceitful and unjust means, bribes, and cheating.

Paul called wealth filthy lucre. There is nothing wrong with money, but the love of it is wrong. Some people worship it as their god and others sell their souls to acquire it. Money can cause people to go astray, and instead of using their wealth for the glory of God and the good of humanity, they use it to destroy themselves in riotous living.

---

[22]Acts 2:13-15.

[23]About 9:00 a.m. See Acts 2:15.

CHAPTER ELEVEN

Bread Cast upon the Water

Cast thy bread upon the waters: for thou shalt find it after many days. Ecc. 11:1.

"Cast your bread upon the waters; for you shall find it after many days" means, "Do good to others and some day when you are in need they will come back to help you."

It often happens that a person returning home in the last stage of a journey, while eating beside a winding stream or a river, throws a few dry loaves of bread upon the water, thinking they will not be needed. Hours later, continuing the journey toward home, the person may become hungry and might find floating on the water the same loaves that had been thrown away and, of course, picks them up and eats them.

At times the road is beset with difficulties and travelers are delayed. There are many winding streams in some lands. The Jordan is a winding river.

But the thought here is that good comes back again to the person who does good. It may not come the same day, but it will come some day when the person is in need. David recompensed Biham, the son of Barzilai, for what his father had done for David.[24] The law of compensation is an immutable law. It is just as sure as the shining of the sun. Good always produces good, and evil produces evil. Man reaps what he sows. Jesus said, "Give, and it shall be given unto you . . ."[25]

The Way of the Wind

As thou knowest not what is the way of the spirit, nor how the bones do grow in the womb of her that is with child: even so thou knowest not the works of God who maketh all. Ecc. 11:5.

The same Aramaic word that means "spirit" also means "wind, pride, rheumatism."[26] The term *ruha* has been mistranslated many times. In

[24]2 Sam. 19:31-40.

[25]Lk. 6:38.

[26]See Lk. 13:11, Eastern Aramaic Peshitta text, Lamsa translation.

this instance *ruha* means "wind." This is because no one knows its way; that is to say, no one knows where it originates or where it goes.

Modern scientific instruments, such as radar, have revealed some of the hidden secrets of the wind. The translators of the King James Version no doubt misunderstood the meaning of the term *ruha*.

Jesus quoted this passage when he said: "The wind blows where it pleases, and you hear its sound; but you do not know whence it comes and whither it goes; such is every man who is born of the Spirit."[27]

The works of God are more mysterious than those of the wind. Things do not happen by of chance. There is a hidden reason in all occurrences.

CHAPTER TWELVE

Old Age

While the sun, or the light, or the moon, or the stars, be not darkened, nor the clouds return after the rain. Ecc. 12:2.

In this instance "sun" symbolizes beauty, glory, and majesty. Stars and moon denote fortune and success. In the Near East when a man's beauty fades and his glory passes away, it is said, "His sun has set and his stars have disappeared behind the horizon." This means that he has lost his good looks, power, and fortune. Clouds symbolize sorrows; they stop the light of the sun. The author of Ecclesiastes is writing about men who are advanced in years and fast declining in strength, fame, beauty, and wealth.

In those days, like today, it was commonly believed that the stars had something to do with a man's rise and decline, and with his birth, strength, and fortune.[28] Astrology is one of the oldest sciences, and is just as ancient as the Bible. The people in the ancient days traveled by the stars and, at times, were warned and guided by them.

Parts of the Body

In the day when the keepers of the house shall tremble, and the strong men

---

[27]Jn. 3:8, Eastern Aramaic Peshitta text, Lamsa translation

[28]Mt. 2:2.

shall bow themselves, and the grinders cease because they are few, and those that look out of the windows be darkened. Ecc. 12:3.

This is one of the most poetic passages in all of King Solomon's writings. The members of the human body are described subtly in allegories. "The keepers of the house" are the legs, "the strong men" are the arms, "the grinders" are the teeth, and "those that look out of the windows" are the eyes. Many of King Solomon's sayings were written in figurative language and were well understood by the readers. In those days, the wise were able to understand proverbs, riddles, dark sayings and their interpretations.

The author of Ecclesiastes is speaking of old age, when legs and arms become feeble and eyes become dim. The people are admonished to remember the Creator while still young, strong, and sound in health, and not to wait until becoming so old and burdened with the physical body that they cannot pray and are too weary and poor to offer sacrifices.

Deafness

And the doors shall be shut in the streets, when the sound of the grinding is low, and he shall rise up at the voice of the bird, and all the daughters of music shall be brought low. Ecc. 12:4.

"The doors" in this verse refer to old age, when an elderly man cannot go out and his hearing becomes so dull that the sound of the grinding of the hand mill and the noise of singing, dancing, and rejoicing of young women is low—that is, when the elderly man can no longer recognize musical tones and melodies.[29]

In the Near East many families live together. Dancing, grinding, and cooking are done under the same roof. The elderly men live together with the young and at times become nervous and greatly disturbed. During the night even the sound of the chirping of a bird may awaken them.

The Almond Tree

Also when they shall be afraid of that which is high, and fears shall be in the way, and the almond tree shall flourish, and the grasshopper shall be a burden,

---

[29]2 Sam. 19:35.

and desire shall fail: because man goeth to his long home, and the mourners go about the streets. Ecc. 12:5.

The almond tree is symbolic of man's maturity and fruitfulness. The almond tree produces abundant blossoms. The middle of the Aramaic text reads: ". . . the almond tree shall blossom, and the locust shall be multiplied and fragrance shall scatter, and trouble shall cease . . ."

"The almond tree shall blossom" means that a man will begin having many children. "The locust" and "fragrance" are symbolic of children, grandchildren, and great-grandchildren, which some of the old men see before they pass away. The daughters marry and spread the fame of the old man abroad. In the Near East some men marry at the age of nine or ten and live to be 120 or 130. By the time they are old, the house is filled with children, grandchildren, and great-grandchildren.

King Ahab and Gideon had 70 male children each. Even after World War I there were some Near Eastern kings and princes with 500 to 600 children.

A human being encounters various troubles, challenges, and struggles from the day of birth until the day of death. And when an individual goes to his or her everlasting home, all troubles and worries are left behind.

Pitcher Broken

Or ever the silver cord be loosed, or the golden bowl be broken, or the pitcher be broken at the fountain, or the wheel broken at the cistern. Ecc. 12:6.

"The pitcher" here symbolizes the earthly life, the body in which the soul dwells. A human being was often likened to a vessel. This is because vessels were made of clay, and a person's body was created from the red earth. In the Near East water was brought from wells, cisterns, and brooks on the heads or the shoulders of women. As a maiden placed the vessel on her shoulder or on her head, often it would fall and break near the well. The maiden then returned home sad and empty-handed. In that part of the world such a vessel was important. Some women even cried over a good vessel. But once it was broken at the well, the fragments were left there.

Silver cord or thread was used for the weaving of costly brocades. It ran through the cloth from one end to the other. When it was cut off, the weaver stopped weaving. The golden bowl was a family heirloom. Allegorically, the thread and the bowl mean life. This is because life is more precious than all man's possessions on earth.

Solomon explains the period of man's old age figuratively. What is implied is this: A man in his declining years loses his potency and is no longer able to have intercourse. All physical organs weaken and therefore cannot function. When speaking of the human anatomy, and particularly of human sexual organs, Near Easterners used metaphors and idiomatic terms of speech.

Words of the Wise

The words of the wise are as goads, and as nails fastened by the masters of assemblies, which are given from one shepherd. Ecc. 12:11.

The Eastern Aramaic text reads: "The words of the wise are as goads, and as nails deeply fastened, which are arranged by workmen and given from one master builder."

In the Near East donkeys were driven by goads. When the animal stopped, the rider jabbed it in the back. All men traveling in a caravan carried goads. King Solomon compared the words of the wise to goads because as the goads caused the animals to move faster, so the words of the wise awaken people's faculties and guide them in the right way. He also likened the words of the wise to nails that were deeply fastened by expert builders who received knowledge from one master builder.

INTRODUCTION TO SONG OF SOLOMON

The title of the book is clearly stated in the first verse, which was added to the book by the copyist or the compiler. For many centuries these songs have been known as the *Song of Solomon, the King of Israel.*

King Solomon was a wise man, poet, and philosopher, who knew every part of his land and every phase of life. He was also a lover of nature. The author of the book is familiar with the beauty of the land in northern Israel and Lebanon. That is why he mentions Tirza, Carmel, and Lebanon. Lebanon is one of the most beautiful lands in the world. Fertile valleys, lush fields, trees, vines, and cedars grace the country. Streams and brooks are also abundant. The regions of Tirza and Galilee are also beautiful and prolific when compared with the stony land of Judah.

The book is rich in poetic philosophy in which deep and sincere love is generously and vividly expressed. Early Christian authorities believed that Solomon's songs were composed about the Christ and his bride, the church. A Jewish interpretation is that the love relationship in this book is employed as a metaphor for the relationship between God and Israel. Be that as it may, the Song of Songs deserves its caption. Its style and beauty have never been surpassed. Indeed, only a wise and experienced king like Solomon, who had made a deep study of nature, the world, and humankind, could have written such a song as this, with its profound and lasting spiritual meaning.[1]

CHAPTER ONE

Sunburn

Look not upon me, because I am black, because the sun hath looked upon me: my mother's children were angry with me; they made me the keeper of the vineyards; but mine own vineyard have I not kept. Sol. 1:6.

---

[1]For many years Jewish and Christian scholars have debated the history and origin of the Song of Solomon. Dating of the book is unknown and the suggested dates are also highly debated. As with the books of Proverbs and Ecclesiastes, biblical historians do not believe King Solomon is the author of the book.

The sun is very hot in Israel and Arabia during the summer months. In that part of the world the days are warm and the nights are cold. Consequently, the vineyard keepers and people in general who live an outdoor life with their flocks are sunburned.

During the summer season when grapes are ripening, the whole family leaves the town home and moves into small cottages or booths that are constructed in the vineyard. They do this to escape the heat and to protect the vineyard from thieves and travelers who might steal the grapes.

"Vineyard" is also used allegorically, meaning "my beloved." Israel was called God's vineyard. "Now I will sing to my well-beloved a song of my beloved concerning his vineyard. My well-beloved had a vineyard on the corner of a fertile land."[2] Metaphorically, the vineyard and the garden also mean "a beloved one" or "wife."

CHAPTER TWO

Apples

Stay me with flagons, comfort me with apples; for I am sick of love. Sol. 2:5.

The Eastern Aramaic text reads: "Sustain me with delicacies, surround me with apples; for I am sick for love." The phrase "sick of love" is incorrect.

Apples were used by Near Eastern poets as a symbol of love. When the bride entered her future home, the bridegroom stood on the roof, and as the bride approached the door of the home, he threw an apple to her. The apple might be caught by one of the young people who was following in the bridal procession.

During wedding feasts an artificial tree was constructed and all its branches were decorated with beautiful apples and delicacies. As the festivities progressed, the tree was broken and the apples and sweet foods were divided among the guests. When a man was in love with a girl, he would give her an apple. Candies were unknown in those ancient days, and dates and other sweet foods were used for confection.

---

[2]Isa. 5:1, Eastern Aramaic Peshitta text, Lamsa translation.

Turtle Dove

The flowers appear on the earth; the time of the singing of birds is come, and the voice of the turtle is heard in our land. Sol. 2:12.

The Eastern Aramaic text reads: "The flowers appear on the earth; the time of pruning has come, and the voice of the turtledove is heard in our land." "The voice of the turtle" is an incorrect translation. The turtledove is like a pigeon.

The significance of the voice of the turtledove points to the fact that spring had come and joy was at hand. Spring is the mating season for birds. Nature, at this time, is so beautiful and friendly. Most marriages were made in the springtime.

Also, a turtledove was offered as a sacrifice for the redemption of the firstborn male. When Jesus of Nazareth was brought to the temple, Joseph and Mary, being poor, could only afford a turtledove.

CHAPTER THREE

The Watchmen

The watchmen that go about the city found me: to whom I said, Saw ye him whom my soul loveth? Sol. 3:3.

In the Near East the night guards patrolled the dark and crooked streets of the walled cities, beating a drum as a warning to the people not to walk in the streets during the night hours.

Only city officials, noblemen, and those who in advance had obtained the name of the night could walk freely. Every night was given a name, and those who failed to know the name of the night were detained by the watchmen. This custom prevailed until after World War I.

Palace in Lebanon

King Solomon made himself a chariot of the wood of Lebanon. He made the pillars thereof of silver, the bottom thereof of gold, the covering of it of purple, the midst thereof being paved with love, for the daughters of Jerusalem.
Sol. 3:9-10.

The Aramaic word *magdla* means "a palace or tower," but the King James Version mistakenly reads "chariot." The Eastern Aramaic text reads: "King Solomon made himself a palace of wood of Lebanon." "He built also the house of the forest of Lebanon; its length was a hundred cubits and its breadth fifty cubits and its height thirty cubits, upon four rows of cedar pillars, with cedar beams upon the pillars."[3]

The reference here is to the house that Solomon built of cedars of Lebanon. Solomon ruled over all the lands from the Great Sea (Mediterranean) to the River Euphrates.

CHAPTER FOUR

Encouraged by His Beloved

Thou hast ravished my heart, my sister, my spouse; thou hast ravished my heart with one of thine eyes, with one chain of thy neck. Sol. 4:9.

The Aramaic text reads *labewteni* and means, "you have encouraged me." The same word also means "comforted or consoled."

Maidens in the Near East are very shy. They seldom see or talk to their fiances. But the more retiring they are, the more they are sought by their lovers. When a girl is in love she may secretly encourage her lover to see her. On such an occasion the girl may make signs with her eyes.

"Honey" a Figure of Speech

Thy lips, O my spouse, drop as the honeycomb: honey and milk are under thy tongue; and the smell of thy garments is like the smell of Lebanon. Sol. 4:11.

"Honey" in this instance is a metaphor meaning "sweet speech." Honey drops gently from the honeycomb, and as it drops, those who see it are eager to eat it. Near Eastern people often say, "His words are like honey; his speech is sweet."

Milk in Semitic languages is symbolic of wisdom, innocence, and sincerity because its appearance is white and pure. Milk is a natural food prepared by God for babies and little children who cannot yet eat other

---

[3]1 Ki. 7:2, Eastern Aramaic Peshitta text, Lamsa translation.

food. Words spoken with sincerity were considered pure like milk and sweet like honey that drips from a honeycomb.

Isaiah says: "Butter and honey shall he eat . . ."[4] "My son, eat thou honey, because it is good; and the honeycomb, which is sweet to thy taste."[5] Words of wisdom are sweet to the ear of the wise, just as honey is sweet to the palate.

Garden, a Wife

A garden enclosed is my sister, my spouse; a spring shut up, a fountain sealed. Sol. 4:12.

The Aramaic term "garden" is used figuratively, meaning "a wife." In the Near East a wife is often called a garden and the husband, keeper of the garden. Even today, Near Eastern poets and composers still use the term garden referring to a wife or a beloved one. "I am come into my garden . . ." means, "I am with my beloved."[6]

CHAPTER FIVE

Visiting at Night

I sleep, but my heart waketh: it is the voice of my beloved that knocketh, saying, Open to me, my sister, my love, my dove, my undefiled: for my head is filled with dew, and my locks with the drops of the night. Sol. 5:2.

In the Near East no man could visit his sweetheart in the daytime. Near Easterners would gossip if they saw a man talking to a young woman, and such gossip was destructive to the reputation of the maiden and her parents. Nevertheless, some lovers dared to visit each other during the dark hours of night when the streets were empty and everyone was asleep.

The dew here is symbolic of late hours when the dew falls on the ground. The two lovers would meet in a secret place near the door, in the

---

[4]Isa. 7:15, K.J.V.
[5]Prov. 24:13, K.J.V.
[6]See Sol. 5:1.

silence of the night.

A Heart Moved by Love

My beloved put in his hand by the hole of the door, and my bowels were moved for him. Sol. 5:4.

In the Near East both doors and keys were made of wood. There was a hole about a foot long and six inches wide between the doorpost and the door. The wooden lock was constructed in this hole in the side of the door. One had to put one's hand into the hole in order to reach the lock. As the wooden key was large and the hole in the lock long, the opening caused a noise. Bandits and thieves used keys made of stiff hair when robbing a home, so those in the house might not be awakened. In this verse, the girl waits on her bed, expecting her beloved to place the key into the lock.

The Aramaic term *rahmeh*, "bowels," has many meanings; we need to understand the context to translate this word correctly into English. Rahmah is singular and rahmeh is plural. The word can mean "friends, bowels, womb, bladder, testicles," and a few other meanings. Metaphorically, however, the word signifies "love, passion, mercy, kindness, affection, compassion, tender-heartedness, benevolence, friendliness."

"My bowels were moved for him" may be translated as, "my heart was moved for him when I heard the noise of the key," or "my passions stirred when I heard my beloved at the door." The translators of the King James Version rendered the word literally as "bowels."

Night Watchmen

The watchmen that went about the city found me, they smote me, they wounded me; the keepers of the walls took away my veil from me. I charge you, O daughters of Jerusalem, if ye find my beloved, that ye tell him, that I am sick of love. Sol. 5:7-8.

All walled cities in the Near East have night watchmen who would guard the shops and marketplaces until dawn. Two or three of them went together about the city, beating on a small drum in a peculiar sound that announced their presence.

When the watchmen would meet strangers in the street, they arrested them. Even inhabitants of the city who were late might be arrested and beaten if they failed to know the number or the sign of the night.

All those who thought that they might have to arrive home late at night had to ask for the sign of the night so that they wouldn't be arrested. Then again, some of the guards were stationed on the wall near the city gates, and the doors of the gate were closed and locked.

At times spies and dangerous men would try to enter the city disguised in women's attire. When the night guards suspected them, they removed their veils. Of course, in modern times in most cities, the night watchmen have been replaced by policemen.

The maid was so much in love with her beloved that she sought him regardless of the dangers and difficulties during the night hours when even men dared not walk abroad and confront the night watchmen.

CHAPTER SIX

Beautiful and Desirable

Thou art beautiful, O my love, as Tirzah, comely as Jerusalem, terrible as an army with banners. Sol. 6:4.

The Eastern Aramaic text reads: "You are beautiful and desirable, O my beloved, comely as Jerusalem, and esteemed [or revered] as one chosen among beauties."

The term "Tirzah" in the King James Version is a mistranslation of the Aramaic word *sebyana,* "delight." Tirzah was the name of the youngest daughter of Zelophehad.[7] The first capitol of the northern kingdom was named Tirzah, and Jeroboam, the founder of the kingdom, dwelt there. King Jeroboam may have beautified the city, but this would have been after the death of King Solomon. Fair women in the Near East were often likened to beautiful cities.

Black Hair

Turn away thine eyes from me, for they have overcome me: thy hair is as a flock of goats that appear from Gilead. Sol. 6:5.

---

[7]Num. 26:33.

Women with black hair were greatly admired in biblical lands and other parts of the Near East. Blond hair was so rare that men or women who had blond hair were looked upon as strangers. The few blond-haired and blue-eyed men and women who are found today in the holy lands and Arabia are the descendants of Roman soldiers and the Crusaders.

Goats in biblical lands are very black. A flock of goats looks beautiful when led by the shepherd to and from the mountain. The black color stands out conspicuously against light brown earth and faded grass. In the same way, a fair maiden with long black hair stands out among women.

Public Chariot

Or ever I was aware, my soul made me like the chariots of Amminadib. Sol. 6:12.

The term *amminadib* is a mis-transliteration of *di amma,* meaning "of the people," that is, "a public chariot." The Eastern Aramaic text reads: "And being unfamiliar with the place, I sat in the public chariot which was ready." Evidently, chariots and wagons were used for transportation during the reign of King Solomon, about 1000 BCE.

The Assyrians and Babylonians used wagons for transport of military supplies, and chariots for war. The Egyptians were noted for the manufacture of beautiful gilded chariots. Joseph sent Egyptian wagons to bring his father, Jacob, and his brothers and their families from the land of Canaan to Egypt about 2000 BCE.[8]

CHAPTER SEVEN

Damascus

Thy navel is like a round goblet, which wanteth not liquor: thy belly is like a heap of wheat set about with lilies. Thy two breasts are like two young roes that are twins. Thy neck is as a tower of ivory; thine eyes like the fishpools in Heshbon, by the gate of Bath-rabbim: thy nose is as the tower of Lebanon which looketh toward Damascus. Sol. 7:2-4.

---

[8]See Gen. 45:19.

The Aramaic word *bartha* (pronounced bath), "daughter," is often used for "a city." For example: "the daughter of Babylon" (*Bath Babel*),[9] "the daughter of Zion,"[10] and "Harken, O daughter."[11]

Barth sagiaey, "the daughter of many," means "the city with many inhabitants." During the time of King Solomon, Damascus was a great metropolis and the oldest city in the world. It was like an emerald encased in a yellow-gold setting, a paradise in the heart of the arid desert. The other Aramaic word for "many" is *rabeh.* In Semitic languages parts of the body were often portrayed metaphorically.

CHAPTER EIGHT

Kissing

O that thou wert as my brother, that sucked the breasts of my mother! when I should find thee without, I would kiss thee; yea, I should not be despised. Sol. 8:1.

In biblical lands girls could not commune with or court their lovers, nor could they kiss them prior to their marriage. The only male a girl could openly converse with was a close relative, and the only one she could kiss was her brother or possibly a close cousin. Even in the modern Near East this custom still prevails.

When girls met their brothers returning from a journey, they would kiss them, but they were not allowed to speak to or to keep company with their lovers or strangers. All arrangements for a marriage were made by the parents.[12]

Under the Apple Tree

Who is this that cometh up from the wilderness, leaning upon her beloved? I raised thee up under the apple tree: there thy mother brought thee forth; there she brought thee forth that bare thee. Sol. 8:5.

---

[9]See Jer. 50:42; 51:33.

[10]Ps. 9:14.

[11]Ps. 45:10, K.J.V.

[12]See Sol. 4:9 and 5:2.

"Under the apple tree" means under the protection of the shadow of an apple tree. During hot summer months in the Near East, babies and small children were put under fig or apple trees to protect them from the sun. The shade of an apple tree was considered cool and refreshing. The sick and the weary also sought the protection of the shadow of trees, especially the apple tree. Jesus said to Nathaniel, "When thou wast under the fig tree, I saw thee."[13] For many centuries trees were worshiped.

The apple is symbolic of love, beauty, and tender care.[14] "Keep me as the apple of thine eye; hide me under the shadow of thy wings."[15] Beloved ones are spoken of as the apple of the eye. "Let not the apple of your eye cease from shedding tears."[16] In the Near East during marriage feasts the bridegroom throws an apple to the bride. This is because an apple is desired more than any other fruit.

Seal

Set me as a seal upon thine heart, as a seal upon thine arm; for love is strong as death; jealousy is cruel as the grave: the coals thereof are coals of fire, which hath a most vehement flame. Sol. 8:6.

The Eastern Aramaic text reads: "Set me as a seal upon your heart, as a seal upon your arm; for love is strong as death; desire is cruel as Sheol; its flashes are flashes of fire and flame."

"Seal upon your heart" means to be in one's mind for good and that the person will always be remembered. "Seal on your arm" means to be loved with all one's strength and might. Seals were precious objects and were well guarded. The arm signifies strength and power. Love is unconquerable, and it must take its course.

Jealousy is a mistranslation. It should read "desire." Desire was considered too strong to be defeated, and it was likened to Sheol.

---

[13]Jn. 1:48, K.J.V.

[14]Dt. 32:10.

[15]Ps. 17:8, K.J.V.

[16]Lam. 2:18, Eastern Aramaic Peshitta text, Lamsa translation.

Physical Immaturity

We have a little sister, and she hath no breasts: what shall we do for our sister in the day when she shall be spoken for? Sol. 8:8.

"She hath no breasts" means that the young girl had not matured bodily. In the Near East physically matured women were known by the size of their breasts. "In the day when she shall be spoken for" means when she is sought in marriage or betrothed. It should read: ". . . in the day when they shall seek her hand."

Near Eastern girls who were ready to be married could not be seen either by their prospective bridegrooms or by the matchmakers. Those who arranged a marriage for a son had to take a chance. It was like buying an article without seeing it. Then again, women could be rejected or divorced on account of certain physical deficiencies. Near Easterners liked heavyset women with large breasts.[17]

The little sister in this verse has been rejected for a marriage because of her lack of breasts. Nonetheless she would be taken care of until the day she has physically matured and is fully ready to become a prospective bride.

Large Breasts

I am a wall, and my breasts like towers: then was I in his eyes as one that found favor. Sol. 8:10.

In the Near East the larger a woman's breasts were, the more they were preferred. Not many years ago, women used to wear many garments just so they could appear well breasted and heavyset. On a wedding day the bride was attired with many garments and covered with a heavy veil.

Moreover, women with large breasts were considered beauties and were desired by kings, princes, and the wealthy classes. This was also true in many European countries and in some parts of South America.

---

[17]See verse 10.

Vineyards Leased

Solomon had a vineyard at Baal-hamon; he let out the vineyard unto keepers; every one for the fruit thereof was to bring a thousand pieces of silver. Sol. 8:11.

The Eastern Aramaic text reads: ". . . and its fruits were abundant." *Baal-hamon* is a translation of the Aramaic word *ebey,* "its produce." Baal was the god of fertility and farming, but the reference here is to the abundant fruits. Solomon's vineyard was very fertile. The Aramaic reads: ". . . he let out the vineyard to keepers; a man offered for its fruits a thousand pieces of silver."

Vineyards, orchards, and large gardens in the Near East belonged to wealthy landowners and princes who seldom bothered with the fruit. When the fruit was ripe, many vineyards, orchards, and produce fields were leased to professional contractors, who took care of them or hired workers to watch over them, gather their fruit, and sell it in the market for a profit.

In Aramaic the vineyard is symbolic of one's beloved, and the song is a vivid poetic description of the relationships of lovers. Near Easterners, in such cases, used poetic and figurative speech, which was easily understood by the uneducated public.

Many followers of Jesus considered this poetry a figurative expression of the relation between Christ and his church. Jesus loved his church so much that he died for it. The Song of Solomon thus has a profound spiritual meaning for those who read it spiritually.

BIBLIOGRAPHY

Freedman, David Noel, Editor in Chief, *Anchor Bible Dictionary,* New York: Doubleday, 1997.

Hitti, Philip K. *The Near East in History,* A 5000 Year Story. Princeton, New Jersey: Prentice Hall, 1964.

Lamsa, George M. *Old Testament Light:* A Scriptural Commentary based on the Aramaic of the Ancient Peshitta Text. Englewood Cliffs, New Jersey: Prentice Hall, 1964.

Sarna, Nahum M., *On the Book of Psalms:* Exploring the Prayers of Ancient Israel. New York: Schocken Books, 1993.

Zeitlan, Irving M. *Ancient Judaism.* Oxford: Polity Press, Basil Blackwell, 1984.

The Jewish Study Bible, Featuring the Jewish Publication Society, Tanakh Translation, Torah, Nevim and Kethuvim, New York, Oxford, University Press, 2004.

The Holy Bible: From Ancient Eastern Manuscripts. George M. Lamsa, translator. A. J. Holman Company, Philadelphia 1957.

ABOUT THE AUTHOR

George M. Lamsa

George M. Lamsa, Th.D., a renowned native Assyrian scholar of the Holy Bible, translator, lecturer, ethnologist, and author, was born August 5, 1892 in a civilization with customs, manners and language almost identical to those in the time of Jesus. His native tongue, Aramaic, was filled with similar idioms and parables, untouched by the outside world in 1900 years.

Until World War 1, his people living in that part of the ancient biblical lands that today is known as Kurdistan, in the basin of the rivers Tigris and Euphrates, retained the simple nomadic life as in the days of the Hebrew patriarchs. Only at the beginning of the 20th century did the isolated segment of the once great Assyrian Empire learn of the discovery of America and the Reformation in Germany.

Likewise, until that same time, this ancient culture of early Christians was unknown to the Western world, and the Aramaic language was thought to be dead. But in this so-called "Cradle of Civilization," primitive biblical customs and Semitic culture, cut off from the world, were preserved.

Lamsa's primary upbringing as a boy was to tend the lambs. But as the first-born in his family, while yet an infant he was dedicated to God by his devout mother. Years after her death, when Lamsa was 12 years of age, her vow was renewed by native tribesmen, an ox killed, and its blood rubbed on his forehead. Lamsa claimed this vow to God had always been part of him. "God's hand," he affirmed, "has been steadfastly on my shoulder, guiding me in the divine work."

Lamsa's formal education and studies began under the priests and deacons of the ancient Church of the East. Later he graduated with the highest honors ever bestowed from the Archbishop of Canterbury's Colleges in Iran and in Turkey, with the degree of Bachelor of Arts. Lamsa never married, but dedicated his life to "God's calling." He spoke eight languages and his lowest grade in any subject was 99.

At the beginning of World War 1, when Turkey began its invasions, Lamsa was forced to flee the Imperial University at Constantinople where he was studying. He went to South America where he endured great hardships during those years. He knew but three words in Spanish at that time—water, work, and bread. As best as he could he existed—in the British Merchant Marine for a time, then working on railroads, in mines, and later in printing shops, a trade he had learned while attending college in Iran.

After arriving in the United States in his early 20s, Lamsa worked by day as a printer, and by night he went to school. He later studied at the Episcopal Theological Seminary in Alexandria, Virginia, and at Dropsie College in Philadelphia.

It was through his struggles, during these years, with the English idioms that Lamsa gradually launched into his "life's work" of translating the Holy Bible from Aramaic into English. Yet many years were to pass before the world received his translations.

First as a lecturer in churches and seminaries, in halls and auditoriums, before statesmen, theologians, groups of artists, actors and others, Lamsa received recognition as a poet-philosopher and as an authority on all phases of Near Eastern civilization.

It was his own inner compulsion, and the urging of hundreds who heard him, that drove him forward and brought about—after 30 years of labor, research and study—his translation of the Holy Bible from a branch of the ancient Aramaic language that Jesus and the earliest Christians used.

There were times, when the idioms in the manuscripts could not be given correct English equivalents, that he was temporarily stopped in his translations. It was Lamsa's firm belief that his translation from Aramaic would bring people closer to the Word of God and would facilitate understanding between the East and the West. For forty years, he produced commentaries and many other works based on the Aramaic language. The last ten years of his life, Dr. Lamsa tutored and prepared Dr. Rocco A. Errico to continue with the Aramaic approach to Scripture. He left this earthly life on September 22, 1975, in Turlock, California.

ABOUT THE AUTHOR

Rocco A. Errico

Dr. Rocco A. Errico is an ordained minister, international lecturer and author, spiritual counselor, and one of the nation's leading Biblical scholars working from the original Aramaic *Peshitta* texts. For ten years he studied intensively with Dr. George M. Lamsa, Th.D., (1890-1975), world-renowned Assyrian biblical scholar and translator of the *Holy Bible from the Ancient Eastern Text.*

Dr. Errico is proficient in Aramaic and Hebrew exegesis, helping thousands of readers and seminar participants understand how the Semitic context of culture, language, idioms, symbolism, mystical style, psychology, and literary amplification—the *Seven Keys* that unlock the Bible—are essential to understanding this ancient spiritual document.

Dr. Errico is the recipient of numerous awards and academic degrees, including a Doctorate in Philosophy from the School of Christianity in Los Angeles; a Doctorate in Divinity from St. Ephrem's Institute in Sweden; and a Doctorate in Sacred Theology from the School of Christianity in Los Angeles. In 1993, the American Apostolic University College of Seminarians awarded him a Doctorate of Letters. He also holds a special title of Teacher, Prime Exegete, *Maplana d'miltha dalaha*, among the Federation of St. Thomas Christians of the order of Antioch. In 2002, Dr. Errico was inducted into the Morehouse College Collegium of Scholars.

Dr. Errico is a featured speaker at conferences, symposia, and seminars throughout the United States, Canada, Mexico and Europe and has been a regular contributor for over 28 years to *Science of Mind Magazine*, a monthly journal founded in 1927. He began his practice as an ordained minister and pastoral counselor in the mid-1950s and during the next three decades served in churches and missions in Missouri, Texas, Mexico, and California. Throughout his public work, Dr. Errico has stressed the nonsectarian, *open* interpretation of Biblical spirituality, prying it free from 2000 years of rigid orthodoxy, which, according to his research, is founded on incorrect translations of the original Aramaic texts.

In 1970, Dr. Errico established the Noohra Foundation in San Antonio, Texas, as a non-profit, non-sectarian spiritual-educational organization devoted to helping people of all faiths to understand the Near Eastern background and Aramaic interpretation of the Bible. In 1976, Dr. Errico relocated the Noohra Foundation in Irvine, California, where it flourished for the next 17 years. For seven years, the Noohra Foundation operated in Santa Fe, New Mexico, and in September 2001, it relocated to Smyrna, Georgia, where Dr. Errico is Dean of Biblical Studies for Dr. Barbara King's School of Ministry—Hillside Chapel and Truth Center in Atlanta.

Under the auspices of the Noohra Foundation, Dr. Errico continues to lecture for colleges, civic groups and churches of various denominations in the United States, Canada, Mexico and Europe.

For a complimentary catalog of Aramaic Bible translations, books, audio and video cassettes, CDs and DVDs, to receive mailings of classes, retreats and future publications, or for any other inquiries, write, call, or email the Noohra Foundation. Those interested in scheduling Dr. Errico for a personal appearance may also contact:

Noohra Foundation
PMB 343
4480 S Cobb Dr SE Ste H
Smyrna, Georgia 30080

Phone: 678-945-4006
Fax: 678-945-4966

email: info@noohra.com or noohrafoundation@yahoo.com
Noohra Foundation website: www.noohra.com

In addition to this commentary, the Noohra Foundation is pleased to offer the following books by Dr. Rocco A. Errico and Dr. George M. Lamsa.

COMMENTARIES BY DR. ERRICO & DR. LAMSA

(NEW TESTAMENT) **Aramaic Light on the Gospel of Matthew, Aramaic Light on the Gospels of Mark and Luke, Aramaic Light on the Gospel of John, Aramaic Light on the Acts of the Apostles, Aramaic Light on Romans through 2 Corinthians, Aramaic Light on Galatians through Hebrews, Aramaic Light on James through Revelation**, (OLD TESTAMENT) **Aramaic Light on Genesis, Aramaic Light on Exodus through Deuteronomy, Aramaic Light on Joshua through 2 Chronicles.**

BOOKS BY DR. ERRICO:

Let There Be Light: The Seven Keys

In this illuminating work, Dr. Errico presents seven key insights to understand the allusions, parables, and teachings of the Bible, opening the door to the ancient Aramaic world from which the Bible emerged.

And There Was Light

Like its predecessor, *Let There Be Light*, this book unlocks puzzling passages with the Seven Keys. The Bible now becomes clearer and more relevant for Western readers, and the teaching ministry and parables of Jesus come alive as never before.

Setting a Trap for God: The Aramaic Prayer of Jesus

Dr. Errico explains the meaning of the Lord's Prayer based on the Aramaic language and ancient culture of the Near East. Discover the way of peace, health, and prosperity as you learn to "set a trap" for the inexhaustible power of God.

The Mysteries of Creation: The Genesis Story

A challenging new look at the processes and mysteries of the primal creation account. Dr. Errico uses his own direct translation from the Aramaic-Peshitta text of Genesis 1:1-31 and 2:1-3.

The Message of Matthew: An Annotated Parallel Aramaic-English Gospel of Matthew

Dr. Errico's translation of the ancient Aramaic Peshitta text of Matthew with illuminating annotations. The English translation is on the left side of the page with footnotes. The Aramaic text is on the right.

Classical Aramaic: Book I (with Fr. Michael Bazzi)

A beginning practical grammar in a self-teachable format that prepares you to read the New Testament in Jesus' own native tongue.

La Antigua Oración Aramea De Jesús: El Padrenuestro

Dr. Errico's own translation into Spanish of his book *The Ancient Aramaic Prayer of Jesus.*

Das Aramaische Vaterunser

German translation and publication of *Setting a Trap for God.*

Es Werde Licht

German translation and publication of *Let There Be Light.*

Otto Accordi Con Dio: il Padre Nostro originario

Italian translation and publication of *Setting a Trap for God.*

BOOKS BY DR. LAMSA

The Holy Bible from the Ancient Eastern Text

The entire Bible translated directly into English from Aramaic, the language of Jesus. There are approximately 12,000 major differences between this English translation and the many traditional versions of the Bible.

Idioms in the Bible Explained and A Key to the Original Gospels

Two books in one. In Book 1 (*Idioms in the Bible Explained*) Dr. Lamsa explains nearly 1000 crucial idioms and colloquialisms of Eastern speech that will enrich reading of the Bible for student and general reader alike.

Book 2 (*A Key to the Original Gospels*) explains how the gospels were written, the reason for two different genealogies, the conflicting stories of the birth of Jesus, and more.

The Shepherd of All: The Twenty-Third Psalm

Based on his own personal experience as a shepherd, Dr. Lamsa interprets what many consider the most beautiful, moving and meaningful psalm in the light of Near Eastern biblical customs.

New Testament Origin

Dr. Lamsa presents his theory for Aramaic as the original written language of the New Testament.

Dr. George M. Lamsa: A Life

This brief biography was dictated by Dr. Lamsa and has an introduction by Dr. Errico.

(To receive a complete catalog or place an order, see information on page 304.)